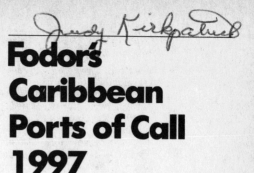

Judy Kirkpatrick

Fodor's
Caribbean
Ports of Call
1997

Reprinted from *Fodor's Worldwide Cruises and Ports of Call 1997*

Fodor's Travel Publications, Inc.
New York • Toronto • London • Sydney • Auckland
http://www.fodors.com/

ISBN 0–679–03317–3

Fodor's Caribbean Ports of Call

Editor: M. T. Schwartzman
Contributors: Robert Blake, Janet Foley, Amy Fried, Herb Hiller, Tracy Patruno, Kate Pennebaker, Melissa Rivers, Heidi Sarna, Jordon Simon, Jonathan Siskin, Dinah A. Spritzer, Simon Worrall, Jane E. Zarem
Creative Director: Fabrizio La Rocca
Cartographer: David Lindroth
Cover Photograph: Bob Krist
Cover Design: John Olenyik
Design: Vignelli Associates

Special Sales

Contents

Index

Maps

Please Write to Us

Everyone who has worked on *Caribbean Ports of Call 1997* has taken enormous care to ensure the accuracy of the text. All prices and opening times we quote are based on information supplied to us at press time. However, the passage of time will always bring changes, so it's always a good idea to call ahead to confirm information in this guide when it matters—particularly if you have to travel far from your ship. Fodor's cannot accept responsibility for any errors that may have occurred.

Was your ship as we described it? Was the food better? The service worse? The cabins smaller? Did our restaurant picks exceed your expectations? Did you find a museum we recommended a waste of time? Positive and negative, we love your feedback. So please send us a letter or postcard (we're at 201 East 50th Street, New York, NY 10022). If you have complaints, we'll look into them and revise our entries when the facts warrant it. We'll look forward to hearing from you. And in the meantime, have a wonderful cruise!

1 Cruise Primer

Choosing Your Cruise

The right ship is one that makes you comfortable. Every ship has its own personality, depending upon its size, when it was built, and its purpose. Big ships are more stable and offer a huge variety of activities and facilities. Smaller ships feel intimate, like private clubs. Each type of ship satisfies a certain type of passenger, and for every big-ship fan there is somebody who would never set foot aboard one of these "floating resorts."

Comparing Ships

In order to compare cruise ships, you need to speak "ship talk." Vessels are generally described according to their passenger capacity, gross registered tonnage, passenger-to-crew ratio, and space ratio. A ship's passenger capacity is usually based on double occupancy, meaning the normal cruise complement of the vessel with two passengers in each cabin. This does not include third or fourth passengers in a cabin, which on some ships can greatly increase the total passenger count. Gross registered tonnage is commonly used to measure a vessel's size. Technically, it is a measurement of the ship's volume, with one cubic foot equal to one gross registered ton. Passenger-to-crew ratio indicates the number of passengers served by each crew member—the lower the ratio, the better the level of service. Space ratio, the ship's tonnage divided by its passenger capacity, allows you to compare a ship's roominess. The higher the ratio, the more spacious a vessel will feel. The roomiest ships have ratios of 40:1 or better; ships with ratios of less than 28:1 may feel cramped.

But when choosing your cruise, the size of the ship isn't the only factor to consider. You also need to find out about the nature of the experience you will have—the lifestyle and activities available by day and after dark, the mealtime hours and dining-room dress codes, how roomy the ship is, and how good the service is apt to be. Equally important are your itinerary, the accommodations, and the cost of the cruise.

Types of Ships

Although all ocean liners are equipped with swimming pools, spas, nightclubs, theaters, and casinos, there are three distinct types: classic liners, cruise liners, and megaships. Many **classic liners**, ships constructed between 1950 and 1969 for transatlantic or other ocean crossings, are still sailing in the fleets of many cruise lines. Beginning in the 1960s, ship lines began to create vessels specifically for cruising. Some of these **cruise liners** were brand new; others were converted ferries or freighters. Vessels known as **megaships**, the biggest cruise ships ever built, first appeared in the late 1980s and, with their immense proportions and passenger capacities, immediately established a new standard of cruise-ship design.

Cruises are also available aboard a number of small ships: cruise yachts, expedition ships, motor-sailing ships, and coastal cruisers.

Classic Liners With their long, sweeping hulls and stepped-back passenger decks, these vessels defined passenger-ship design for decades. Now serving cruise duty, they were originally configured to keep passengers happy during long ocean crossings. Typically, their cabins and closets are larger than those on vessels built for cruising. Deck space is sheltered, with fully or partially enclosed promenades that allow you to relax on deck even during foul weather. A few are still steam powered, without the vibrations sometimes associated with diesel power. Rich wood panels the walls, and fixtures may be the original brass. Smaller ships may feel cramped because of low ceilings in the lobby and corridors. But on the most opulent vessels, public spaces designed to inspire still do. There are balconies above the dining room, where musicians can serenade diners; stained glass graces the cinemas and other public spaces; and grand staircases lead from one deck to another. Such traditional features have proved so enduring they have been incorporated in the plans for some of today's newest vessels.

Although classic ships typically carry between 600 and 1,000 passengers and register between 20,000 and 30,000 tons, a couple of them are among the largest passenger ships afloat.

Cruise Liners When shipbuilders stopped constructing vessels for transportation and started designing them for vacationing, the cruise liner entered the scene. On these ships, outdoor deck space is plentiful; stateroom space is not. Many have a wraparound outdoor promenade deck that allows you to stroll or jog the perimeter of the ship. Older cruise liners resemble the transatlantic ships from which they are descended: Decks are stacked one atop the other in steps, and the hull amidships may appear to droop, so the bow and stern seem to curve upward. In the newest cruise liners, traditional meets trendy. You find atrium lobbies and expansive sun and sports decks, picture windows instead of portholes, and cabins that open onto private verandas. The smallest cruise liners carry 500 passengers and are no bigger than 10,000 tons, while the largest accommodate 1,500 passengers, exceed 50,000 tons, and are stuffed with diversions—almost like megaships.

Megaships The centerpiece of most megaships is a three-, five-, or seven-story central atrium. However, these giant vessels are most easily recognized by their boxy profile: The hull and superstructure rise straight out of the water, as many as 14 stories tall, topped out by a huge sun or sports deck with a jogging track and swimming pool, which may be Olympic size. Some megaships, but not all, also have a wraparound promenade deck. Like the latest cruise liners, picture windows are standard equipment, and cabins in the top categories have private verandas. From their casinos and discos to their fitness centers, everything is proportionally bigger and more extravagant than on other ships. Between 1,500 and 2,500 passengers can be accommodated, and tonnage ranges from 60,000 to 70,000 or more.

Cruise Yachts At the opposite end of the spectrum from the megaship is the tiny cruise yacht. These intimate vessels carry from 100 to 300 passengers, register between 4,000 and 15,000 tons, and are like miniature ocean liners, with big-ship amenities such as fitness centers, casinos, lounges, and swimming pools. What sets these yachts apart from typical ocean liners is that passengers are treated like royalty. Cabins are all outside suites equipped with every creature comfort on the high seas—from VCRs and stocked minibars to marble baths. Built into the stern of some of these vessels are retractable platforms, which are lowered for water sports when the ship is at anchor in calm waters.

Expedition Ships Vessels of this type are designed to reach into the most remote corners of the world. Shallow drafts allow them to navigate up rivers, close to coastlines, and into shallow coves. Hulls may be hardened for sailing in Antarctic ice. Motorized rubber landing craft known as Zodiacs, kept on board, make it possible for passengers to put ashore almost anywhere. However, because the emphasis during cruises aboard expedition ships tends to be on learning and exploring, the ships don't have casinos, showrooms, multiple bars and lounges, and other typical ocean-liner diversions. Instead, they have theaters for lectures, well-stocked libraries, and enrichment programs, led by experts, as entertainment. The smallest expedition ships carry fewer than 100 passengers and register just over 2,000 tons. The largest carries nearly 200 people and registers 9,000 tons.

Motor-Sail Vessels A number of cruise vessels were designed as sailing ships. With their sails unfurled, they are an impressive sight. But since they must keep to a schedule, they cannot rely solely on wind power. So all are equipped with engines as well. Usually they employ both means of propulsion, a technique known as motor sailing, to put on a good show and make the next port on time. These vessels range from small windjammers carrying a handful of passengers to rather large clipper-style ships that approach the size of a small ocean liner and accommodate almost 400 passengers.

Coastal Cruisers Designed more for exploring than entertaining, these yachtlike ships are able to sail to remote waterways and ports. Some have forward gangways for bow landings or carry a fleet of Zodiac landing craft. Unlike larger expedition ships, they do not have ice-hardened hulls. Registering no more than 100 tons and carrying only about 100 passengers, coastal cruisers offer few onboard facilities and public spaces—perhaps just a dining room and a multipurpose lounge.

The Cruise Experience

Your cruise experience will be shaped by several factors, and to determine whether a particular ship's style will suit you, you need to do a bit of research. Is a full program of organized activities scheduled by day? What happens in the evening? Are there one or two seatings in the dining room? If there is more than one, you will not be allowed to arrive and exit as the spirit moves you but instead must show up promptly when service begins—and clear out within a specified time. What kind of entertainment is offered after dark? And how often do passengers dress up for dinner? Some cruises are fancier than others.

Although no two cruises are quite the same, even aboard the same ship, the cruise experience tends to fall into three categories.

Formal Formal cruises embody the ceremony of cruising. Generally available on ocean liners and cruise yachts sailing for seven days or longer, formal cruises recall the days when traveling by ship was an event in itself. By day, shipboard lifestyle is generally unstructured, with few organized activities. Tea and bouillon may be served to the accompaniment of music from a classical trio in the afternoon. Ashore, passengers may be treated to a champagne beach party. Meals in the dining room are served in a single seating, and passengers are treated to the finest cuisine afloat. Jackets and ties for men are the rule for dinner, tuxedos are not uncommon, and the dress code is observed faithfully throughout the evening. Pianists, cabaret acts, and local entertainers provide nighttime diversion. Service is extremely attentive and personalized. Passenger-to-crew and space ratios are best. Because these cruises tend to attract destination-oriented passengers, shore excursions —such as private museum tours—sometimes are included in the fare, as are pre- or post-cruise land packages and sometimes even tips.

Semiformal   Semiformal cruises are a bit more relaxed than their formal counterparts. Meals are served in two seatings on ocean liners or one seating on small ships, menu choices are plentiful, and the cuisine is on a par with that available in better restaurants. Men tend to wear a jacket and tie to dinner most nights. Adding a distinct flair to the dining room is the common practice of staffing the restaurant with waiters of one nationality. Featured dishes may be prepared table side, and you often are able, with advance notice, to order a special diet, such as kosher, low salt, low cholesterol, sugar-free, or vegetarian. There is a daily program of scheduled events, but there's time for more independent pursuits; passengers with similar interests are often encouraged to meet at appointed times for chess or checkers, deck games, and other friendly contests. Production-style shows are staged each evening, but the disco scene may not be too lively. Passenger-to-crew and space ratios assure good service and plenty of room for each passenger. Look for semiformal cruises aboard classic liners, cruise liners, megaships, and a few expedition ships on voyages of seven days or longer.

Casual   Casual cruises are the most popular. Shipboard dress and lifestyle are informal. Meals in the dining room are served in two seatings on ocean liners and one seating on specialty ships; menus are usually not extensive, and the food is good but not extraordinary; your options may be limited if you have special dietetic requirements. Men dress in sport shirts and slacks for dinner most nights, in jackets and ties only two or three evenings of a typical seven-day sailing. Aboard casual ocean liners, activities are more diverse than on formal and semiformal ships, and there is almost always something going on, from bingo to beer-chugging contests. Las Vegas–style variety shows or Broadway revues headline the evening entertainment. Discos bop into the wee hours. Passenger-to-crew and space ratios are generally good, but service tends to be less personal. On small ships, activities on board will be limited as indicated in Types of Ships, *above.*

Look for casual cruises aboard classic liners, cruise liners, and megaships sailing three- to seven-day itineraries to fun-and-sun destinations; expedition ships; motor-sailing ships; and coastal cruisers calling on more unusual ports.

How Long to Sail

Short cruises are ideal for first-time cruisers and families with children. In just two to five days you can get a quick taste of cruising. You'll have the chance to sail aboard some of the newest ships afloat, built exclusively for these runs. Short itineraries may include stops at one or two ports of call, or none at all. The most popular short cruises are three- and four-day sailings to the Bahamas or Key West and Cozumel out of Miami.

After you have experienced a long weekend at sea, you may want to try a **weeklong cruise.** With seven days aboard ship, you get twice as much sailing time and a wider choice of destinations— as many as four to six ports, depending on whether you choose a loop or one-way itinerary (*see* Ship Itineraries, *below*). Since cruises are priced by a per diem rate multiplied by the number of days aboard ship, a weeklong cruise probably costs twice as much as a short cruise.

For some people, seven days is still too short— just when you learn your way around the ship, it's time to go home. On **10- or 11-day sailings,** you get more ports as well as more time at sea, but you won't pay as much as on **two-week sailings.** Many experienced cruisers feel it's just not worth the effort to board a ship for anything less than 14 days, so they opt for either a single 14-day itinerary or sign up for two seven-day trips back-to-back, combining sailings to eastern and western Caribbean ports of call, for example— and taking advantage of the discounts offered by some lines for consecutive sailings.

Ship Itineraries

In choosing the best cruise for you, a ship's itinerary is another important factor. The length of the cruise will determine the variety and number of ports you visit, but so will the type of itinerary and the point of departure. Some cruises, known as **loop cruises,** start and end at the same point and usually explore ports close to one another; **one-way cruises** start at one port and end at another and range farther afield.

Most cruises to the Caribbean are loop cruises. Sailings out of San Juan, Puerto Rico, can visit up to six ports in seven days, while loop cruises out of Florida can reach up to four ports in the same time.

Note: Cruise itineraries listed in Chapter 3 are for the late-1996 to mid-1997 cruise season but are subject to change. Contact your travel agent or the cruise line directly for up-to-the-minute itineraries.

Hints for Passengers with Children

Children aboard cruise ships are a common sight these days. To serve this growing market, a number of cruise lines have expanded their facilities and programs aimed at children. Many offer a discount for younger cruisers.

Discounts   Discounted fares range from free passage on off-peak sailings to reduced per diems during high season. Some cruise lines, such as Celebrity Cruises, Dolphin Cruise Line, Majesty Cruise Line, Norwegian Cruise Line, and Royal Olympic Cruises allow children under two to sail without charge. Airfares and shore excursions also are frequently discounted. For single parents sailing with their children, Premier Cruise Lines offers a reduced single supplement of 25% (normally the charge is 100%).

Activities and   Lines that frequently sail with children aboard
Supervision   may have costumed staff to entertain younger passengers. Premier Cruise Lines has Looney Tunes favorites, such as Bugs Bunny and Daffy Duck, running around its ships. Aboard Dolphin Cruise Line or Majesty Cruise Line you can sail with the Flintstones or Jetsons. Many other lines now have supervised play areas for children and teenagers, at least during summer vacation and holiday periods. Programs include arts and crafts, computer instruction, games and quizzes, kids' movies, swimming-pool parties, scavenger hunts, ship tours, magic shows,

snorkeling lessons, kite flying, cooking classes, and teaching sessions on the history of the ports to be visited. Find out in advance whether there are special programs for your child's age group, how many hours of supervised activities are scheduled each day, whether meals are included, and what the counselor-to-child ratio is. Royal Caribbean Cruise Line and Celebrity Cruises have programs for children in three separate age groups; Norwegian Cruise Line and Carnival Cruise Lines' Camp Carnival programs are divided into four age groups; and Premier Cruise Lines has a kids' program for five age groups.

Some ships provide day care and baby-sitting for younger children at no extra charge, while others charge a nominal hourly rate. On many ships, baby-sitting is by private arrangement (at a negotiated price). If you plan to bring an infant or toddler, be sure to request a crib, high chair, or booster seat in advance and bring plenty of diapers and formula.

Ships with two dinner seatings routinely assign passengers with children to the earlier seating; some lines will not permit children to eat in the dining room on their own. If your kids are picky eaters, check ahead to see if special children's menus are offered.

Publications Several excellent sources on family travel exist. But above all, call the line and determine exactly what children's programs will be available during your sailing, and talk it over with your travel agent.

The most comprehensive guide on family cruising is *Great Cruise Vacations With Your Kids*, formerly titled *Cruising with Children*, which contains the nitty-gritty details—from pricing to kids' programs to crib availability—on over 35 cruise lines. It is published by **Travel With Your Children** (TWYCH, 40 5th Ave., New York, NY 10011, tel. 212/477–5524) and is available in bookstores for $9.95. TWYCH's quarterly newsletter *Family Travel Times* (annual subscription $40), features a column on cruising.

Agency to Los Angeles–based **CruiseMasters** (*see* Agen-
Contact cies to Contact *in* Booking Your Cruise, *below*)
has developed an expertise in family cruising
and offers brochures and tip sheets about cruising, ports, and sightseeing, written from the
perspective of families and children.

Hints for Passengers with Disabilities

The official position of the International Council
of Cruise Lines, which represents cruise lines in
Washington, is that the Americans with Disabilities Act does not apply to cruise ships. The
council argues that most cruise ships, as for-
eign-flag vessels, are not subject to domestic
U.S. laws governing construction and design.
However, the council is working with the International Maritime Organization (IMO), which
sets safety and design standards, to make
cruise ships as accessible as possible. Nevertheless, disclaimers on every cruise brochure allow
ships to refuse passage to anyone whose disability might endanger others. Most ships require
that you travel with an able-bodied companion
if you use a wheelchair or have mobility problems.

If you have a mobility problem, even though you
do not use a wheelchair, tell your travel agent.
Each cruise line sets its own policies; choose
the line that is most accommodating. Also be
careful to select a ship that is easy to get around.
Ships vary even within the fleet of the same
line. Follow up by making sure that the cruise
line is fully informed of your disabilities and
any special needs, and ask if the ship has a full-
time physician on board. (Virtually all major
cruise ships have a doctor on call.) Get written
confirmation of any promises that have been
made to you about a special cabin or transfers to
and from the airport. The line may request a letter from your doctor stating that you need neither a wheelchair nor a companion, or that you
will not require special medical attention on
board.

If you have any type of chronic health problem
that may require medical attention, notify the
ship's doctor soon after you board so he or she

will be prepared to treat you appropriately, if necessary.

Passengers in Wheelchairs The latest cruise ships have been built with accessibility in mind, and many older ships have been modified to accommodate passengers in wheelchairs. The key areas to be concerned about are public rooms, outer decks, and, of course, your cabin. If you need a specially equipped cabin, book as far in advance as possible and ask specific questions of your travel agent or a cruise-line representative. Specifically, ask how your cabin is configured and equipped. Is the entrance level or ramped? Are all doorways at least 30 inches wide (wider if your wheelchair is not standard size)? Are pathways to beds, closets, and bathrooms at least 36 inches wide and unobstructed? In the bathroom, is there 42 inches of clear space in front of the toilet and are there grab bars behind and on one side of it and in the bathtub or shower? Ask whether there is a three-prong outlet in the cabin, and whether the bathroom has a handheld showerhead, a bath bench, or roll-in shower or shower stall with fold-down seat, if you need them.

The best cruise ship for passengers who use wheelchairs is one that ties up right at the dock at every port, at which time a ramp or even an elevator is always made available. Unfortunately, it's hard to ascertain this in advance, for a ship may tie up at the dock at a particular port on one voyage and, on the next, anchor in the harbor and have passengers transported to shore via tender. Ask your travel agent to find out which ships are scheduled to dock on which cruises. If a tender is used, some ships will have crew members carry the wheelchair and passenger from the ship to the tender. Unfortunately, other ships point-blank refuse to take wheelchairs on tenders, especially if the water is choppy. At some ports, ships always tender because docking facilities are unavailable. For more information about where and whether ships dock or tender, *see* Coming Ashore for each port *in* Chapter 2.

Passengers with Vision Impairments Some ships allow guide dogs to accompany passengers with vision impairments; however, if your cruise is scheduled to visit foreign ports (as most do), you may not be able to take a guide dog ashore, depending on the country. To avoid potential quarantine upon returning to the United States, guide dogs should have their shots updated within seven days of sailing, and owners should carry the dog's valid health and rabies certificates.

Pregnant Women Considering advanced pregnancy a disability, cruise lines may refuse passage to pregnant women. "Advanced" usually refers to the third trimester. If you are pregnant, check on the cruise line's policy before you book passage.

Passengers with Diabetes Check with individual cruise lines to find out if a ship stocks insulin and other diabetic supplies and if a physician is on board. A good resource, chock-full of travel tips, is the quarterly newsletter *The Diabetic Traveler* (Box 8223 RW, Stamford, CT 06905, tel. 203/327–5832, $18.95 per yr). Back issues are available and include one dedicated to cruise vacations ($3, Autumn 1992).

Organizations Several organizations provide travel information for people with disabilities, usually for a membership fee, and some publish newsletters and bulletins. Among them are the **Information Center for Individuals with Disabilities** (29 Stanhope St., Box 256, Boston, MA 02217, tel. 617/450–9888; in MA, 800/462–5015; TTY 617/424–6855); **Mobility International USA** (Box 10767, Eugene, OR 97440, tel. and TTY 503/343–1284, fax 503/343–6812), the U.S. branch of an international organization based in Belgium (*see below*) that has affiliates in 30 countries; **MossRehab Hospital Travel Information Service** (tel. 215/456–9600, TTY 215/456–9602); **Society for the Advancement of Travel for the Handicapped** (SATH, 347 5th Ave., New York, NY 10016, tel. 212/447–7284; membership $35); and **Travelin' Talk** (Box 3534, Clarksville, TN 37043, tel. 615/552–6670, fax 615/552–1182).

In the United Kingdom Important information sources include the **Royal Association for Disability and Rehabilitation** (RADAR, 12 City Forum, 250 City Rd., London EC1V 8AF, tel. 0171/250–3222), which publishes travel information for people with disabilities in Britain, and **Mobility International** (Rue de Manchester 25, B1070 Brussels, Belgium, tel. 00–322–410–6297), an international clearinghouse of travel information for people with disabilities.

Travel Agencies and Tour Operators **Accessible Journeys** (35 W. Sellers Ave., Ridley Park, PA 19078, tel. 610/521–0339 or 800/846–4537, fax 610/521–6959) arranges escorted trips for travelers with disabilities and provides licensed health-care professionals to accompany those who require aid. **Flying Wheels Travel** (143 W. Bridge St., Box 382, Owatonna, MN 55060, tel. 507/451–5005 or 800/535–6790) is a travel agency specializing in domestic and worldwide cruises for people with mobility problems.

Publications *Wheels and Waves: A Cruise-Ferry Guide for the Physically Handicapped* ($13.95 plus $3 shipping, tel. 800/637–2256) describes more than 200 ships, including 100 with accessible cabins. It is a publication of Wheels Aweigh (17105 San Carlos Blvd., Fort Myers, FL 33931).

Several publications are available from the Consumer Information Center (Pueblo, CO 81009, tel. 719/948–3334): "Fly Smart" (include Dept. 575B in address), a free pocket-size brochure, details flight safety tips. "Fly-Rights" (Dept. 133B), is a booklet that includes a section on air-travel rights for passengers with disabilities ($1.75).

Travelin' Talk Directory (*see* Organizations, *above*) was published in 1993. This 500-page resource book ($35 check or money order with a money-back guarantee) is packed with information for travelers with disabilities. Twin Peaks Press (Box 129, Vancouver, WA 98666, tel. 360/694–2462 or 800/637–2256) publishes the *Directory of Travel Agencies for the Disabled* ($19.95), which lists more than 370 agencies worldwide, and *Wheelchair Vagabond* ($14.95), a collection of personal travel tips. Add $3 shipping for the first book, $1.50 for each additional. *Cruise Travel Magazine* (World Publishing Co., Box 342, Mt. Morris, IL 61054, tel. 815/734–4151 or 800/877–5893; $9.97 per yr) published an in-depth article and chart on cruising for people with disabilities in its January 1996 issue. Back issues are available. "Cruising for the Physi-

cally Challenged" (tel. 800/882–9000) is a free
booklet published by World Wide Cruises Inc.,
offering practical travel tips in a Q&A format.

Hints for Older Passengers

For older travelers, cruise vacations strike an
excellent balance: They offer a tremendous variety of activities and destinations in one convenient package. You can do as much or as little as
you want, meet new people, see new places, enjoy shows and bingo, learn to play bridge, or
take up needlepoint—all within a safe, familiar
environment. Cruises are *not* a good idea for
those who are bedridden, have a serious medical
condition that is likely to flare up on board, or
are prone to periods of confusion or severe memory loss.

No particular rules apply to senior citizens on
cruises. Those who want a leisurely, relaxed
pace will probably be happiest on ships that attract a higher percentage of older passengers:
luxury ocean liners, cruise yachts, and expedition ships on voyages of longer than seven days.
Passengers who are less than spry should look
for a ship where the public rooms are clustered
on one deck and select a cabin near an elevator
or stairway amidships. Do not book a cabin with
upper and lower berths.

Only a couple of cruise lines, notably Royal Caribbean and Premier, have reduced rates for
senior citizens, but senior citizens may be able
to take advantage of local discounts ashore.
When in port, showing proof of age often results
in reduced admissions, half fares on public
transportation, and special dining rates.

Several cruise lines employ "gentleman hosts,"
who act as dancing and bridge partners for single ladies traveling alone. Look into Cunard
Line, Holland America Line, Royal Olympic
Cruises, and Silversea Cruises.

Organization The **National Council of Senior Citizens** (1331 F
St. NW, Washington, DC 20004, tel. 202/347–
8800; membership $12 annually) offers dis-
counts on cruises, along with such nontravel
perks as magazines and newsletters.

Tour Operators	**Saga International Holidays** (222 Berkeley St., Boston, MA 02116, tel. 617/262–2262 or 800/343–0273) caters to those over age 50 who like to travel in groups. **SeniorTours** (508 Irvington Rd., Drexel Hill, PA 19026, tel. 800/227–1100) arranges cruises.
Publication	"The Mature Traveler" (Box 50400, Reno, NV 89513, tel. 702/786–7419; $29.95), a monthly newsletter, lists discounts on cruises.

Hints for Gay and Lesbian Passengers

Organization	The **International Gay Travel Association** (Box 4974, Key West, FL 33041, tel. 800/448–8550, IGTA@aol.com), which has over 1,100 travel-industry members, will provide you with names of travel agents and cruise lines that specialize in gay travel.
Tour Operators and Travel Agencies	Some of the largest agencies serving gay travelers are **Advance Damron Vacations** (10700 Northwest Fwy., #160, Houston, TX 77092, tel. 713/682–2650 or 800/695–0880), **Islanders/Kennedy Travel** (183 W. 10th St., New York, NY 10014, tel. 212/242–3222 or 800/988–1181), **Now Voyager** (4406 18th St., San Francisco, CA 94114, tel. 415/626–1169 or 800/255–6951), **Pied Piper** (tel. 212/239–2412 or 800/874–7312), and **Yellowbrick Road** (1500 W. Balmoral Ave., Chicago, IL 60640, tel. 312/561–1800 or 800/642–2488). **R.S.V.P. Travel Productions** (tel. 800/328–7787) operates many gay cruises, and **Olivia Cruises & Resorts** (tel. 800/631–6277) provides the same service for lesbian travelers.
Publication	"Out & About" (tel. 800/929–2268; $49 for 10 issues) is a monthly newsletter that reports on gay-friendly cruise lines as well as other gay travel opportunities in a roundup-style format. A cruise, tour, and events calendar is published quarterly.

Booking Your Cruise

Using a Travel Agent

Since nearly all cruises are sold through travel agents, the agent you choose to work with can be just as important as the ship you sail on. So how do you know if an agent or agency is right for you? Talk to friends, family, and colleagues who have used an agency to book a cruise. The most qualified agents are members of CLIA (Cruise Lines International Association) and the NACOA (National Association of Cruise-Only Agencies), as well as ASTA (American Society of Travel Agents). Agents who are CLIA Accredited Cruise Counsellors or Master Cruise Counsellors have had extensive cruise and ship inspection experience; agents who are NACOA members are also experienced cruisers. If you're undecided about a ship or line, an agent's personal account of his or her own cruise can be invaluable. However, keep in mind that agencies often have partnerships with certain cruise lines. In some cases, the agency may actually block space on a ship; in other cases, the agency agrees to sell a certain amount of space. Either way, the agency gets a favorable rate from the cruise line; the agency can then afford to offer a "discounted" price to the public. But since agents often receive higher commissions on these cruises, they might steer you toward a cruise that might not be for you. *A good travel agent puts your needs first.*

Larger agencies often have more experienced cruisers on their staff and can provide the biggest discounts. Smaller agencies may compete with their personalized service. Whether you choose a large or small agency, a good agent takes the time to learn as much as possible about you and your cruise companion(s). An agent who asks a few cursory questions before handing you a brochure is a mere order taker; an agent who asks you to fill out a questionnaire about your personal interests is a professional. A travel agent might not know what ship is right for you; a good agent *will* know which ones are wrong.

Of course, you want the best price. When it comes down to it, the top agencies can more or less get you the same price on most cruises, because they'll guarantee that if the cruise line lowers the price in a promotion, you'll get the better deal. So look for an agency that offers this guarantee. But the overall value of your cruise depends on an agency's service, and agencies that are willing to go the extra mile for their clients by providing free cruise-discount newsletters, cabin upgrades, dollar-stretching advice, and 24-hour service in case of a problem are your best bet.

Cruise-Only Travel Agents As the name implies, "cruise-only" travel agencies specialize in selling cruises. However, these agencies can sell you air tickets and other travel arrangements, too, as part of your cruise package. Sometimes, your choice may be limited to a package put together by the cruise line. Increasingly, though, cruise-only agencies are putting together their own custom-designed cruise vacations.

Full-Service Travel Agents Full-service agents have broad travel experience, but may be less knowledgeable about cruise lines than their cruise-only counterparts. If you know exactly what line and ship you want to sail on and are more concerned about your pre- or post-cruise land arrangements, a full-service agent may be more helpful. (But keep in mind that full-service agencies may not have the same discounts as cruise-only agencies.) If you choose to use a full-service agency, look for one that has a cruise desk with agents who sell only cruises. Then, you get the best of both worlds.

Spotting Swindlers Always be on the lookout for a scam. Although reputable agencies far outnumber crooks, a handful of marketeers use deceptive and unethical tactics. The best way to avoid being fleeced is to pay for your cruise with a credit card, from deposit to full payment. That way, if an agency goes out of business before your cruise departs, you can cancel payment on services not rendered. Two tip-offs that an agency may be a bad apple: It doesn't accept credit cards and it asks for a deposit that is more than what the cruise line has requested (check the brochure). To avoid a disreputable agency, make sure the one you choose has been in business for at least five years. Check its reputation with the local Better Business Bureau or consumer protection agency *before* you pay any deposits. If a cruise price seems too good to be true, it could mean the agency is desperate to bring in money and may close its doors tomorrow, so don't be tempted by agencies that claim they can beat any price. Be wary of bait-and-switch tactics: If you're told that an advertised bargain cruise is sold out, don't be persuaded to book a more expensive substitute. Also, if you're told that your cruise reservation was canceled because of over-booking and that you must pay extra for a con-firmed rescheduled sailing, demand a full re-fund. Finally, if ever you fail to receive a voucher or ticket on the promised date, place an inquiry immediately.

Getting the Best Cruise for Your Dollar

By selecting the right agent, you have the greatest chance of getting the best deal. But having a basic knowledge of how and why cruises are discounted can only benefit you in the end. Since your vacation experience can vary greatly depending on the ship and its ports of call, it's best to pick your vessel and itinerary first, and then try to get the best price. Remem-ber, it's only a deal if the cruise you book, no matter what the price, meets your expectations.

Like everything in retail, each cruise has a bro-chure list price. But like the sticker price on a new car, nobody actually pays this amount. These days, if you asked any 10 cruise passen-gers on any given ship what they paid, they would give you 10 different answers. Discounts from cruise lines and agencies can range from 5% on a single fare to 50% on the second fare in a cabin.

Approach deep discounts with skepticism. Fewer than a dozen cabins may be offered at the discounted price, they may be inside cabins, and the fare may not include air transportation or transfers between the airport and the ship. Fi-nally, do the math. A promotion might sound catchy, but if you divide the price by the number of days you'll be cruising and include the cost of air and accommodations, you might find that the deal of the century is really a dud.

Deals and Discounts
Seasonal Discounts

Cruise-brochure prices are typically divided into three categories based on the popularity of sailing dates and weather: high season, shoulder season, and low-season. Obviously, prices will be higher for a Caribbean sailing in December than for the same sailing in August. Before you take advantage of a low-season rate, have your agent check on the specific weather conditions and on other factors (such as mosquitoes) in your cruise destination.

Early-Bird Specials Almost all cruise lines provide a discount for passengers who book and put down a deposit far in advance; an additional discount may be provided if payment is made in full at the time of booking. These discounts, given to passengers who book at least six months before departure, range from 10% to 50% off the brochure rate. (Brochures are usually issued a year or more in advance of sailing dates.) Most early-booking discounts in the Caribbean include round-trip airfare. Booking a popular cruise early is the best way to get the best price; there will likely be no last-minute deals on these sailings. The other advantage of booking far in advance is that you're more likely to get the cabin and meal seating you want. On most cruises, the cheapest and most expensive cabins sell out first.

Last-Minute Savings In recent years, cruise lines have provided fewer and fewer last-minute deals. However, if a particular cruise is not selling well, a cruise line may pick certain large cruise-only travel agencies to unload unsold cabins. These deals, sometimes referred to by agents as "distressed merchandise," are typically available three weeks to three months before the cruise departs. These specials are unadvertised, but may be listed in the agencies' newsletters and on their cruise telephone hot lines (*see* Agencies to Contact, *below*). Keep in mind that your choice of cabin and meal seating is limited for such last-minute deals. Distressed merchandise on older ships, those built before the 1980s, may be limited to smaller cabins in undesirable areas of the ship. Last-minute deals may only be available in certain regions.

Mixed Bag Besides the major discounts mentioned above, agencies and cruise lines might attract passengers with price promotions such as "Sail for 12 Days and Pay for Only 10," "Free Hotel Stay with Your Cruise," and "Two Sail for the Price of One." Read the fine print before you book. The offer may be a bargain—or just slick advertising. How can you tell? Compare the advertised price to the standard early-booking discount, and check if the promotion includes airfare. Free or discounted air on cruise-only prices are common for Caribbean sailings. Also check on senior-citizen discounts and "cruise dollars" accrued on participating credit cards. Cruise lines that target families sometimes take on a third or fourth cabin passenger for free. Some of the best cruise prices are available on repositioning cruises (*see* Ship Itineraries, *above*).

Payment

Once you have made a reservation for a cabin, you will be asked to put down a deposit. Handing money over to your travel agent constitutes a contract, so before you pay, review the cruise brochure to find out the provisions of the cruise contract. What is the payment schedule and cancellation policy? Will there be any additional charges before you can board your ship, such as transfers, port fees, or local taxes? If your air connection requires you to spend an evening in a hotel near the port before or after the cruise, is there an extra cost?

If possible, pay your deposit and balance with a credit card. This gives you some recourse if you need to cancel, and you can ask the credit-card company to intercede on your behalf in case of problems.

Deposit Most cruises must be reserved with a refundable deposit of $200–$500 per person, depending upon how expensive the cruise is; the balance is due 45–75 days before you sail. If the cruise is less than 60 days away, however, you may have to pay the entire amount immediately.

Cancellation Your entire deposit or payment may be refunded if you cancel your reservation between 45 and 75 days before departure; the grace period varies from line to line. If you cancel later than that, you will forfeit some or all of your deposit (*see* Protection, *below*). An average cancellation charge is $100 one month before sailing, $100 plus 50% of the ticket price between 15 and 30 days prior to departure, and $100 plus 75% of the ticket price between 14 days and 24 hours ahead of time. If you simply fail to show up when the ship sails, you will lose the entire amount. Many travel agents also assess a small cancellation fee. Check their policy.

Protection Cruise lines sell two types of policies that protect you in the event of cancellation or trip interruption. **Waivers** provide a full refund if you cancel your trip for any reason, usually up to 72 hours before sailing; the cost to cover a seven-day cruise is about $75. **Insurance,** sold by an insurance broker and through travel agencies, protects against cancellation for specified reasons plus trip delay, interruption, medical expenses, emergency evacuation, and lost, stolen, or damaged luggage; the cost to cover a seven-day cruise is about $99. The insurance does not cover cancellations, interruptions, or delays caused by a preexisting medical condition. Keep in mind that a waiver is only available at the time of booking; insurance policies are best purchased after you have paid a significant portion of your cruise, which you will lose in the case of cancellation. Neither insurance nor waivers protect you against cruise-line default. For that, you'll need special default insurance, sold only by a select number of companies, such as Travel Guard (*see* Insurance, *below*). These companies also cover preexisting medical conditions.

Agencies to Contact The agencies listed below specialize in booking cruises, have been in business at least five years, and emphasize customer service as well as price.

Cruise Only **Cruise Fairs of America** (2029 Century Park E, Suite 950, Los Angeles, CA 90067, tel. 310/556–2925 or 800/456–4386, fax 310/556–2254), established in 1987, has a fax-back service for information on the latest deals. The agency also publishes a free twice-yearly newsletter with tips on cruising.

Cruise Headquarters (4225 Executive Sq., #1600, La Jolla, CA 92037, tel. 619/453–1201 or 800/424–6111, fax 619/453–0653), established in 1988, specializes in luxury cruises and personalized shoreside arrangements.

Cruise Holidays of Kansas City (7000 N.W. Prairie View Rd., Kansas City, MO 64151, tel. 816/741–7417 or 800/869–6806, fax 816/741–7123), a franchisee of Cruise Holidays, a cruise-only agency with outlets throughout the United States, has been in business since 1988. The agency mails out a free newsletter to clients every other month with listings of cruise bargains.

Cruise Line, Inc. (150 N.W. 168th St., N. Miami Beach, FL 33169, tel. 305/653–6111 or 800/777–0707, fax 305/576–0073), established in 1983, publishes *World of Cruising* magazine three times a year and a number of free brochures, including "Guide to First Time Cruising," "Guide to Family Cruises," and "Guide to Cruise Ship Weddings and Honeymoons." The agency has a 24-hour hot line with prerecorded cruise deals that are updated weekly.

Cruise Pro (2527 E. Thousand Oaks Blvd., Thousand Oaks, CA 91362, tel. 805/371–9884 or 800/222–7447; in CA, 800/258–7447; fax 805/371–9084), established in 1983, has special discounts listed in its three-times-per-month mailings to members of its Voyager's Club ($15 to join).

Cruise Quarters of America (1241 E. Dyer Rd., Suite 110, Santa Ana, CA 92705, tel. 714/754–0280 or 800/648–2444, fax 714/850–1974), established in 1986, is a division of Associated Travel International, one of the country's largest travel companies, and has a VIP club (tel. 800/517–5391) for upscale cruise planning.

CruiseMasters (3415 Sepulveda Blvd., Suite 645, Los Angeles, CA 90034, tel. 310/397–7175 or 800/242–9000, fax 310/397–3568), established in 1987, gives each passenger a personalized, bound guide to their ship's ports of call. The guides provide money-saving tips and advice on whether to opt for a prepackaged port excursion or strike out on your own. The agency's Family Cruise Club serves parents cruising with their children. A World Cruise Desk is dedicated to booking very long cruises.

Cruises of Distinction (93 Dorsa Ave., Livingston, NJ 07039, tel. 201/716–0088 or 800/634–3445, fax 201/716–9893), established in 1984, publishes a free 80-page cruise catalog four times a year. For a fee of $39, which is credited to your first cruise booking, you can receive notification of unadvertised specials by mail or fax.

Don Ton Cruise Tours (3151 Airway Ave., E–1, Costa Mesa, CA 92626, tel. 714/545–3737 or 800/

318–1818, fax 714/545–5275), established in 1972, features a variety of special-interest clubs, including a short-notice club, singles club, family cruise club, and adventure cruise club. The agency is also experienced in personalized pre- and post-cruise land arrangements.

Golden Bear Travel (16 Digital Dr., Novato, CA 94949, tel. 415/382–8900; outside CA, 800/551–1000; fax 415/382–9086) acts as general sales agent for a number of foreign cruise ships and specializes in longer, luxury cruises. Its Cruise Value club sends members free twice-a-month mailings with special prices on "distressed merchandise" cruises that are not selling well. The agency's Mariner Club runs escorted cruises for passengers who would like to travel as part of a group.

Kelly Cruises (1315 W. 22nd St., Suite 105, Oak Brook, IL 60521, tel. 708/990–1111 or 800/837–7447, fax 708/990–1147), established in 1986, publishes a quarterly newsletter highlighting new ships and special rates. Passengers can put their name on a free mailing list for last-minute deals.

Vacations at Sea (4919 Canal St., New Orleans, LA 70119, tel. 504/482–1572 or 800/749–4950, fax 504/486–8360), established in 1983, puts together its own pre- and post-cruise land packages and hosted tours, such as Caribbean golf cruises.

Full Service **Ambassador Tours** (120 Montgomery St., Suite 400, San Francisco, CA 94104, tel. 415/981–5678 or 800/989–9000, fax 415/982–3490), established in 1955, does 80% of its business in cruises. Three times a year, the agency distributes a free 32-page catalog, which lists discounts on cruises and land packages.

Time to Travel (582 Market St., San Francisco, CA 94104, tel. 415/421–3333 or 800/524–3300, fax 415/421–4857), established in 1935, does 90% of its business in cruises. It mails a free listing of cruise discounts to its clients three to five times a month. Time to Travel specializes in pre- and post-cruise land arrangements and claims its staff of 19 has been nearly everywhere in the world.

Trips 'n Travels, (1024 Kane Concourse, Bay Harbor, FL 33154, tel. 305/864–2222 or 800/

331–2745, fax 305/861–8809) does 80% of its business in cruises. The agency's concierge service arranges theater tickets and so forth in ports of call. Its free cruise-bargain newsletter is mailed out to clients six times per year.

White Travel Service (127 Park Rd., West Hartford, CT 06119, tel. 203/233–2648 or 800/547–4790, prerecorded cruise hot line with discount listings 203/236–6176, fax 203/236–6177), founded in 1972, does most of its business in cruises.

Before You Go

Tickets, Vouchers, and Other Travel Documents

After you make the final payment to your travel agent, the cruise line will issue your cruise tickets and vouchers for airport–ship transfers. Depending on the airline, and whether you have purchased an air-sea package, you may receive your plane tickets or charter-flight vouchers at the same time; you may also receive vouchers for any shore excursions, although most cruise lines issue these aboard ship. Should your travel documents not arrive when promised, contact your travel agent or call the cruise line directly. If you book late, tickets may be delivered directly to the ship.

Once aboard, you may be asked to turn over your passport for group immigration clearance (*see* Passports and Visas, *below*; Embarkation *in* Arriving and Departing, *below*) or to turn over your return plane ticket so the ship's staff may reconfirm your flight home. Otherwise, keep travel documents in a safe place, such as the safe in your cabin or at the purser's office.

Passports and Visas

U.S. Citizens   American citizens boarding ships in the United States usually need neither a passport nor visas to call at ports in the Caribbean. However, carrying a passport is always a good idea, and entry requirements do change, so read your cruise documents carefully to see what you'll need for embarkation. (You don't want to be turned away at the pier!) If you are boarding a ship outside the United States, you'll need the appropriate entry requirements for that country.

On cruises to some countries, you may be required to obtain a visa in advance. Check with your travel agent or cruise line about specific requirements. If you do need a visa for your cruise, your travel agent should help you obtain it through a visa service by mail or directly from the consulate or embassy. (There may be a charge of up to $25 for this service, added to the visa charge.)

Passport Renewal You can pick up new and renewal application forms at any of the 13 U.S. Passport Agency offices and at some post offices and courthouses. Although passports are usually mailed within four weeks of your application's receipt, allow five weeks or more from April through summer. Call the Department of State Office of Passport Services' information line (tel. 202/647–0518) for fees, documentation requirements, and other details.

If your passport is lost or stolen abroad, report the loss immediately to the nearest embassy or consulate and to the local police. If you can provide the consular officer with the information contained in the passport, he or she will usually be able to issue you a new passport promptly. For this reason, keep a photocopy of the data page of your passport separate from your money and traveler's checks. Also leave a photocopy with a relative or friend at home.

Non-U.S. Citizens If you plan to cruise from an American gateway, such as Miami or Los Angeles, and return to the United States at the end of the trip, you may need a passport from your own country, along with a B-2 visa, which allows multiple entries into the United States.

Canadians An identity card will be sufficient for entry and reentry into the United States. Passport application forms are available at 28 regional passport offices as well as post offices and travel agencies. Whether for a first or a subsequent passport, you must apply in person. Children under 16 may be included on a parent's passport but must have their own to travel alone. Passports are valid for five years and are usually mailed within two to three weeks of an application's receipt. For fees, documentation requirements, and other information, in English or French, call the passport office (tel. 819/994–3500 or 800/567–6868).

U.K. Citizens British citizens need a valid passport to enter the United States. However, if you will be boarding your ship within 90 days, you probably won't need a visa. You will need to fill out the Visa Waiver Form 1-94W, supplied by the airline. Applications for new and renewal passports are available from main post offices as well as at six passport offices, located in Belfast, Glasgow, Liverpool, London, Newport, and Peterborough. You may apply in person at all passport offices, or by mail to all except the London office. Children under 16 may travel on an accompanying parent's passport. All passports are valid for 10 years. Allow a month for processing.

What to Pack

You will naturally pack differently for the tropics than for an Alaskan cruise, but even if you're heading for warmer climates, take along a sweater in case of cool evening ocean breezes or overactive air-conditioning. In the Caribbean, a rain slicker may come in handy. Make sure you take at least one pair of comfortable walking shoes for exploring port towns. Shorts or slacks are convenient for shore excursions, but remember that in Latin America women are expected to dress modestly and men to wear slacks.

Generally speaking, plan on one outfit for every two days of cruising, especially if your wardrobe contains many interchangeable pieces. Ships often have convenient laundry facilities as well. And don't overload your luggage with extra toiletries and sundry items; they are easily available in port and in the ship's gift shop (though usually at a premium price). Soaps, and sometimes shampoos and body lotion, are often placed in your cabin compliments of the cruise line.

Take an extra pair of eyeglasses or contact lenses in your carry-on luggage. If you have a health problem that requires a prescription drug, pack enough to last the duration of the trip or have your doctor write a prescription using the drug's generic name, because brand names vary from country to country. Always carry prescription drugs in their original packaging to avoid problems with customs officials. Don't pack them in luggage that you plan to check in case your bags go astray. Pack a list of the offices that supply refunds for lost or stolen traveler's checks.

Electricity   Most cruise ships use U.S.-type 110V, 60-cycle electricity and grounded plugs, but others employ 220V, 50-cycle current and are fitted with European- or English-type outlets. In that case, to use U.S.-purchased electric appliances on board, you'll need an adapter plug. Unless the appliance is dual-voltage and made for travel, you'll also need a converter. For a copy of the free brochure "Foreign Electricity is No Deep Dark Secret," send a stamped, self-addressed envelope to adapter-converter manufacturer Franzus Company (Customer Service, Dept. B50, Murtha Industrial Park, Box 142, Beacon Falls, CT 06403, tel. 203/723–6664).

Luggage

Allowances   Cruise passengers can bring aboard as much
On Board Ship   luggage as they like and are restricted only by the amount of closet space in their cabin. If you are flying to your point of embarkation, be aware of the airline's luggage policies. Because luggage is often tossed about and stacked as it is moved between ship and airport, take suitcases that can take abuse.

In Flight   Free airline baggage allowances depend on the airline, the route, and the class of your ticket; ask in advance. In general, on domestic flights and on international flights between the United States and foreign destinations, you are entitled to check two bags. A third piece may be brought aboard, but it must fit easily under the seat in front of you or in the overhead compartment. In the United States, the Federal Aviation Administration gives airlines broad latitude to limit carry-on allowances and tailor them to different aircraft and operational conditions. Charges for excess, oversize, or overweight pieces vary.

If you are flying between two destinations outside the United States, note that baggage allowances may be determined not by piece but by weight; again, ask your airline about their specific restrictions.

Safeguarding Your Luggage When your cruise documents arrive, they will often include luggage tags bearing the name of your ship. Place one on each piece of luggage before leaving home: These tags will identify your luggage to cruise-line officials if there is an automatic luggage-pull service at the airport on arrival. Also tag your bags inside and out with your name, address, and phone number. (If you use your home address, cover it so that potential thieves can't see it.) Put a copy of your itinerary inside each bag, so you can easily be tracked, and itemize your bags' contents and their worth in case they go astray.

When you check in for your pre- or post-cruise flight, make sure that the tag attached by baggage handlers bears the correct three-letter code for your destination. If your bags do not arrive with you, or if you detect damage, immediately file a written report with the airline before you leave the airport.

Insurance

Travel insurance can protect your monetary investment, replace your luggage and its contents, or provide for medical coverage should you fall ill during your trip. Most travel agencies and many insurance agents sell specialized health-and-accident, flight, trip-cancellation, and luggage insurance, as well as comprehensive policies with some or all of these features. Comprehensive policies may also reimburse you for delays due to weather—an important consideration if you're traveling during the winter months. Some health-insurance policies do not cover preexisting conditions, but waivers may be available in specific cases. Coverage is sold by the companies listed below; these companies act as the policy's administrators. The actual insurance is usually underwritten by a well-known name, such as The Travelers or Continental Insurance.

Before you make any purchase, review your existing health and home-owner policies to find out whether they cover expenses incurred while traveling.

Companies to Contact Travel insurance covering baggage, health, and trip cancellation or interruption is available from **Access America, Inc.** (Box 90315, Richmond, VA 23286, tel. 804/285–3300 or 800/284–8300), **Carefree Travel Insurance** (Box 9366, 100 Garden City Plaza, Garden City, NY 11530, tel. 516/294–0220 or 800/323–3149), **Tele-Trip** (Mutual of Omaha Plaza, Box 31716, Omaha, NE 68131, tel. 800/228–9792), **Travel Guard International** (1145 Clark St., Stevens Point, WI 54481, tel. 715/345–0505 or 800/826–1300), **Travel Insured International** (Box 280568, East Hartford, CT 06128, tel. 203/528–7663 or 800/243–3174), and **Wallach & Company** (107 W. Federal St., Box 480, Middleburg, VA 22117, tel. 703/687–3166 or 800/237–6615).

U.K. Residents Most tour operators, travel agents, and insurance agents sell policies covering accidents, medical expenses, personal liability, trip cancellation, and loss or theft of personal property. You can also buy an annual travel-insurance policy valid for every trip (usually of less than 90 days) you make during the year in which it's purchased. Make sure you will be covered if you have a preexisting medical condition or are pregnant. The Association of British Insurers, a trade association representing 450 insurance companies, advises extra medical coverage for visitors to the United States.

For advice by phone or the free booklet "Holiday Insurance," which sets out what to expect from a holiday-insurance policy and gives price guidelines, contact the association (51 Gresham St., London EC2V 7HQ, tel. 0171/600–3333; 30 Gordon St., Glasgow G1 3PU, tel. 0141/226–3905; Scottish Provident Bldg., Donegall Sq. W, Belfast BT1 6JE, tel. 01232/249176; call for other locations).

Arriving and Departing

If you have purchased an air-sea package, you will be met by a cruise-company representative when your plane lands at the port city and then shuttled directly to the ship in buses or minivans. Some cruise lines arrange to transport your luggage between airport and ship—you don't have to hassle with baggage claim at the start of your cruise or with baggage check-in at the end. If you decide not to buy the air-sea package but still plan to fly, ask your travel agent if you can use the ship's transfer bus anyway; if you do, you may be required to purchase a round-trip transfer voucher ($5–$20). Otherwise, you will have to take a taxi to the ship.

If you live close to the port of embarkation, bus transportation may be available. If you are part of a group that has booked a cruise together, this transportation may be part of your package. Another option for those who live close to their point of departure is to drive to the ship. The major U.S. cruise ports all have parking facilities.

Embarkation

Check-In On arrival at the dock, you must check in before boarding your ship. (A handful of smaller cruise ships handle check-in at the airport.) An officer will collect or stamp your ticket, inspect or even retain your passport or other official identification, ask you to fill out a tourist card, check that you have the correct visas, and collect any unpaid port or departure tax. Seating assignments for the dining room are often handed out at this time, too. You may also register your credit card to open a shipboard account, although that may be done later at the purser's office.

After this you may be required to go through a security check and to pass your hand baggage through an X-ray inspection. These are the same machines in use at airports, so ask to have your photographic film inspected visually.

Although it takes only five or 10 minutes per family to check in, lines are often long, so aim for off-peak hours. The worst time tends to be immediately after the ship begins boarding; the later it is, the less crowded. For example, if boarding begins at 2 PM and continues until 4:30, try to arrive after 3:30.

Boarding the Ship Before you walk up the gangway, the ship's photographer will probably take your picture; there's no charge unless you buy the picture (usually $6). On board, stewards may serve welcome drinks in souvenir glasses—for which you're usually charged between $3 and $5 cash.

You will either be escorted to your cabin by a steward or, on a smaller ship, given your key by a ship's officer and directed to your cabin. Some elevators are unavailable to passengers during boarding, since they are used to transport luggage. You may arrive to find your luggage outside your stateroom or just inside the door; if it doesn't arrive within a half hour before sailing, contact the purser. If you are among the unlucky few whose luggage doesn't make it to the ship in time, the purser will trace it and arrange to have it flown to the next port.

Visitors' Passes Some cruise ships permit passengers to invite guests on board prior to sailing, although most cruise lines prohibit all but paying passengers for reasons of security and insurance liability. Cruise companies that allow visitors usually require that you obtain passes several weeks in advance; call the lines for policies and procedures.

Most ships do not allow visitors while the ship is docked in a port of call. If you meet a friend on shore, you won't be able to invite him or her back to your stateroom.

Disembarkation

The last night of your cruise is full of business. On most ships you must place everything except your hand luggage outside your cabin door, ready to be picked up by midnight. Color-coded tags, distributed to your cabin in a debarkation packet, should be placed on your luggage before the crew collects it. Your designated color will later determine when you leave the ship and help you retrieve your luggage on the pier.

Your shipboard bill is left in your room during the last day; to pay the bill (if you haven't already put it on your credit card) or to settle any questions, you must stand in line at the purser's office. Tips to the cabin steward and dining staff are distributed on the last night.

The next morning, in-room breakfast service is usually not available because stewards are too busy. Most passengers clear out of their cabins as soon as possible, gather their hand luggage, and stake out a chair in one of the public lounges to await the ship's clearance through customs. Be patient—it takes a long time to unload and sort thousands of pieces of luggage. Passengers are disembarked by groups according to the color-coded tags placed on luggage the night before; those with the earliest flights get off first. If you have a tight connection, notify the purser before the last day, and he or she may be able to arrange faster preclearing and debarkation for you.

Customs and Duties

U.S. Customs Before your ship lands, each individual or family must fill out a customs declaration, regardless of whether anything was purchased abroad. If you have fewer than $1,400 worth of goods, you will not need to itemize purchases. Be prepared to pay whatever duties are owed directly to the customs inspector, with cash or check.

U.S. Customs now preclears a number of ships sailing in and out of Miami and other ports—it's done on the ship before you disembark. In other ports you must collect your luggage from the dock, then stand in line to pass through the inspection point. This can take up to an hour.

Allowances. You may bring home $400 worth of foreign goods duty-free if you've been out of the country for at least 48 hours and haven't already used the $400 exemption, or any part of it, in the past 30 days. Note that these are the *general* rules, applicable to most countries; if you're returning from a cruise that called in the U.S. Virgin Islands, the duty-free allowance is higher—$1,200.

Alcohol and Tobacco. Travelers 21 or older may bring back 1 liter of alcohol duty-free, provided the beverage laws of the state through which they reenter the United States allow it. In the case of the U.S. Virgin Islands, 5 liters are allowed. In addition, 100 non-Cuban cigars and 200 cigarettes are allowed, regardless of your age. From the U.S. Virgin Islands, 1,000 cigarettes are allowed, but only 200 of them may have been acquired elsewhere. Antiques and works of art more than 100 years old are duty-free.

Gifts. Duty-free, travelers may mail packages valued at up to $200 to themselves, up to $100 to others with a limit of one parcel per addressee per day (including alcohol or tobacco products or perfume valued at up to $5); mark the package "For Personal Use" or "Unsolicited Gift" and write the nature of the gift and its retail value on the outside.

For More Information. For a copy of "Know Before You Go," a free brochure detailing what you may and may not bring back to the United States, rates of duty, and other pointers, contact the **U.S. Customs Service** (Box 7407, Washington, DC 20044, tel. 202/927–6724).

Canadian Customs

Allowances. If you've been out of Canada for at least seven days, you may bring in C$500 worth of goods duty-free. If you've been away less than seven days but more than 48 hours, the duty-free exemption drops to C$200. You cannot pool exemptions with family members. Goods claimed under the C$500 exemption may follow you by mail; those claimed under the lesser exemption must accompany you.

Alcohol and Tobacco. Alcohol and tobacco products may be included in the seven-day and 48-hour exemption. If you meet the age requirements of the province or territory through which you reenter Canada, you may bring in, duty-free, 1.14 liters (40 imperial ounces) of wine or liquor *or* two dozen 12-ounce cans or bottles of beer or ale. If you are 16 or older, you may bring in, duty-free, 200 cigarettes, 50 cigars or cigarillos, and 400 tobacco sticks or 400 grams of manufactured tobacco. Alcohol and tobacco must accompany you on your return.

Gifts. An unlimited number of gifts valued up to C$60 each may be mailed to Canada duty-free. These do not count as part of your exemption. Label the package "Unsolicited Gift—Value Under $60." Alcohol and tobacco are excluded.

For More Information. For additional information, including details of duties on items that exceed your duty-free limit, contact Revenue Canada (2265 St. Laurent Blvd. S, Ottawa, Ontario K1G 4K3, tel. 613/993–0534) for a copy of the free brochure "I Declare/Je Déclare." For recorded information (within Canada only), call 800/461–9999.

U.K. Customs **Allowances.** When returning from cruises that called at countries outside the European Union, you may import duty-free 200 cigarettes, 100 cigarillos, 50 cigars or 250 grams of tobacco; 1 liter of spirits or 2 liters of fortified or sparkling wine or liquer; 2 liters of still table wine; 60 milliliters of perfume; 250 milliliters of toilet water; plus £136 worth of other goods, including gifts and souvenirs.

For More Information. For further information or a copy of "A Guide for Travellers," which details standard customs procedures as well as what you may bring into the United Kingdom from abroad, contact HM Customs and Excise (Dorset House, Stamford St., London SE1 9NG, tel. 0171/202–4227).

U.S. Customs for Foreigners If you hold a foreign passport and will be returning home within hours of docking, you may be exempt from all U.S. Customs duties. Everything you bring into the United States must leave with you when you return home. When you reach your own country, you will have to pay appropriate duties there.

2 Ports of Call

Going Ashore

Traveling by cruise ship presents an opportunity to visit many different places in a short time. The flip side is that your stay will be limited in each port of call. For that reason, cruise lines invented shore excursions, which maximize passengers' time by organizing their touring for them. There are a number of advantages to shore excursions: In some destinations, transportation may be unreliable, and a ship-packaged tour is the best way to see distant sights. Also, you don't have to worry about being stranded or missing the ship. The disadvantage is that you will pay more for the convenience of having the ship do the legwork for you. Of course, you can always book a tour independently, hire a taxi, or use foot power to explore on your own.

Disembarking

When your ship arrives in a port, it either ties up alongside a dock or anchors out in a harbor. If the ship is docked, passengers just walk down the gangway to go ashore. Docking makes it easy to go back and forth between the shore and the ship.

Tendering If your ship anchors in the harbor, however, you will have to take a small boat—called a launch or tender—to get ashore. Tendering is a nuisance. When your ship first arrives in port, everyone wants to go ashore. Often, in order to avoid a stampede at the tenders, you must gather in a public room, get a boarding pass, and wait until your number is called. This continues until everybody has disembarked. Even then, it may take 15–20 minutes to get ashore if your ship is anchored far offshore. Because tenders can be difficult to board, passengers with mobility problems may not be able to visit certain ports. The larger the ship, the more likely it will use tenders. It is usually possible to learn before booking a cruise whether the ship will dock or anchor at its ports of call. (For more information about where and whether ships dock, tender, or both, *see* Coming Ashore for each port, *below*.)

Before anyone is allowed to walk down the gangway or board a tender, the ship must first be cleared for landing. Immigration and customs officials board the vessel to examine passports and sort through red tape. It may be more than an hour before you're actually allowed ashore. You will be issued a boarding pass, which you must have with you to get back on board.

Returning to the Ship

Cruise lines are strict about sailing times, which are posted at the gangway and elsewhere as well as announced in the daily schedule of activities. Be certain to be back on board at least a half hour before the announced sailing time or you may be stranded. If you are on a shore excursion that was sold by the cruise line, however, the captain will wait for your group before casting off. If the ship must leave without you, the cruise company will fly you, at its expense, to the next port. That is one reason many passengers prefer ship-packaged tours.

If you are not on one of the ship's tours and the ship does sail without you, immediately contact the cruise line's port representative, whose name and phone number are often listed on the daily schedule of activities. You may be able to hitch a ride on a pilot boat, though that is unlikely. Passengers who miss the boat must pay their own way to the next port of call.

The Bahamas

The Bahamas is an archipelago of more than 700 islands that begins in the Atlantic Ocean off the coast of Florida and stretches in a great southeasterly arc for more than 750 miles to the Caribbean Sea. Each island is bordered by soft, white-sand beaches lined with whispering casuarinas and swaying palms. Offshore, the islands are fringed by coral reefs and surrounded by a palette of blue and green waters of unbelievable clarity.

Fewer than 250,000 people live in the Bahamas, most of them in the two major urban resort centers of Nassau and Freeport. The Bahamas are one of cruising's most popular destinations.

Three- and four-day cruises from Florida to Nassau and Freeport are a big hit among young and budget-conscious travelers. Many cruise lines also include a port call in the Bahamas as part of a longer sailing, sometimes for a beach party or barbecue at one of several isolated Bahamian islands. For some passengers, these excursions are the highlight of a cruise. One of the best such destinations is Blue Lagoon Island (also called Sale Cay). It is used by Dolphin and Premier. (For seasonal itineraries, *see* Chapter 3.)

A cruise to the Bahamas is ideal for first-time cruisers, shopping fanatics, beach bums, and party goers. You can sail and scuba dive all day and, if your ship ties up overnight, gamble and dance well into the evening. But don't expect an unspoiled paradise: Nassau and Freeport/Lucaya are crowded and far less scenic than most Caribbean islands.

When to Go Winter, from mid-December through April, is the traditional high season. However, Bahamas cruises are offered all year, and the weather remains consistently mild, in the 70s and 80s. The Goombay Summer, from June through August, is filled with social, cultural, and sporting events. June through October is the rainy season, and humidity is high.

Currency The Bahamian dollar is held at a par with the U.S. dollar, and the two currencies are used interchangeably. Be sure to request U.S. dollars and coins when you receive change, however. Traveler's checks and major credit cards are accepted by most fine restaurants and stores.

Passports and Visas U.S., Canadian, and British citizens do not need passports or visas if they have proof of citizenship; however, a passport is preferable.

Telephones and Mail Long-distance credit-card and collect calls can be made from most public phones. Airmail rates to the United States and Canada are 55¢ for first-class letters and 40¢ for postcards.

Shore Excursions Many ships offer excursions to a casino for round-the-clock gaming action and various other forms of entertainment, including elaborate floor shows and topless revues. Some ships stay overnight in Freeport or Nassau.

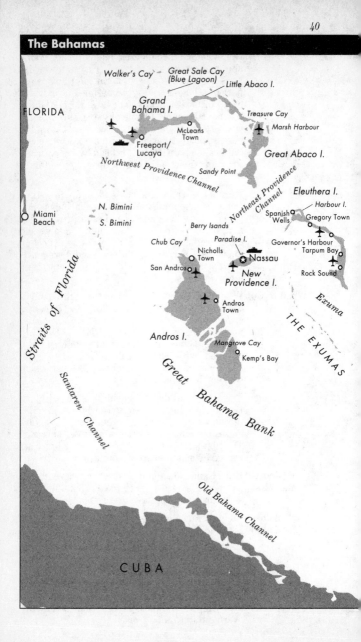

The Bahamas

FLORIDA

Walker's Cay
Great Sale Cay
(Blue Lagoon)
Little Abaco I.
Grand Bahama I.
Treasure Cay
Marsh Harbour
McLeans Town
Freeport/Lucaya
Great Abaco I.
Northwest Providence Channel
Sandy Point

Miami Beach

N. Bimini
S. Bimini

Berry Isands

Northeast Providence Channel

Eleuthera I.
Harbour I.
Spanish Wells
Gregory Town
Governor's Harbour
Tarpum Bay
Rock Sound

Chub Cay
Paradise I.
Nicholls Town
Nassau
San Andros
New Providence I.

Straits of Florida

Andros Town

Andros I.
Mangrove Cay
Kemp's Bay

THE EXUMAS

Exuma

Great Bahama Bank

Santaren Channel

Old Bahama Channel

CUBA

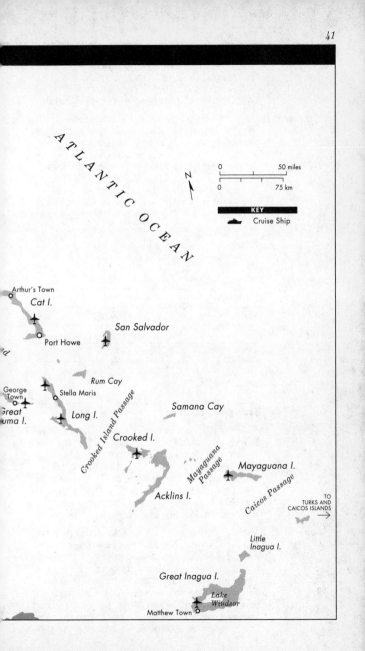

In addition, many ships offer shopping excursions. Both Freeport and Nassau have a host of malls and stores (*see below*). Water sports are a major draw, and most ships offer snorkeling or boat trips to outlying islands, as well as fishing.

Shopping Duty-free bargains in the Bahamas include imported china, crystal, leather, electronics, sweaters, liquor, watches, and perfume. Figure a 25% savings on most goods and a 35%–60% savings on liquor. Though no store will deliver to your ship, most shopping is within a 10-minute walk of the pier. Most stores are open Monday–Saturday 9–5; some close at noon on Thursday.

Dining Most Bahamian restaurants have adopted the European custom of adding a service charge to your bill—usually 15%, sometimes as little as 10%.

Category	Cost*
$$$	over $30
$$	$20–$30
$	under $20

per person for a three-course meal, excluding drinks and service

Freeport/Lucaya

Freeport is on Grand Bahama Island, the fourth-largest island in the archipelago. Its 530-square-mile interior is heavily forested with palmettos, casuarinas, and Caribbean pines. The 96-mile southern coastline is made up of sheltered harbors bordered by miles of unspoiled white-sand beaches and fringed with a nearly unbroken line of spectacular reefs.

Virtually unknown and unpopulated a generation ago, Grand Bahama was developed in the early 1950s. Modern, well-planned Freeport is the centerpiece of Grand Bahama. Its boulevards and shops are linked by a palm-lined road to Lucaya, a suburb set among thousands of acres of tropical greenery that sprawls along canals and ocean beach. Scattered here and there are hotels, the International Bazaar, four golf courses, two casinos, and Port Lucaya, the new shopping mall/tourist area.

Shore Excursions
The following is a good choice in Freeport. It may not be offered by all cruise lines. Time and price are approximate.

Freeport Shopping & Sightseeing Tour. This bus trip covers about 26 miles round-trip, stopping along the way for a half hour at the Garden of the Groves and for shopping at the International Bazaar. *3 hrs. Cost: $12.*

Coming Ashore
The cruise-ship harbor is an industrial center in the middle of nowhere. A cab from the cruise-ship piers to downtown costs $10 for two passengers. A Bahamas Ministry of Tourism office is at the port, but depending on where your ship is berthed, it may be a short walk across the parking lot or a long hike. You'll also find a Ministry of Tourism Information Center at the International Bazaar on West Sunrise Highway. Pick up maps, brochures, and information from either office.

Getting Around
Everything in Freeport/Lucaya is far apart, so you need to sign up for a shore excursion, take a cab, or rent a car or moped.

By Bus
Buses serve downtown Freeport and Lucaya; the fare is about 75¢. Service between Freeport and Lucaya costs $1.

By Car
Car rentals average $60–$85 daily, and a significant deposit is required. In Lucaya, contact **Avis** (tel. 242/373–1102).

By Bicycle, Moped, or Scooter
Rental mopeds and bicycles are available dockside in Freeport. Rates for bicycles start at about $10 per day, with a $50 deposit; scooters cost $40 per day with a $50–$100 deposit. Helmets are mandatory.

By Taxi
Metered taxis meet all the incoming cruise ships. Rates are $2 for the first ¼ mile and 30¢ for each additional ¼ mile. A taxi tour costs $12–$18 an hour, but rates for longer trips are negotiable. Always settle the fare in advance. Taxis are also available in most major tourist areas. Try **Freeport Taxi** (tel. 242/352–6666).

Exploring
Freeport/
Lucaya

Numbers in the margin correspond to points of interest on the Freeport/Lucaya map.

You will enjoy driving or riding around Freeport/Lucaya as long as you remember to drive on the left. Broad, landscaped "dual carriageways"—British for highways—and tree-lined streets wind through parks, past lovely homes, and along lush, green fairways.

❶ **Churchill Square** and the Freeport town center is where residents shop and tend to business. If you're hungry, **Mum's Coffee Shop and Bakery,** at 7 Yellow Pine Street, has delicious homemade breads, soups, and sandwiches. Head north on the Mall to Settler's Way East, then turn right **❷** and follow the tree-lined highway to the **Rand Memorial Nature Center.** The 100-acre park, composed of natural woodland, preserves more than 400 indigenous varieties of subtropical plants, trees, and flowers. It is also a sanctuary for thousands of native and migratory birds. A mile of well-marked nature trails leads to a 30-foot waterfall. Guided walks are conducted by the resident naturalists.

Leaving the nature center, continue east on Settler's Way, then turn south (right) onto West **❸** Beach Road to the **Garden of the Groves** (admission free; closed Wed.). The 11-acre park features some 5,000 varieties of rare and familiar subtropical and tropical trees, shrubs, plants, and flowers. Well-marked paths lead past clearly identified plants, a fern gully and grotto, and a tiny, stone interdenominational chapel.

From here, head for the sea, then turn right onto Royal Palm Way and drive until you come to **❹** the **Underwater Explorers Society** (UNEXSO), the famous scuba-diving school of the Bahamas, which trains more than 2,500 divers annually. *Tel. 242/373–1244. Dive lesson and 1 dive $89; snorkeling trip including all equipment $15. Open daily 8–6.*

❺ Within walking distance is **Lucayan Harbour,** with a 50-slip marina at which *El Galleon* is moored. This replica of a 16th-century Spanish galleon offers day and dinner cruises.

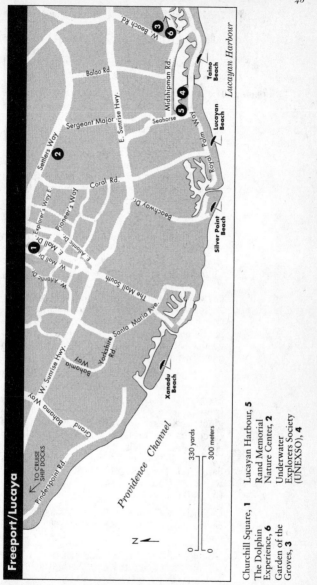

Freeport/Lucaya

Churchill Square, **1**
The Dolphin Experience, **6**
Garden of the Groves, **3**
Lucayan Harbour, **5**
Rand Memorial Nature Center, **2**
Underwater Explorers Society (UNEXSO), **4**

Providence Channel

Lucayan Harbour

Taino Beach

Lucayan Beach

Silver Point Beach

Xanadu Beach

W. Beach Rd.

Balao Rd.

Sergeant Major

E. Sunrise Hwy.

Settlers Way

Coral Rd.

Explorer's Way E.

Pioneer's Way

E. Mall Dr.

E. Atlantic Dr.

W. Mall Dr.

W. Atlantic Dr.

The Mall South

W. Sunrise Hwy.

Bohemia Way

Yorkshire Rd.

Santa Maria Ave.

Grand Bahama Way

Pindersport Rd.

TO CRUISE SHIP DOCKS

Midshipman Rd.

Seahorse

Royal Palm

Beachway Dr.

330 yards

300 meters

N

❻   The **Dolphin Experience** at Sanctuary Bay is the world's largest dolphin sanctuary. A $25 ferry ride from the UNEXSO dive shop takes you there to see the dolphins and take pictures. For $59, you can wade into the waist-deep water and cavort with the dolphins for about 20 minutes.

Shopping   The **International Bazaar and Straw Market** is on West Sunrise Highway, next to the Princess Casino. You enter through the 35-foot, red-lacquer Torii Gate, traditional symbol of welcome in Japan. Within the bazaar are a straw market and exotic shops with merchandise from around the world. Most items are priced at 20%–40% below U.S. *retail* prices, which means that you may or may not be getting a bargain when compared with prices in discount stores at home. Two dozen countries are represented in the 10-acre bazaar, with nearly a hundred shops. The vendors in the straw market expect you to haggle over the price, but don't bargain in the stores. For a less touristy experience, go to **Churchill Square** and the Freeport town center. An open-air produce market offers mangoes, papayas, and other fruit for snacking as you walk. To the east of Freeport is **Port Lucaya,** an attractive waterfront marketplace with 85 shops, boutiques, restaurants, and lounges. You'll need to drive or take a taxi to get here from downtown Freeport.

Sports   One of the most famous scuba schools and NAUI
Diving   centers in the world is the **Underwater Explorers Society** (UNEXSO), adjacent to Port Lucaya (*see* Exploring Freeport/Lucaya, *above*). Beginners can learn to dive for $89, which includes three hours of professional instruction in the club's training pools, and a shallow reef dive. For experienced divers, there are three trips daily (tel. 242/373–1244 or 800/992–3483, or write to UNEXSO, Box F-2433, Freeport, Grand Bahama).

Fishing   Contact **Reef Tours** (tel. 242/373–5880). Boat charters cost $300 for a half day, $600 for a full day.

Golf   Grand Bahama's four championship 18-hole courses are among the best in the Caribbean: **Bahamas Princess Hotel & Golf Club** (2 courses, tel. 242/352–6721), **Fortune Hills Golf & Coun-**

try Club (tel. 242/373–4500), and **Lucayan Golf & Country Club** (tel. 242/373–1066). Fees are about $35 for nine holes.

Parasailing
Windsurfing Contact the **Clarion Atlantik Beach** (Royal Palm Way, tel. 242/373–1444) or **Bahamas Sea Adventures** (at the Radisson Hotel, tel. 242/373–3923). Parasail rides cost $20–$25 for seven minutes. Windsurfing boards cost $10–$15 an hour; private lessons cost $25–$30.

Tennis Cruise passengers are welcome at several hotels. Try **Xanadu Beach Resort** (3 clay courts, tel. 242/352–6782) and the **Lucayan Beach Resort & Casino** (4 courts, tel. 242/373–7777). Court time costs $5 an hour.

Beaches The closest beach to the cruise-ship dock is **Xanadu Beach,** which has a mile of white-sand beach. South of Port Lucaya stretch three delightful beaches: **Fortune Beach, Smith's Point,** and **Taino Beach,** where sunbathers will also find the Stone Crab (tel. 242/373–1442)—a popular seafood restaurant.

Dining
$$ **Pub on the Mall.** Opposite the International Bazaar, this splendid English pub has authentic atmosphere and decor. The Prince of Wales Lounge serves good fish-and-chips and steak-and-kidney pie. Bass Ale is on tap. Baron's Hall serves superb dinners at night—try the coquilles St. Jacques, Cornish game hen, or roast beef with Yorkshire pudding. *At Ranfurly Circus, tel. 242/352–5110. AE, MC, V.*

$ **Pusser's Co. Store and Pub.** Fashioned after an old Welsh pub, this amiable establishment overlooking Port Lucaya is part bar, part restaurant, and part maritime museum. It has a nautical decor with antique copper measuring cups and Tiffany lamps suspended from the wood-beam ceiling. Locals swap tall tales and island gossip with tourists over rum-based Pusser's Painkillers. Solid English fare is favored: shepherd's pie, fisherman's pie, steak-and-ale pie. *Port Lucaya Marketplace, tel. 242/373–8450. AE, MC, V.*

Nassau

The 17th-century town of Nassau, the capital of the Bahamas, has witnessed Spanish invasions and hosted pirates, who made it their headquarters for raids along the Spanish Main. The new American Navy seized Ft. Montagu here in 1776, when they won a victory without firing a shot.

The cultural and ethnic heritage of old Nassau includes the Southern charm of British loyalists from the Carolinas, the African tribal traditions of freed slaves, and a bawdy history of blockade-running during the Civil War and rum-running in the Roaring Twenties. Over it all is a subtle layer of civility and sophistication, derived from three centuries of British rule.

Reminders of the island's British heritage are everywhere in Nassau. Court justices sport wigs and scarlet robes. The police wear colonial garb: starched white jackets, red-striped navy trousers, tropical pith helmets. Traffic keeps to the left, and the language has a British-colonial lilt, softened by a slight drawl. New Providence Island's charm, however, is often lost in its commercialism. Downtown Nassau's colonial facade is barely visible, painted over with duty-free-shop signs. Away from town, high-rise resorts and glittering casinos line the beaches. Lovely Old Nassau sold its soul to keep the tourists coming, and come they do in ever-increasing numbers.

Shore Excursions   The following are good choices in Nassau. They may not be offered by all cruise lines. Times and prices are approximate.

Undersea Creatures   **Coral World.** A 100-foot observation tower soars above the landscape, but the real views are of turtles, stingrays, and starfish. Budget about three hours, but you can stay as long as you want—the ferry back to the cruise-ship docks leaves every half hour. *Cost: $21 ($24 with ferry transfers).*

Snorkeling Adventure. The Bahamas is an underwater wonderland. On this tour you can learn to snorkel, then join an escorted tour or set off on your own. *2½–3 hrs. Cost: $20–$25.*

Coming Ashore   Cruise ships dock at one of three piers on Prince George's Wharf. Taxi drivers who meet the ships may offer you a $2 ride into town, but the historic government buildings and duty-free shops lie just outside the dock area. The one- or two-block walk takes 5 to 10 minutes. As you leave the pier, look for a tall pink tower: Diagonally across from here is the tourist information office. Stop in for maps of the island and downtown Nassau. On most days you can join a free one-hour walking tour conducted by well-trained guides. Outside the office, an ATM dispenses U.S. dollars.

Getting Around
By Bus — Jitney service runs to most points on the island. Walk from the pier to Frederick Street between Bay Street and Woodes Rogers Walk to catch a bus. The fare is 75¢ and buses run until 8:30 PM.

By Carriage — Across from the docks, along Rawson Square, surreys drawn by straw-hatted horses will take you through the old city and past some nearby historic sites. The cost is $10 for two for 25 minutes, but verify prices before getting on.

By Car — Car-rental rates begin at $50 a day; a substantial deposit is required. **Hertz** (tel. 242/327–6866) has an office in downtown Nassau.

By Ferry — A ferry commutes between the dock area and Paradise Island ($2 round-trip). Another goes to Coral World ($3 round-trip).

By Scooter — Scooters may be rented as you exit Prince George's Wharf. Rates average $25 per half day, $40 per full day. Helmets are mandatory.

By Touring Car or Taxi — As you disembark from your ship you will find a row of taxis and luxurious air-conditioned limousines. The latter are Nassau's fleet of tour cars, useful and comfortable for a guided tour of the island. Taxi fares are fixed at $2 for the first ¼ mile, 30¢ each additional ¼ mile. Sightseeing tours cost about $20–$25 per hour.

Exploring Nassau — *Numbers in the margin correspond to points of interest on the Nassau map.*

❶ ❷ As you leave the cruise wharf, you enter **Rawson Square**. Directly across Bay Street is **Parliament Square**. Dating from the early 1800s and patterned after southern U.S. colonial architecture, this cluster of yellow, colonnaded buildings with green shutters is striking. In the center of the square is a statue of the young Queen Victoria, and the **Bahamas House of Parliament**.

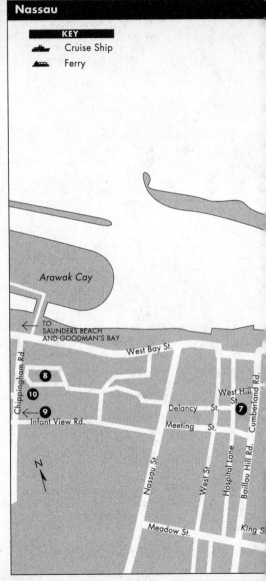

Ardastra Gardens
and Zoo, **9**
Ft.
Charlotte, **8**
Ft. Fincastle, **4**
Graycliff, **7**
Gregory
Arch, **6**
Nassau Botanic
Gardens, **10**
Parliament
Square, **2**
Queen's
Staircase, **3**
Rawson
Square, **1**
Water
Tower, **5**

Nassau

KEY

⛴ Cruise Ship

⛴ Ferry

Arawak Cay

← TO
SAUNDERS BEACH
AND GOODMAN'S BAY

West Bay St.

Chippingham Rd.

8

10

← **9**
Infant View Rd.

West Hill
St.

Delancy St. **7**

Meeting St.

Cumberland Rd.

Baillou Hill Rd.

Hospital Lane

Nassau St.

West St.

N

Meadow St.

King S

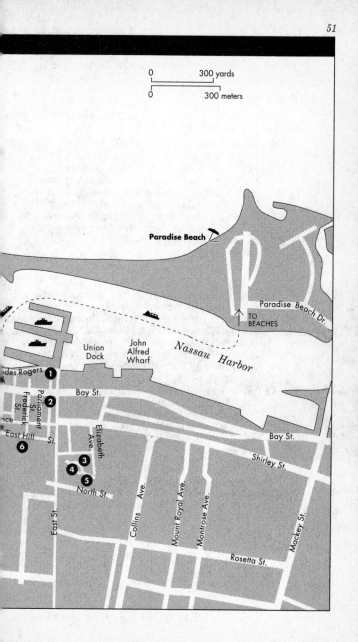

0   300 yards

0   300 meters

Paradise Beach

Paradise Beach Dr.

TO
BEACHES

Nassau Harbor

odes Rogers ❶

Union
Dock

John
Alfred
Wharf

Parliament
St.

Bay St.

❷

Frederick
St.

nce

East Hill

❻

Elizabeth
Ave.

St.

❸

❹

❺

North St.

Bay St.

Shirley St.

Collins Ave.

Mount Royal Ave.

Montrose Ave.

Mackey St.

East St.

Rosetta St.

❸ At the head of Elizabeth Avenue is the **Queen's Staircase,** a famous Nassau landmark. Its 66 steps, hewn from the coral limestone cliff by slaves in the late 18th century, were designed to provide a direct route between town and **Ft. Fincastle** at the top of the hill. The staircase was named more than a hundred years later, in honor of the 66 years of Queen Victoria's reign.

❹ Climb the staircase to reach **Ft. Fincastle.** The fort, shaped like the bow of a ship, was built in 1793. It never fired a shot in anger but served as a lookout and signal tower. For a really spectacular view of the island of New Providence, climb the 225 steps (or ride the elevator) to the top of ❺ the nearby **Water Tower.** Rising to 126 feet, more than 200 feet above sea level, the tower is the highest point on the island.

Head back toward the harbor to Parliament Street. At No. 48 you'll find **Green Shutters,** a charming Bahamian house from 1865, converted into an English-style pub (*see* Dining, *below*). On East Hill Street, you'll see historic mansions. Just beyond the **Bank House,** on the north side of the street, is a broad flight of stairs that leads down to Prince Street. Here are two historic churches, **St. Andrew's Kirk, Presbyterian** (1810) and **Trinity Methodist** (1866). Continue west along Prince Street. As you pass Market ❻ Street look up the hill for a good view of **Gregory Arch,** the picturesque entrance to **Grant's Town.** Known as the "over-the-hill" section of Nassau, Grant's Town was laid out in the 1820s by Governor Lewis Grant as a settlement for freed slaves.

On Duke Street, follow the high Government House wall around the corner to Baillou (pronounced blue) Hill Road. Take West Hill Street; ❼ across Baillou Hill is the **Graycliff** hotel, a superb example of Georgian colonial architecture, dating from the mid-1700s, that now houses a gourmet restaurant.

Next, visit the most interesting fort on the island, ❽ **Ft. Charlotte,** built in 1787 replete with a waterless moat, a drawbridge, ramparts, and dungeons. Like Ft. Fincastle, no shots were ever fired in anger from this fort. Ft. Charlotte is located at the top of a hill and commands a fine view of Nassau Harbor and Arawak Cay, a small, man-made island that holds huge storage tanks of fresh water barged in from Andros Island. *Off W. Bay St. at Chippingham Rd., tel. 242/322–7500. Admission free. Local guides conduct tours Mon.–Sat. 8:30–4.*

9 A block farther west, on Chippingham Road, are the **Ardastra Gardens and Zoo,** with 5 acres of tropical greenery and flowering shrubs, an aviary of rare tropical birds, and exotic animals from different parts of the world. The gardens are renowned for the pink, spindly legged, marching flamingos that perform daily at 11, 2, and 4. The flamingo, by the way, is the national bird of the Bahamas. *Near Ft. Charlotte, off Chippingham Rd., tel. 242/323–5806. Admission: $7.50. Open daily 9–5.*

10 Across the street is the **Nassau Botanic Gardens.** On its 18-acre grounds are 600 species of flowering trees and shrubs; two freshwater ponds with lilies, water plants, and tropical fish; and a small cactus garden that ends in a grotto. The many trails wandering through the gardens are perfect for leisurely strolls. *Near Ft. Charlotte, off Chippingham Rd., tel. 242/323–5975. Admission: $1. Open daily 8–4:30.*

Shopping   *Forbes* magazine once claimed that the two cities in the world with the best buys on wristwatches were Hong Kong and Nassau. Most of the stores selling these and other duty-free items are clustered along an eight-block stretch of Bay Street in Old Nassau or spill over onto a few side streets downtown. Most stores are open Monday–Saturday 9–5; some close at noon on Thursday. The straw market is open seven days a week. Most shops accept major credit cards.

If you're interested in old-fashioned maps and prints, seek out **Balmain Antiques** (tel. 242/323–7421). Though located on Bay Street, it's a little hard to find: The doorway to the second-floor gallery is set off from the sidewalk on the side of the building.

Sports   Contact **Chubasco Charters** (tel. 242/322–8148)
Fishing   or **Brown's Charters** (tel. 242/324–1215). Boat charters cost $300 for a half day, $600 for a full day.

Golf Three excellent 18-hole championship courses are open to the public: **Crystal Palace Golf Course** (opposite the Wyndham Ambassador Hotel, tel. 242/327–6000, 800/222–7466 in the United States), **Paradise Island Golf Club** (eastern end of Paradise Island, tel. 242/363–3925, 800/321–3000 in the United States), and **South Ocean Beach & Golf Resort** (adjacent to Divi Bahamas Beach Resort, tel. 242/362–4391). Fees are $45–$70 for 18 holes, $22–$27 for nine holes.

Parasailing Windsurfing is available at **Le Meridien Royal**
Windsurfing **Bahamian Hotel** (tel. 242/327–6400). Board rental costs $12 an hour; lessons cost $30. Parasailing is available from **Sea Sports Ltd.** (in front of the Nassau Beach Hotel, tel. 242/327–6058). A six-minute ride costs $30.

Beaches **Paradise Beach,** the Bahamas' most famous beach, stretches for more than a mile on the western end of Paradise Island. The $3 admission includes a welcome drink, towels, and the use of changing rooms and locker. The **Western Esplanade** sweeps westward from the British Colonial Hotel on Bay Street (a 10-minute walk from the cruise-ship pier). It's just across the street from shops and restaurants, and it has rest rooms, a snack bar, and changing facilities. A little farther west, just past the bridge that leads to Coral World, is **Saunders Beach. Goodman's Bay,** a bit farther west of Saunders, is popular with Bahamians for picnics and cookouts on weekends and holidays.

Dining **Graycliff.** Situated in a magnificent, 200-year-
$$$ old colonial mansion, Graycliff is filled with antiques and English country-house charm. The outstanding Continental and Bahamian menu includes beluga caviar, grouper *au poivre vert,* and chateaubriand, with elegant pastries and flaming coffees for dessert. The wine cellar is excellent. *W. Hill St., across from Government House, tel. 242/322–2796 or 800/633–7411. Reservations essential. Jacket required. AE, DC, MC, V.*

$$ **Green Shutters.** Shades of Fleet Street! This very British pub is a cozy place awash with wood paneling. Steak-and-kidney pie, bangers and mash, and shepherd's pie are featured alongside such island favorites as cracked conch and Baha-

mian crawfish tail. *48 Parliament St., tel. 242/ 325-5702. AE, MC, V.*

$$ Poop Deck. Coiled rope wraps around beams, life preservers hang on the walls, and port and starboard lights adorn the newel posts of this favorite haunt of Nassau residents. Tables overlook the harbor and Paradise Island. Cuisine is exceptional Bahamian-style seafood, served in a festive, friendly atmosphere. The food is spicy, the wine list extensive. Save room for guava duff, a warm guava-layered local dessert, and a Calypso coffee, spiked with secret ingredients. *E. Bay St. (an 8-min cab ride from pier), tel. 242/393-8175. AE, DC, MC, V.*

$ Shoal Restaurant and Lounge. Saturday mornings at 9 you'll find hordes of jolly Bahamians digging into boiled fish and johnnycake, the marvelous specialty of the house. A bowl of this peppery dish, filled with chunks of boiled potatoes, onions, and grouper, keeps the locals coming back to this dimly lit, basic, and off-the-tourist-beat "Ma's kitchen," where standard Nassau dishes, including peas 'n' rice and cracked conch, are served. If it suits you, you'll find native mutton here, too, which is sometimes hard to find. *Nassau St., tel. 242/323-4400. Reservations not accepted. AE.*

Nightlife Some ships stay late into the night or until the next day so that passengers can enjoy Nassau's nightlife. You'll find nonstop entertainment nightly along Cable Beach and on Paradise Island. All the larger hotels offer lounges with island combos for listening or dancing, and restaurants with soft guitar or piano background music.

Casinos The three casinos on New Providence Island— **Crystal Palace Casino, Paradise Island Resort and Casino,** and **Ramada Inn Casino**—open early in the day, remain active into the wee hours of the morning, and offer Continental gambling and a variety of other entertainment. Visitors must be 18 or older to enter a casino, 21 or older to gamble.

Discos **Club Waterloo** (tel. 242/393-7324), on East Bay Street, is one of Nassau's most swinging nightspots. Disco and rock can be heard nightly at **Club Pastiche** (tel. 242/363-3000), at the Paradise Island Resort and Casino.

The **Drum Beat Club** (tel. 242/322–4233) on West Bay Street, just up from the Best Western British Colonial Hotel, features the legendary Peanuts Taylor, still alive and well and beating away at those tom-toms; his band and gyrating dancers put on two shows nightly at 8:30 and 10:30.

Caribbean

Nowhere in the world are conditions better suited to cruising than in the ever-warm, treasure-filled Caribbean Sea. Tiny island nations, within easy sailing distance of one another, form a chain of tropical enchantment that curves from Cuba in the north all the way down to the coast of Venezuela. There is far more to life here than sand and coconuts, however. The islands are vastly different, with their own cultures, topographies, and languages. Colonialism has left its mark, and the presence of the Spanish, French, Dutch, Danish, and British is still felt. Slavery, too, has left its cultural legacy, blending African overtones into the colonial/Indian amalgam. The one constant, however, is the weather. Despite the islands' southerly position, the climate is surprisingly gentle, due in large part to the cooling influence of the trade winds.

The Caribbean is made up of the Greater Antilles and the Lesser Antilles. The former consists of those islands closest to the United States: Cuba, Jamaica, Hispaniola (Haiti and the Dominican Republic), and Puerto Rico. (The Cayman Islands lie south of Cuba.) The Lesser Antilles, including the Virgin, Windward, and Leeward islands and others, are greater in number but smaller in size, and constitute the southern half of the Caribbean chain. Cruise lines often include Caracas, Venezuela, and Mexico's Yucatán Peninsula in their Caribbean itineraries as well.

More cruise ships ply these waters than any others in the world. There are big ships and small ships, fancy ships and party ships. In peak season, it is not uncommon for several ships to disembark thousands of passengers into a small town on the same day—a phenomenon not always enjoyed by locals. Despite some overcrowding, however, the abundance of cruise ships in the area allows you to choose the itinerary that suits you best. Whether it's shopping or scuba diving, fishing or sunbathing, you're sure to find the Caribbean cruise of your dreams. (For seasonal itineraries, *see* Chapter 3.)

When to Go Average year-round temperatures throughout the Caribbean are 78°F–85°F, with a low of 65°F and a high of 95°F; downtown shopping areas always seem to be unbearably hot. High season runs from December 15 to April 14; during this most fashionable, most expensive, and most crowded time to go, reservations up to a year in advance are necessary for many ships. A low-season (summer) visit offers certain advantages: Temperatures are virtually the same as in winter (even cooler on average than in parts of the U.S. mainland), island flora is at its height, and the water is smoother and clearer. Some tourist facilities close down in summer, however, and many ships move to Europe, Alaska, or the northeastern United States.

Hurricane season runs from June through October. Although cruise ships stay well out of the way of these storms, hurricanes and tropical storms—their less-powerful relatives—can affect the weather throughout the Caribbean for days, and damage to ports can force last-minute itinerary changes.

Currency Currencies vary throughout the islands, but U.S. dollars are widely accepted. Don't bother changing more than a few dollars into local currency for phone calls, tips, and taxis.

Passports and Visas American citizens boarding ships in the United States usually need neither a passport nor visas to call at ports in the Caribbean. However, carrying a passport is always a good idea. Citizens of Canada and the United Kingdom should consult with their travel agent or cruise line regarding any documentation they may need for a Caribbean cruise.

Shore Excursions Typical excursions include a bus tour of the island or town, a visit to a local beach or liquor factory, boat trips, snorkeling or diving, and charter fishing. As far as island tours go, it's al-

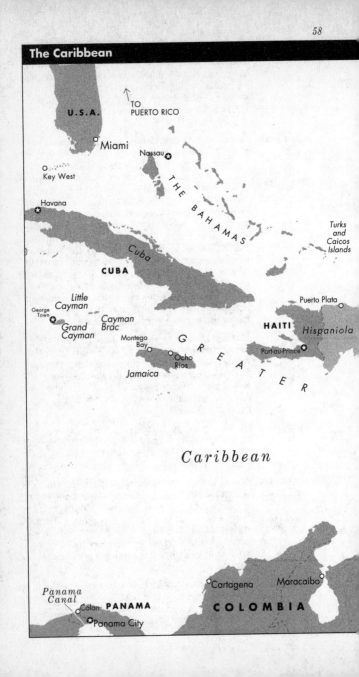

The Caribbean

U.S.A.

TO PUERTO RICO

Miami

Key West

Nassau

THE BAHAMAS

Havana

Cuba

Turks and Caicos Islands

CUBA

Little Cayman

George Town

Grand Cayman

Cayman Brac

Puerto Plata

HAITI

Hispaniola

Montego Bay

G R E A T E R

Ocho Rios

Port-au-Prince

Jamaica

Caribbean

Cartagena

Maracaibo

Panama Canal

Colon

PANAMA

Panama City

COLOMBIA

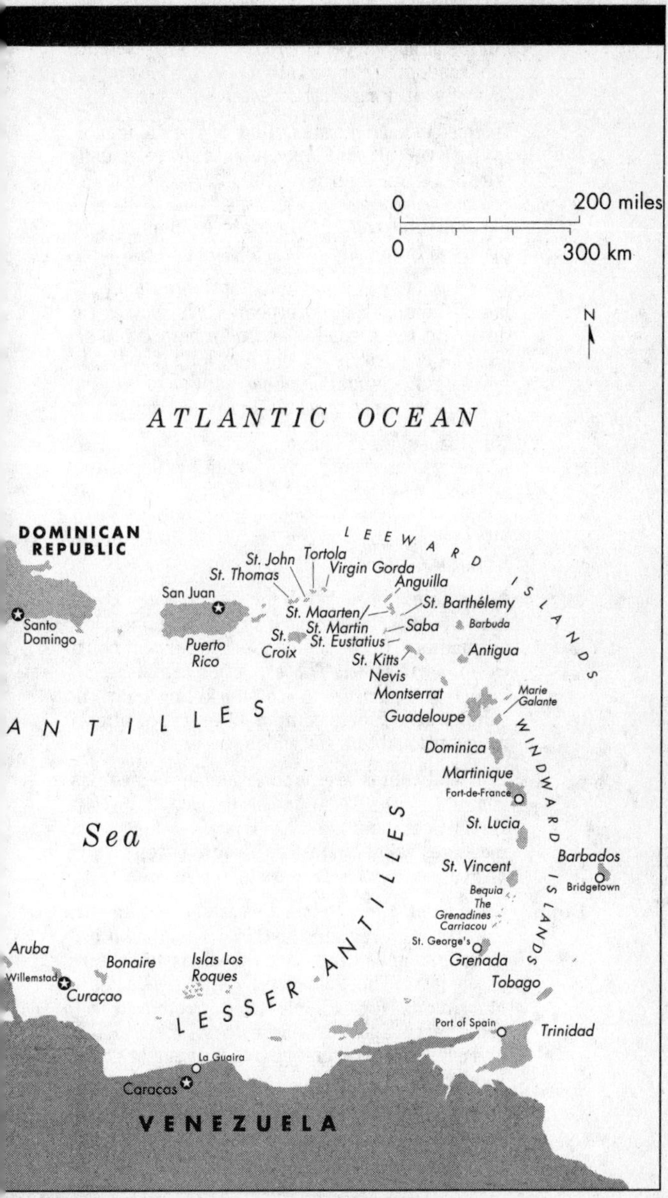
0
200 miles
0
300 km
N
ATLANTIC OCEAN
DOMINICAN REPUBLIC
Santo Domingo
San Juan
Puerto Rico
LEEWARD ISLANDS
St. John
Tortola
St. Thomas
Virgin Gorda
Anguilla
St. Barthélemy
St. Maarten/
St. Martin
Saba
Barbuda
St. Croix
St. Eustatius
St. Kitts
Nevis
Antigua
Montserrat
Marie Galante
Guadeloupe
ANTILLES
Dominica
WINDWARD ISLANDS
Martinique
Fort-de-France
St. Lucia
Sea
Barbados
Bridgetown
St. Vincent
Bequia
The Grenadines
Carriacou
St. George's
Grenada
Tobago
Aruba
Bonaire
Islas Los Roques
Willemstad
Curaçao
LESSER ANTILLES
Port of Spain
Trinidad
La Guaira
Caracas
VENEZUELA

ways safest to take a ship-arranged excursion, but it's almost never cheapest. You also sacrifice the freedom to explore at your own pace and the joys of venturing off the beaten path.

If you seek adventure, find a knowledgeable taxi driver or tour operator—they're usually within a stone's throw of the pier—and wander around on your own. A group of four to six people will find this option more economical and practical than will a single person or a couple.

Renting a car is also a good option on many islands—again, the more people, the better the deal. But get a good island map before you set off, and be sure to find out how long it will take you to get around. The boat will leave without you unless you're on a ship-arranged tour.

Conditions are ideal for water sports of all kinds; scuba diving, snorkeling, windsurfing, sailing, waterskiing, and fishing excursions abound. Your shore-excursion director can usually arrange these activities for you individually if the ship offers no formal excursion.

Many ships throw beach parties on a private island or an isolated beach in the Bahamas, the Grenadines, or (depending on the current political climate) Haiti. These parties are either included in your fare, with snorkeling gear and other water-sports equipment extra, or offered as an optional tour for which you pay.

Golf and tennis are popular among cruise passengers, and several lines—particularly NCL, Royal Caribbean, and Seabourn—offer special packages ashore. Most golf courses rent clubs, although many passengers bring their own.

Dining Cuisine on the Caribbean's islands is hard to classify. The region's history as a colonial battleground and ethnic melting pot creates plenty of variety. The gourmet French delicacies of Martinique, for example, are far removed from the hearty Spanish casseroles of Puerto Rico and even farther from the pungent curries of St. Lucia.

The one quality that defines most Caribbean cooking is its essential spiciness. Seafood is naturally quite popular. Some of it is even unique to

the region, such as Caribbean lobster: Clawless
and tougher than other types, it is more like
crawfish than Maine lobster. And no island
menu is complete without at least a half dozen
dishes featuring conch, a mollusk similar to es-
cargot that is served in the form of chowders,
fritters, salads, and cocktails. Dress is generally casual—though in Caracas men should not
wear shorts.

Category	Cost*
$$$	over $30
$$	$15–$30
$	under $15

*per person for a three-course meal, excluding
drinks, service, and sales tax*

Antigua

Some say Antigua has so many beaches that you
could visit a different one every day for a year.
Most have snow-white sand, and many are
backed by lavish resorts offering sailing, diving, windsurfing, and snorkeling.

The larger of the British Leeward Islands, Antigua was the headquarters from which Lord
Horatio Nelson made his forays against the
French and pirates in the late 18th century. A
decidedly British atmosphere still prevails, un-
derscored by a collection of pubs that will raise
the spirits of every Anglophile. Cruise passengers with a taste for history will want to explore
English Harbour and its carefully restored
Nelson's Dockyard, as well as tour an 18th-cen-
tury Royal Naval base, old forts, historic
churches, and tiny villages. Hikers can wander
through a tropical rain forest lush with pineap-
ples, bananas, and mangoes. Those of an archaeological bent will head for the megaliths of
Greencastle to seek out some of the 30 excavations of ancient Indian sites.

About 4,000 years ago Antigua was home to a
people called the Siboney. They disappeared
mysteriously, and the island remained uninhab-
ited for about 1,000 years. When Columbus
sighted the 108-square-mile island in 1493, the

Arawaks had already set up housekeeping. The English moved in 130 years later, in 1623. Then a sequence of bloody battles involving the Caribs, the Dutch, the French, and the English began. Africans had been captured as slaves to work the sugar plantations by the time the French ceded the island to the English in 1667. On November 1, 1981, Antigua, with its sister island 30 miles to the north, Barbuda, achieved full independence. The combined population of the two islands is about 90,000—only 1,200 of whom live on Barbuda.

Currency   Antigua uses the Eastern Caribbean (E.C.) dollar, commonly known as beewees. Figure about E.C. $2.70 to U.S. $1. U.S. dollars are generally accepted, but you may get your change in beewees.

Telephones   Calling the United States is a simple matter of dialing 1 to reach **AT&T**'s USADirect.

Shore   The following is a good choice in Antigua. It may
Excursions   not be offered by all cruise lines. Times and prices are approximate.

Island Sights   **Nelson's Dockyard and Clarence House.** Driving through Antigua's lush countryside, you will visit the 18th-century residence of the duke of Clarence. Then visit Nelson's Dockyard, a gem of Georgian British maritime architecture and a must for history buffs and Anglophiles. *3 hrs. Cost: $30–$40.*

If you want to feel like Indiana Jones, opt for a tour with **Tropikelly** (tel. 809/461–0383). You'll be given an insider's look at the whole island by four-wheel-drive, complete with deserted plantation houses, rain-forest trails, ruined sugar mills and forts, and even a picnic lunch with drinks. The highlight is the luxuriant tropical forest around the island's highest point, Boggy Peak. *5 hrs. Cost: $60.*

Coming   Though some ships dock at the deep-water har-
Ashore   bor in downtown St. John's, most use the town's Heritage Quay, a multimillion-dollar complex with shops, condominiums, a casino, and a food court. Most St. John's attractions are an easy walk from Heritage Quay; the older part of the city is eight blocks away. A tourist information booth is in the main docking building.

Getting Around Avoid public buses. They're unreliable and hard to find. If you don't want to explore St. John's on foot, hire a taxi. If you intend to tour beyond this port city consider renting a car or hiring a taxi driver/guide.

By Car To rent a car, you'll need a valid driver's license and a temporary permit, which is available through the rental agent for $12. Rentals average about $50 per day, with unlimited mileage. Driving is on the left, and Antiguan roads are generally unmarked and full of potholes. Rental agencies are on High Street in St. John's, or they can be called from the terminal. Contact **Budget** (tel. 809/462–3009 or 800/648–4985), **Carib Car Rentals** (tel. 809/462–2062), or **National** (tel. 809/462–2113 or 800/468–0008), all in St. John's.

By Taxi Taxis meet every cruise ship. They are unmetered; fares are fixed, and drivers are required to carry a rate card. Tip drivers 10%. All taxi drivers double as guides, and you can arrange an island tour for about $20 per person, for up to four passengers. A tour of the Royal Dockyard takes about three hours and costs up to $60 for four. The most reliable and informed driver-guides are at **Capital Car Rental** (High St., St. John's, tel. 809/462–0863).

Exploring Antigua *Numbers in the margin correspond to points of interest on the Antigua map.*

❶ **St. John's** is home to about 40,000 people (nearly half the island's population). The city has seen better days, but there are some notable sights.

At the far south end of town, where Market Street forks into Valley and All Saints roads, locals jam the **marketplace** every Friday and Saturday to buy and sell fruits, vegetables, fish, and spices. Be sure to ask before you aim a camera, and expect the subject of your shot to ask for a tip.

If you have a serious interest in archaeology, see the historical displays at the **Museum of Antigua and Barbuda.** The colonial building that houses the museum is the former courthouse, which dates from 1750. *Church and Market Sts., tel. 809/462–1469. Admission free. Open weekdays 8:30–4, Sat. 10–1.*

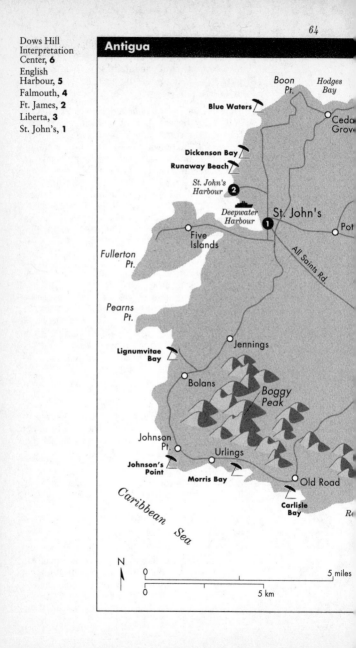

64

Antigua

Boon
Pt.

Hodges
Bay

Blue Waters

Ced
Grov

Dickenson Bay

Runaway Beach

*St. John's
Harbour* **2**

*Deepwater
Harbour*

St. John's **1**

Pot

All Saints Rd

Five
Islands

*Fullerton
Pt.*

*Pearns
Pt.*

**Lignumvitae
Bay**

Jennings

Bolans

*Boggy
Peak*

Johnson
Pt.

Urlings

**Johnson's
Point**

Morris Bay

Old Road

**Carlisle
Bay**

Re

*Caribbean
Sea*

N

0 ——————— 5 miles

0 ——————— 5 km

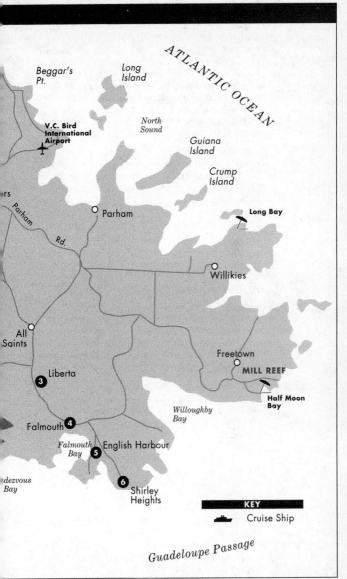

Beggar's Pt.

Long Island

ATLANTIC OCEAN

V.C. Bird International Airport

North Sound

Guiana Island

Crump Island

rs

Parham Rd.

Parham

Long Bay

Willikies

All Saints

Freetown

MILL REEF

3 Liberta

Half Moon Bay

Willoughby Bay

Falmouth **4**

Falmouth Bay **5** English Harbour

Rendezvous Bay

6 Shirley Heights

KEY	
🚢	Cruise Ship

Guadeloupe Passage

Two blocks east of the Museum of Antigua and Barbuda on Church Street is **St. John's Cathedral.** The Anglican church sits on a hilltop, surrounded by its churchyard. At the south gate are figures said to have been taken from one of Napoléon's ships. A previous structure on this site was destroyed by an earthquake in 1843, so the interior of the current church is completely encased in pitch pine to forestall heavy damage from future quakes. *Between Long and Newcastle Sts., tel. 809/461–0082. Admission free.*

A favorite car excursion is to follow Fort Road northwest out of town. After 2 miles you'll come ② to the ruins of **Ft. James,** named for King James II. If you continue on this road, you'll arrive at **Dickenson Bay,** with its string of smart, expensive resorts on one of the many beautiful beaches you will pass.

In the opposite direction from St. John's, 8 miles ③ south on All Saints Road is **Liberta,** one of the first settlements founded by freed slaves. East of the village, on Monk's Hill, are the ruins of Ft. George, built in 1669.

④ **Falmouth,** 1½ miles farther south, sits on a lovely bay, backed by former sugar plantations and sugar mills. St. Paul's Church, dating from the late 18th and early 19th centuries, held services for the military in Nelson's time; it has been restored and is now used for Sunday worship.

⑤ **English Harbour,** the most famous of Antigua's attractions, lies on the coast just south of Falmouth. The Royal Navy abandoned the station in 1889, but it has been restored as Nelson's Dockyard, which epitomizes the colonial Caribbean. Within the compound are crafts shops, hotels, a marina, and restaurants. The Admiral's House Museum has several rooms displaying ship models, a model of English Harbour, and various artifacts from Nelson's days. *Tel. 809/463–1053. Admission: $2. Open daily 8–6.*

The English Harbor area has a number of other attractions. On a ridge overlooking Nelson's Dockyard is Clarence House, built in 1787 and once the home of the duke of Clarence. As you leave the dockyard, turn right at the crossroads in English Harbour and drive up to Shirley

Heights for a spectacular harbor view. Nearby,
 the **Dows Hill Interpretation Center** chronicles
the island's history and culture from Amerindi-
an times to the present. A highlight of the center is its multimedia presentation in which
illuminated displays, incorporating lifelike figures and colorful tableaux, are presented with
running commentary, television, and music—
resulting in a cheery, if bland, portrait of Antiguan life. *Admission: E.C. $15. Open daily 9–
5.*

Shopping **Redcliffe Quay** and **Heritage Quay** are waterfront markets with boutiques, restaurants, and
snack bars. The main tourist shops in St. John's
are along **St. Mary's, High,** and **Long streets.** In
general, shops are open Monday–Saturday
8:30–noon and 1–4; some shops close for the day
at noon on Thursday and Saturday. The duty-
free shops of Heritage Quay cater to tourists
and often have more flexible hours; however,
you may find better deals at Redcliffe Quay.

At Redcliffe Quay, **Decibels** offers a veritable
United Nations of craftwork, from Creole
houses to Mexican raku pottery. For batiks, sarongs, and swimwear, try **Jacaranda. Base** is
where you'll find striped cotton-and-Lycra
beachwear from English designer Steven Giles;
his creations are all the rage on the island. At
the **Goldsmitty,** Hans Smit turns gold and pre-
cious and semiprecious stones into one-of-a-kind
works of art. **Windjammer Clothing** sells nauti-
cally inspired attire for men and women. **Noreen
Phillips,** across Redcliffe Street, creates glitzy
appliqued and beaded eveningwear inspired by
the colors of the sea and sunset.

In downtown St. John's, the **Map Shop** (St.
John's St.) has a wonderful collection of antique
maps and nautical books and charts, and **CoCo
Shop** sells Sea Island cotton designs, Daks
clothing, and Liberty of London fabrics. The **Ci-
gar Shop** (Heritage Quay) has Cuban cigars.
(These cannot be legally brought into the
United States.) You'll also find a wide range of
duty-free shops and factory-outlet stores, from
Body Shop to **Benetton, Polo** to **Gucci.**

Sports *Golf*	You'll find an 18-hole course at **Cedar Valley Golf Club** (tel. 809/462–0161).

Scuba Diving Antigua has plenty of wrecks, reefs, and marine life. **Dockyard Divers** (St. Johns, tel. 809/464–8591), run by British ex–merchant Captain A. G. Finchman, is one of the oldest and most reputable diving-snorkeling outfits on the island.

Beaches Antigua's 366 beaches are public, and many are dotted with resorts that provide water-sports-equipment rentals and a place to grab a cool drink. Since most hotels have taxi stands, you can get back to the ship easily. The following are just a few excellent possibilities: **Carlisle Bay**, where the Atlantic meets the Caribbean Sea, is a long, snow-white beach with the Curtain Bluff resort as a backdrop. A large coconut grove adds to its tropical beauty. **Dickenson Bay** has a lengthy stretch of powder-soft white sand and a host of hotels that cater to water-sports enthusiasts (most will rent snorkeling gear, sailboats, and Windsurfers to cruise passengers with a refundable deposit). **Half Moon Bay**, a ¾-mile crescent of shell-pink sand, is another great place for snorkeling and windsurfing. **Johnsons Point** is a deliciously deserted beach of bleached white sand on the southwest coast.

Dining *In restaurants a 10% service charge is usually added to the bill.*

$$ **Admiral's Inn.** Known simply as "The Ads" to yachtsmen around the world, this historic inn in the heart of English Harbour is a must for Anglophiles and mariners. Dine on curried conch, fresh snapper with lime, or lobster thermidor while taking in the splendid harbor views. *Nelson's Dockyard, tel. 809/460–1027. Reservations essential. AE, MC, V.*

$$ **Redcliffe Tavern.** Set amid the courtyards of Redcliffe Quay, on the second floor of a colonial warehouse, this appealing restaurant has an inventive menu that is part northern Italian, part Continental, part Creole, and all fresh. Antique water-pumping equipment, salvaged from all over the island, adds to the unusual dining experience. *Redcliffe Quay, St. John's, tel. 809/461–4557. AE, MC, V.*

Aruba

Though the "A" in the ABC (Aruba, Bonaire, Curaçao) Islands is small—only 19.6 miles long and 6 miles at its widest—the island's national anthem proclaims "the greatness of our people is their great cordiality," and this is no exaggeration. Once a member of the Netherlands Antilles, Aruba became independent within the Netherlands in 1986, with its own royally appointed governor, a democratic government, and a 21-member elected parliament. Long secure in a solid economy, with good education, housing, and health care, the island's population of about 81,500 regards tourists as welcome guests and treats them accordingly. Waiters serve you with smiles and solid eye contact. English is spoken everywhere. In addition to the ships that call at Aruba on southern Caribbean itineraries, the island is the home port for Seawind's *Seawind Crown*.

The island's distinctive beauty lies in the stark contrast between the sea and the countryside: rocky deserts, cactus jungles, secluded coves, and aquamarine panoramas with crashing waves. It's famous mostly, however, for its casinos.

Currency Arubans accept U.S. dollars, so you've no need to exchange money, except for pocket change for bus fare or pay phones. Local currency is the Aruban florin (AFl). At press time, U.S. $1 will get you AFl 1.77 cash or AFl 1.79 in traveler's checks. Note that the Netherlands Antilles florin used in Bonaire and Curaçao is not accepted on Aruba.

Telephones International calls are placed at the phone center in the cruise terminal. To reach the United States, dial 001, the area code, and the local number.

Shore Excursions The following are good choices on Aruba. They may not be offered by all cruise lines. Times and prices are approximate.

Island Sights **Aruba Town and Countryside Drive.** A comprehensive town-and-country bus tour takes in all the island sights. After the tour, passengers may stay in town, on the beach, or at the casino. *3 hrs. Cost: $25.*

Undersea *Creatures*	**Atlantis Submarine.** Aboard a 65-foot submarine, passengers dive 50–90 feet below the surface along Aruba's Barcadera Reef. *1½ hrs. Cost: $68.*

Glass-Bottom Boat Tour. The view of undersea creatures is less dramatic than aboard the *Atlantis* submarine, but the price is less expensive, too. *1½ hrs. Cost: $25.*

Coming Ashore Ships tie up at the Aruba Port Authority cruise terminal; inside are a tourist information booth and duty-free shops. From here, you're a five-minute walk from various shopping districts and downtown Oranjestad. Just turn right out of the cruise-terminal entrance.

Getting Around
By Bus Buses run hourly between the beach hotels and Oranjestad. They also stop across the street from the cruise terminal on L.G. Smith Boulevard. Round-trip fare is $1.50, exact change.

By Car It's easy to rent a car, Jeep, or motorbike in Aruba, and most roads are in excellent condition. Contact **Avis** (tel. 297/8–28787), **Budget** (tel. 297/8–28600), or **Hertz** (tel. 297/8–24545). Rates begin at about $45 a day.

By Taxi Taxis can be flagged down on the street. Because cabs have no meters, rates are fixed but should be confirmed before you get in. All drivers have participated in the government's Tourism Awareness Programs and have received a Tourism Guide Certificate. An hour tour of the island by taxi will cost about $35 for up to four people.

Exploring Aruba *Numbers in the margin correspond to points of interest on the Aruba map.*

❶ Aruba's charming capital, **Oranjestad,** is best explored on foot. If you're interested in Dutch architecture, begin at the corner of Oude School Straat and go three blocks toward the harbor to Wilhelminastraat, where some of the buildings date back to Oranjestad's 1790 founding. Walk west and you'll pass old homes, a government building, and the Protestant church. When you reach Shuttestraat again, turn left and go one block to Zoutmanstraat.

The small **Archaeology Museum** in Oranjestad has two rooms of Indian artifacts, farm and domestic utensils, and skeletons. *Zoutmanstraat 1, tel. 297/8–28979. Admission free. Open weekdays 8–noon and 1:30–4:30.*

Ft. Zoutman, the island's oldest building, was built in 1796 and used as a major fortress in skirmishes between British and Curaçao troops. The Willem III tower was added in 1868. The fort's Historical Museum displays island relics and artifacts in an 18th-century Aruban house. *Oranjestraat, tel. 297/8–26099. Admission: $1.25. Open weekdays 9–noon and 1:30–4:30.*

Just behind the St. Francis Roman Catholic Church is the **Numismatic Museum,** displaying coins and paper money from more than 400 countries. *Zuidstraat 27, tel. 297/8–28831. Admission free. Open weekdays 7:30–noon and 1–4:30.*

The "real" Aruba—or what's left of its wild, untamed beauty—can be experienced only by taking a car or taxi into the countryside. (Be aware that there are no public bathrooms anywhere, except in a few restaurants.)

❷ The 541-foot peak of **Hooiberg** (Haystack Hill) is located mid-island; you can climb 562 steps to the top for an impressive view. To get there from Oranjestad, turn onto Caya C.F. Croes (shown on island maps as 7A) toward Santa Cruz; the peak will be on your right.

For a shimmering panorama of blue-green sea, drive east on L.G. Smith Boulevard toward San Nicolas. Turn left where you see the drive-in theater. At the first intersection, turn right, then follow the curve to the right to ❸ **Frenchman's Pass,** a dark, luscious stretch of highway arbored by overhanging trees. Legend claims the French and native Indians warred here during the 17th century for control of the island.

Near Frenchman's Pass are the cement ruins of ❹ the **Balashi Gold Mine** (follow the directions to Frenchman's Pass, above, and then take the dirt road veering to the right), a lovely place to picnic, listen to the parakeets, and contemplate the towering cacti. A gnarled divi-divi tree stands guard at the entrance.

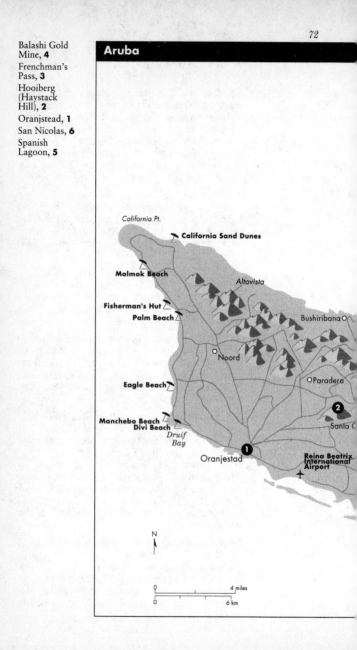

Aruba

California Pt.

California Sand Dunes

Malmok Beach

Altovista

Fisherman's Hut

Palm Beach

Bushiribana

Noord

Eagle Beach

Paradera

Manchebo Beach
Divi Beach
Druif Bay

2

Santa C

Oranjestad

1

Reina Beatrix International Airport

N

0   4 miles
0   6 km

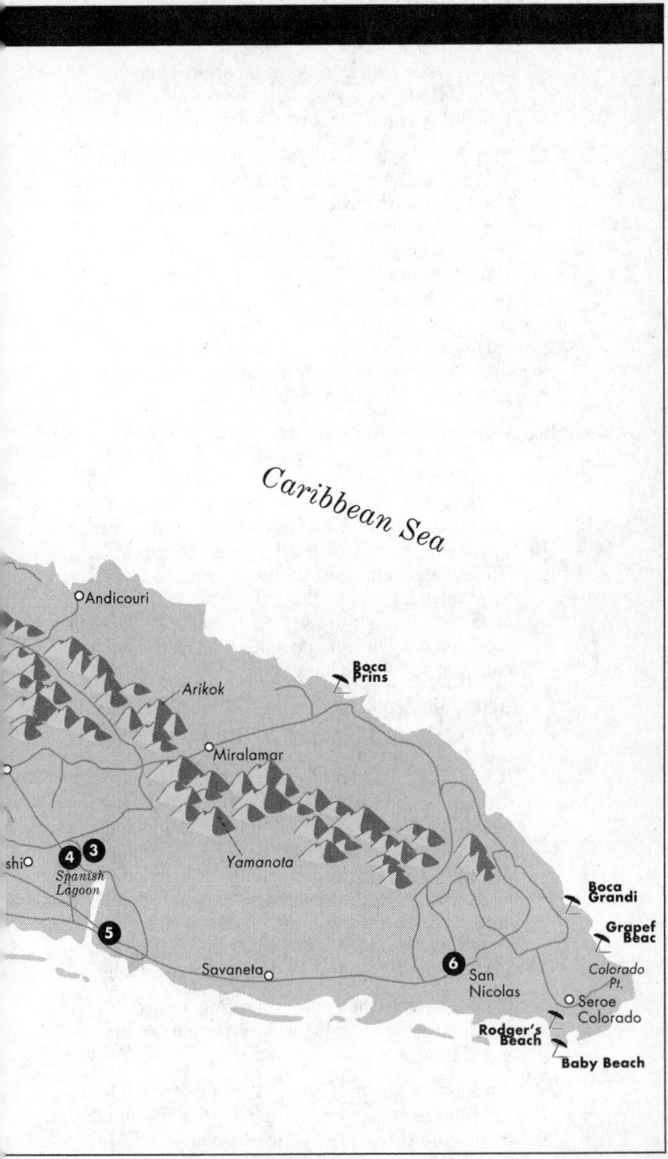

Caribbean Sea

Andicouri

Arikok

Boca
Prins

Miralamar

Yamanota

shi

4 **3**

Spanish
Lagoon

5

Savaneta

6 San
Nicolas

Boca
Grandi

Grapef
Beac

Colorado
Pt.

Seroe
Colorado

Rodger's
Beach

Baby Beach

❺ The area called **Spanish Lagoon** is where pirates once hid to repair their ships (follow L.G. Smith Boulevard, which crosses straight over the lagoon). It's a picturesque place for a picnic or to enjoy the island scenery.

❻ **San Nicolas** is Aruba's oldest village. In the 1980s, the town, with its oil refinery, was a bustling port with a rough-and-tumble quality; now it's dedicated to tourism, with the Main Street promenade full of interesting kiosks. Charlie's Bar (Zeppenfeldstraat 56) on the main street is a popular tourist lunch spot, good for both gawking at the thousands of license plates, old credit cards, baseball pennants, and hard hats covering every inch of the walls and ceiling, and for gorging on "jumbo and dumbo" shrimp.

Shopping Caya G.F. Betico Croes in Oranjestad is Aruba's chief shopping street. The stores are full of Dutch porcelains and figurines, as befits the island's Netherlands heritage. Also consider the Dutch cheeses (you are allowed to bring up to one pound of hard cheese through U.S. Customs), hand-embroidered linens, and any product made from the native plant aloe vera, such as sunburn cream, face masks, and skin fresheners. There is no sales tax, and Arubans consider it rude to haggle.

Artesania Aruba (L.G. Smith Blvd. 178, tel. 297/8–37494) has charming home-crafted pottery and folk objets d'art. **Aruba Trading Company** (Caya G.F. Betico Croes 12, tel. 297/8–22602) discounts brand-name perfumes and cosmetics (first floor), and jewelry and men's and women's clothes (second floor) up to 30%. **Gandleman's Jewelers** (Caya G.F. Betico Croes 5–A, tel. 297/8–34433) sells jewelry, including a full line of watches. **Wulfsen & Wulfsen** (Caya G.F. Betico Croes 52, tel. 297/8–23823) is one of Holland's best stores for fine-quality clothes and shoes.

Sports Contact **De Palm Tours** in Oranjestad (tel. 297/8–24400 or 297/8–24545) for information on fishing charters.
Fishing

Golf An all-new, 18-hole, par-71 golf course, Tierra del Sol (Malmokweg, tel. 297/8–67800), opened in 1995 on the northwest coast near the California Lighthouse. Designed by Robert Trent

Jones, the course combines Aruba's native beauty, such as the flora, cacti, and rock formations, with the lush greens of the world's best courses. The $115 greens fee includes a golf cart. Club rentals are $25–$40. The **Aruba Golf Club** near San Nicolas (tel. 297/8–42006) has a nine-hole course with 20 sand and five water traps, roaming goats, and lots of cacti. Greens fees are $7.50 for nine holes, $10 for 18. Caddies and rental clubs are available.

Hiking **De Palm Tours** (tel. 297/8–24400 or 297/8–24545) offers a guided three-hour trip to remote sites of unusual natural beauty accessible only on foot. The fee is $25 per person, including refreshments and transportation; a minimum of four people is required.

Horseback Riding At **Rancho El Paso** (tel. 297/8–63310), one-hour jaunts ($15) take you through countryside flanked by cacti, divi-divi trees, and aloe-vera plants; two-hour trips ($30) go to the beach as well. Wear lots of sunblock.

Water Sports **De Palm Tours** (tel. 297/8–24400 or 297/8–24545) has a near monopoly on water sports, including equipment and instruction for scuba diving, snorkeling, and windsurfing. However, **Pelican Watersports** (tel. 297/8–31228 or 297/8–24739) and **Red Sail Sports** (tel. 297/8–61603), may offer cheaper rates on water-sports packages, including snorkeling, sailing, windsurfing, fishing, and scuba diving.

Beaches Beaches in Aruba are not only beautiful but clean. On the north side the water is too choppy for swimming, but the views are great. **Palm Beach**—which stretches behind the Americana, Aruba Palm Beach, Holiday Inn, Hyatt, Radisson, and Wyndham hotels—is the center of Aruban tourism, offering the best in swimming, sailing, and fishing. In high season, however, it's packed. **Manchebo Beach,** by the Bucuti Beach Resort, is an impressively wide stretch of white powder and Aruba's unofficial topless beach. On the island's eastern tip, tiny **Baby Beach** is as placid as a wading pool and only 4 or 5 feet deep—perfect for tots and bad swimmers. Thatched shaded areas provide relief from the sun. You'll see topless bathers here from time to time as well.

Dining *Restaurants usually add a 10%–15% service charge.*

$$$ **Chez Mathilde.** This, Aruba's most elegant and romantic restaurant, occupies one of the last surviving 19th-century houses on the island. The French-style menu is continually being re-created. Feast on artfully presented baked escargots with herbs and garlic, rich bouillabaisse with garlic croutons and cream and cognac to taste, grilled Canadian salmon with a delicate balsamic dressing, or filet mignon in a signature pepper sauce prepared table-side. Then, too, there are crêpes Suzette and a chocolate gâteau to tempt the taste buds. *Havenstraat 23, Oranjestad, tel. 297/8–34968. Reservations essential. AE, MC, V. No lunch Sun.*

$–$$ **Boonoonoonoos.** The name—say it just as it looks!—means extraordinary, which is a bit of hyperbole for this Austrian-owned Caribbean bistro in the heart of town. The specialty here is Pan-Caribbean cuisine: The roast chicken Barbados is sweet and tangy, marinated in pineapple and cinnamon and simmered in fruit juices. The Jamaican jerk ribs (a 300-year-old recipe) are tiny but spicy, and the satin-smooth hot pumpkin soup drizzled with cheese and served in a pumpkin shell may as well be dessert. Avoid the place if it's crowded, since the service and the quality of the food deteriorate. *Wilhelminastraat 18A, Oranjestad, tel. 297/8–31888. AE, MC, V. No lunch Sun.*

$ **Le Petit Café.** The motto here is "Romancing the Stone"—referring to tasty cuisine cooked on hot stones. The low ceiling and hanging plants make this an intimate lunch spot for shoppers. Alfresco dining in the bustling square lets diners keep an eye on things, but fumes from nearby traffic tend to spoil the meal. Jumbo shrimp, sandwiches, ice cream, and fresh fruit dishes are light delights. *Emmastraat 1, Oranjestad, tel. 297/8–26577. AE, DC, MC, V. No lunch Sun.*

Barbados

Barbados is a sophisticated island with a life of its own that continues long after cruise passengers have packed up their suntan oils and returned to their ships. A resort island since the

1700s, Barbados has slowly cultivated a civilized attitude toward tourists.

Under uninterrupted British rule for 340 years—until independence in 1966—Barbados retains a very British atmosphere. Afternoon tea is a ritual and cricket is the national sport. The atmosphere, though, is hardly stuffy; people still operate on "island time."

Barbadian beaches along the island's south and west coasts are spectacular, and all are open to the public. On the rugged east coast, where "Bajans" themselves have vacation homes, the Atlantic surf pounds against gigantic boulders. The northeast is dominated by rolling hills and valleys covered by impenetrable acres of sugarcane. Elsewhere on the island are historic plantations, stalactite-studded caves, a wildlife preserve, and tropical gardens, which are linked by almost 900 miles of good roads. Bridgetown, the capital, is a busy city with more traffic than charm.

Currency One Barbados dollar (BDS$) equals about U.S. 50¢. Both currencies are accepted everywhere on the island. Always ask which currency is being quoted.

Telephones Public phones are at the cruise-ship terminal. Use the same dialing procedure as in the United States, or dial for assistance for collect and credit-card calls.

Shore Excursions The following are good choices on Barbados. They may not be offered by all cruise lines. Times and prices are approximate.

Island Sights **Harrison's Cave.** After a bus tour of the island's central parishes, passengers board an electric tram for a one-hour tour of this series of limestone caves. A highlight is the 40-foot underground waterfall that plunges into a deep pool. *3 hrs. Cost: $33.*

Undersea Creatures **Atlantis Submarine.** A 50-foot sub dives as deep as 150 feet below the surface for an exciting view of Barbados's profuse marine life. Most passengers find this trip to the depths to be a thrilling experience. *1½ hrs. Cost: $70.*

Coming Ashore Up to eight ships at a time can dock at Bridgetown's Deep Water Harbour, on the northwest side of Carlisle Bay. The cruise-ship terminal has duty-free shops and a post office, telephone station, tourist information desk, and taxi stand. To get downtown, follow the Careenage. By foot, it will take you about 15 minutes, or you can take a cab for $1.50 each way. Taxi tours of the island are available for $16 per hour.

Getting Around
By Bus
The bus system is good, connecting Bridgetown with all parts of the island, but the buses can be crowded. Service is frequent, but somewhat irregular, so leave plenty of time to make it back to the ship. The fare is BDS$1.50 wherever you go.

By Car
Barbados is a pleasure to tour by car, provided you take along a map and don't mind asking directions. Driving is on the left. You'll need an international driver's license or Barbados driving permit to rent a car; get one at the rental agency for $5 with your valid home license. Contact **National** (tel. 809/426–0603) or **P&S Car Rentals** (tel. 809/424–2052). Cars with automatic transmission cost $65–$70 per day. Gas costs about $3 a gallon.

By Taxi
Taxis await ships at the pier. The fare to Paradise, Brandon, or Brighton beaches runs $3–$5; to Holetown it's $7. Drivers accept U.S. dollars and expect a 10% tip. Taxis operate at a fixed hourly rate of $16, and drivers will cheerfully narrate a tour.

Exploring Barbados
Numbers in the margin correspond to points of interest on the Barbados map.

Bridgetown
❶
The narrow strip of sea known as the Careenage made early **Bridgetown** a natural harbor. Here, working schooners were careened (turned on their sides) to be scraped of barnacles and repainted. Today, the Careenage serves mainly as a berth for pleasure yachts.

At the center of the bustling city is **Trafalgar Square.** The monument to Lord Nelson predates its London counterpart by about two decades. Also here are a war memorial and a three-dolphin fountain commemorating the advent of running water in Barbados in 1865.

The **House of Assembly** and **Parliament buildings** house the third-oldest Parliament of the British Commonwealth and are adjacent to Trafalgar Square. A series of stained-glass windows depicting British monarchs adorns these Victorian Gothic government buildings.

George Washington is said to have worshiped at **St. Michael's Cathedral** on his only trip outside the United States. The structure was nearly a century old when he visited in 1751; destroyed twice by hurricanes, it was rebuilt in 1780 and again in 1831.

Queen's Park, northeast of downtown Bridgetown, is the site of an immense baobab tree more than 10 centuries old. The historic Queen's Park House, former home of the commander of the British troops, has been converted into a theater and a restaurant. *Open daily 9–5.*

The intriguing **Barbados Museum** (about a mile south of downtown Bridgetown on Highway 7) has artifacts dating to Arawak days (around 400 BC), mementos of military history and everyday life in the 19th century, wildlife and natural history exhibits, a well-stocked gift shop, and a good café. *Garrison Savannah, tel. 809/427–0201. Admission: BDS$10. Open Mon.–Sat. 9–5, Sun. 2–6.*

Central Barbados
Folkestone Marine Park (north of Holetown on Highway 1) has a museum of marine life and a snorkeling trail around Dottin's Reef. Non-swimmers can ride in a glass-bottom boat. A barge sunk in shallow water is home to myriad fish. *Holetown, St. James, tel. 809/422-2314. Admission: BDS$1. Closed Mon.*

❸ Harrison's Cave, a series of beautiful limestone caverns, complete with subterranean streams and a 40-foot waterfall, can be toured by electric tram. *Hwy. 2, St. Thomas, tel. 809/438–6640. Admission: BDS$15. Open daily 9–6.*

❹ Welchman Hall Gully offers another opportunity to commune with nature, with acres of labeled flowers, the occasional green monkey, and great peace and quiet. *Hwy. 2, tel. 809/438–6671. Admission: BDS$10. Open daily 9–5.*

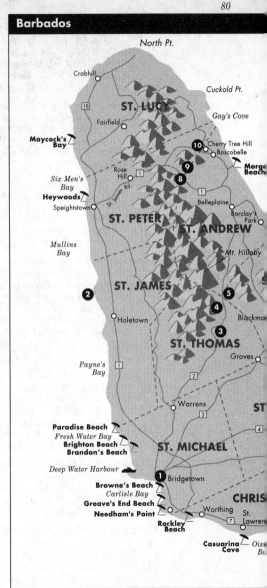

Barbados

North Pt.

Crabhill

Cuckold Pt.

ST. LUCY

Gay's Cove

Fairfield

Maycock's Bay

Cherry Tree Hill

Boscobelle

Rose Hill

Morg Beach

Six Men's Bay

Heywoods

Speightstown

St. James Rd.

ST. PETER

Belleplaine

Barclay's Park

ST. ANDREW

Mullins Bay

Mt. Hillaby

ST. JAMES

Holetown

Blackma

ST. THOMAS

Groves

Payne's Bay

Warrens

ST

Paradise Beach

Fresh Water Bay

Brighton Beach

Brandon's Beach

Deep Water Harbour

ST. MICHAEL

Bridgetown

Browne's Beach

Carlisle Bay

Greave's End Beach

Needham's Point

Rockley Beach

Worthing

St. Lawren

CHRIS

Casuarina Cove

Ois Ba

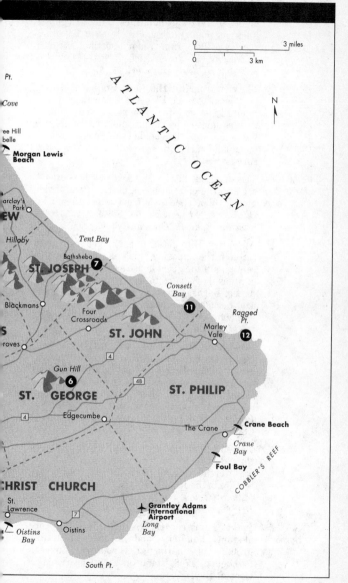

0   3 miles
0   3 km

N

Pt.

Cove

ee Hill
belle

Morgan Lewis Beach

A T L A N T I C O C E A N

arclay's Park

EW

Hilloby

Tent Bay

Bathsheba

ST. JOSEPH ⑦

Consett Bay

⑪

Blackmans

Four Crossroads

ST. JOHN

Ragged Pt.

Marley Vale

⑫

roves

Gun Hill

⑥

4

4B

ST. GEORGE

ST. PHILIP

4

Edgecumbe

The Crane

➤ **Crane Beach**

Crane Bay

COBBLER'S REEF

Foul Bay

CHRIST CHURCH

St. Lawrence

7

✈ **Grantley Adams International Airport**

Long Bay

Oistins Bay

Oistins

South Pt.

At the **Flower Forest,** you can meander through eight acres of fragrant bushes, canna and ginger lilies, puffball trees, and more than 100 other species of flora in a tranquil setting. *Hwy. 2, Richmond, St. Joseph, tel. 809/433–8152. Admission: BDS$10. Open daily 9–5.*

 The view from **Gun Hill Signal Station** is so pretty it seems unreal. Fields of green and gold extend all the way to the horizon, and brilliant flowers surround a picturesque gun tower. The white limestone lion behind the garrison is a famous landmark. *St. George, tel. 809/429–1358. Admission: BDS$8.*

Northern Barbados/ East Coast The small but fascinating **Andromeda Gardens,** set into the cliffs overlooking the ocean, holds unusual plant specimens from around the world. *Bathsheba, St. Joseph, tel. 809/433–9384. Admission: BDS$10. Open daily 9–5.*

At **Farley Hill** national park, you can roam through the imposing ruins of a once-magnificent plantation great house and its surrounding gardens, lawns, and towering royal palms. This part of Barbados has been dubbed the Scotland area because of its rugged landscape. *St. Peter, no phone. Admission: BDS$3 per car; walkers free. Open daily 8:30–6.*

You'll encounter herons, land turtles, screeching peacocks, innumerable green monkeys, geese, brilliantly colored parrots, a kangaroo, and a friendly otter at the **Barbados Wildlife Reserve.** The fauna roam freely, so step carefully and keep your hands to yourself. *Farley Hill, St. Peter, tel. 809/422–8826. Admission: BDS$20. Open daily 10–5.*

Named for a former owner, **St. Nicholas Abbey** is the oldest house on the island (circa 1650) and well worth visiting for its stone and wood architecture in the Jacobean style. *Near Cherry Tree Hill, St. Lucy, tel. 809/422–8725. Admission: BDS$5. Open weekdays 10–3:30.*

Southern Barbados In the eastern corner of St. John Parish, the coral-stone buildings and serenely beautiful grounds of **Codrington Theological College,** founded in 1748, stand on a cliff overlooking Consett Bay.

⑫ The appropriately named **Ragged Point Lighthouse** is where the sun first shines on Barbados and its dramatic Atlantic seascape.

Shopping Barbados is a free port, and duty-free shopping is found mostly in department stores and boutiques along **Broad Street** in Bridgetown and in stores at the cruise-ship terminal. To purchase items duty-free, you must show your passport.

For antiques and fine memorabilia, try **Greenwich House Antiques** (tel. 809/432–1169), in Greenwich Village, Trents Hill, St. James Parish. **Antiquaria** (tel. 809/426–0635), on Spring Garden Highway, St. Michael's Row, next to the Anglican cathedral in Bridgetown, is another good place to search for antiques.

Exclusive designs in "wearable art" by Carol Cadogan are available at **Cotton Days Designs** in Ramsgate Cottage, Lower Bay Street, opposite St. Patrick's Cathedral in Bridgetown (tel. 809/427–7191), and on the Wharf in Bridgetown. **Origins—Colours of the Caribbean** (tel. 809/436–8522), on the Wharf in Bridgetown, is worth visiting for its original—and expensive—handmade clothing and accessories.

At Bridgetown's **Pelican Village Handicrafts Center** (tel. 809/426–4391), on the Princess Alice Highway near the Cheapside Market, you can watch goods and crafts being made before you purchase them; rugs and mats are good buys.

Stores are generally open weekdays 9–5 and Saturdays 8–1.

Sports **Blue Jay Charters** (tel. 809/422–2098) has a 45-
Fishing foot, fully equipped fishing boat with a knowledgeable crew. Call for information on fishing charters.

Golf Several courses are open to cruise passengers: **Almond Beach Village** (9 holes $12.50, tel. 809/422–4900), **Club Rockley Barbados** (9 holes $22.50, tel. 809/435–7873), **Royal Westmoreland Golf Club** (18 holes $90, tel. 809/422–4653), and **Sandy Lane Club** (18 holes $120, tel. 809/432–1145).

Horseback Riding The **Caribbean International Riding Center** (St. Joseph, tel. 809/433–1246) offers one- or two-hour scenic trail rides for cruise-ship passengers. Prices begin at BDS$55, and transportation is included.

Water Sports Waterskiing, snorkeling, and parasailing are available on most beaches of St. James and Christ Church parishes. Windsurfing is best learned on the south coast at **Benston Windsurfing Club Hotel** (Maxwell, Christ Church Parish, tel. 809/428–9095). For scuba divers, Barbados is a rich and varied underwater destination. Two good dive operators are the **Dive Shop Ltd.** (Aquatic Gap, St. Michael, near Grand Barbados Beach Resort, tel. 809/426–9947) and **Dive Boat Safari** (Barbados Hilton, St. Michael, tel. 809/427–4350).

Beaches All beaches in Barbados are open to cruise passengers. The west coast has the stunning coves and white-sand beaches dear to the hearts of postcard publishers, plus calm, clear water for snorkeling, scuba diving, and swimming. **Payne's Bay**, south of Holetown, is the site of several fine resorts—including the Sandy Lane Hotel, which welcomes passengers to its beach. **Greave's End Beach** is south of Bridgetown at Aquatic Gap. In Worthing, on the south coast, **Sandy Beach** has shallow, calm waters and a picturesque lagoon. It's ideal for families. If you don't mind a short drive along Highway 7, the **Crane Beach Hotel,** where the Atlantic meets the Caribbean, is a great find. Waves pound in, but a reef makes it safe for good swimmers, and the sands are golden. For refreshment, there's the hotel's dining room on the cliff above.

Dining *A 5% tax and 10% service charge are added to most restaurant bills. When no service charge is added, tip waiters 10%–15%.*

$ **Bonito Beach Bar & Restaurant.** When you tour the rugged east coast, plan to arrive in Bathsheba at lunchtime and stop here for a wholesome West Indian meal, a fresh-fruit punch, and a spectacular view of the pounding Atlantic surf. *Coast Rd., Bathsheba, tel. 809/433–9034. No credit cards.*

$ **Waterfront Cafe.** A sidewalk table overlooking the Careenage is the perfect place to enjoy a

drink, snack, burger, or "Bajan" meal. It's a
popular gathering place for locals and tourists
alike. *Bridge House, Bridgetown, tel. 809/427–
0093. MC, V.*

Caracas/La Guaira, Venezuela

The busy harbor of La Guaira is the port for
nearby Caracas, the capital of Venezuela. Most
passengers go directly from the dock into air-
conditioned excursion buses for the 15-mile (45-
minute) drive into the big city. Those who want
to explore historical La Guaira will find the colonial zone most interesting.

Caracas is a bustling, multiethnic, cosmopolitan
city of 6 million people. It isn't the safest spot in
the world, so passengers should travel in groups
if touring the capital city on their own. In La
Guaira, too, it's best to explore in a group or
with a local taxi driver/guide: the colonial district is filled with "bandidos." And unless you
want to stick out like a sore thumb, and a rather
rude one at that, men should wear long slacks,
and women should wear slacks or a short-sleeve
dress.

Due to its rapid growth, Caracas is a hodge-
podge of styles. Many of the buildings, such as
Centro Banaven, a black, glass-sided box, display innovative touches; but there is also a
healthy share of neoclassical buildings, such as
the 19th-century Capitol and the 20th-century
Fine Arts Museum, as well as heavier, neo-
Gothic structures. The colonial dwellings of La
Guaira are fascinating symbols of affluence long
gone: Few have been restored, and they stand in
silent, weathered testimony to the passage of
time.

Currency   The monetary unit is the bolivar (Bs). At press
time the dollar exchange stood at Bs 100 on the
free market. Store owners prefer U.S. dollars,
however, and may even give you a discount for
paying in greenbacks.

Telephones   International calls, which are quite expensive,
are best made from a CANTV office. Ask at the
cruise terminal for the nearest one. For operator-assisted international calls, dial 122. AT&T
now offers a collect-call service to the United

States: Dialing 800/11120 connects you directly with an English-speaking operator.

Shore Excursions The following are good choices in Caracas. They may not be offered by all cruise lines. Times and prices are approximate.

Angel Falls and Canaima Lagoon. A jet ride carries you into the lush jungle interior and over Angel Falls—at 3,212 feet, the world's highest waterfall. After landing, you travel by canoe to a resort jungle camp to see another waterfall and the rich vegetation up close. Lunch is followed by a swim in a lagoon, with enough time to hike and explore. Not all ships offer this unforgettable tour. If yours doesn't, ask your shore-excursion director if it can be arranged for you. *9 hrs. Cost: $200.*

Caracas. If you want to see the city, a shore excursion is a much better choice than hiring a car. This half-day tour will show you all you need to see, and still leave you time to explore the area around the ship. *4 hrs. Cost: $30.*

Coming Ashore Cruise ships dock at a modern terminal with souvenir stands and shops inside. Taxi drivers will quote negotiable prices for the round-trip ride to Caracas. Pay no more than $60, and never pay in advance or you may be left stranded. If you plan to explore La Guaira, it's best to hire an English-speaking driver/guide. Although the colonial zone is just a short distance east of the cruise-ship terminal, the walk along the highway is neither particularly scenic nor safe. Pay no more than $15–$20 to see the sights and return to the ship.

Getting Around
By Subway The modern and handsome Metro, with its elegant French cars, covers 13 miles between Propatria in the west and Palo Verde in the east. A million passengers a day ride the quiet, rubber-wheeled trains in air-conditioned comfort. It is such a pleasant experience that some city-tour shore excursions include a jaunt on the subway as a highlight. Individual fares are from Bs 13 to Bs 16.

By Taxi Taxis are the best means of independent exploration. Private tours can be arranged just inside the cruise-ship terminal.

Exploring
La Guaira
Begin a quick survey of the colonial district at **Plaza Vargas**, on the main shore road. Locals gather here around the statue of José Maria Vargas, a Guaireño who was Venezuela's third president. Across the plaza is Calle Bolívar, running between the shore road and the mountains. Lined by the cool and cavernous warehouses of another century's trade and by one- and two-story houses with their colonial windows and red-tile roofs, the street funnels the sea breezes like voices from a more gracious age. Have your driver/guide wait for you at the plaza while you walk down this narrow street.

With your back to the water (you'll be facing the mountains), turn right out of Plaza Vargas to find one of the best-preserved colonial buildings: **Boulton Museum,** a pink house with an ample wood balcony. It will be on your left as you walk down Calle Bolívar. Inside is a treasury of paintings, maps, documents, pistols, and other miscellany collected by the family of John Boulton, occupants of the house for more than 140 years. Unfortunately, the museum is now closed.

At the foot of Calle Bolívar, turn right and pass the post office. Next door is one of the most important old buildings in La Guaira, **Casa Guipuzcoana.** Built in 1734, it was the colony's largest civic structure, housing first the Basque company that held a trading monopoly for 50 years, then the customs office. Restored as a cultural center, it is now the Vargas District Town Hall. Follow the main shore road back to Plaza Vargas, where your driver should be waiting for you.

Exploring
Caracas
Numbers in the margin correspond to points of interest on the Caracas map.

❶ Caracas radiates from its historic center, **Plaza Bolívar.** The old Cathedral, City Hall, and Foreign Ministry (or Casa Amarilla) all face Plaza Bolívar, a pleasant, shady square with benches, pigeons, and the fine equestrian statue of Simón Bolívar, who was born only a block away. Nearby also are the Capitol, the presidential offices in Miraflores Palace, and the 30-story twin towers of the Simón Bolívar Center in El Silencio.

Caracas

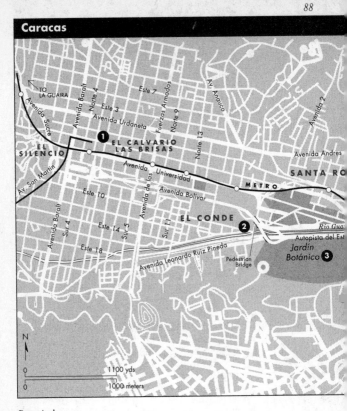

Botanical
Gardens, **3**

Bulevar de
Sabana
Grande, **4**

Parque
Central, **2**

Plaza
Bolívar, **1**

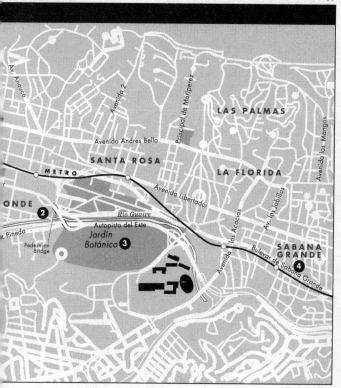

❷ The symbol of modern Caracas is the concrete **Parque Central**, with its two 56-story skyscrapers. Built over 16 years, the office and apartment complex was finished in 1986. Designed for 10,000 people, with seven condominiums and two towers, Parque Central encompasses not only shops, supermarkets, and restaurants, but also schools, a swimming pool, a convention center, a hotel, and the Museum of Contemporary Art. A pedestrian bridge links Parque Central to the Museum of Natural Sciences, the Museum of Fine Arts, and Los Caobos Park. Beyond this bower of mahogany trees, once a coffee plantation, lies the circular fountain of Plaza Venezuela.

❸ Across the *autopista* (highway) from Plaza Venezuela are the **Botanical Gardens** and the City University campus. In its courtyards and buildings are a stained-glass wall by Fernand Léger; murals by Léger and Mateo Manaure; sculptures by Antoine Pevsner, Jean Arp, and Henry Laurens; and, in the Aula Magna Auditorium, acoustic "clouds" by Alexander Calder.

The great fountain with colored lights in Plaza Venezuela is part of the urban renewal undertaken by the Caracas Metro. The Metro has changed the face of Caracas. When entire avenues were torn up, architects and landscapers converted the commercial street of Sabana Grande into a pedestrian boulevard of shops, popular sidewalk cafés, potted plants, and chess tables.

❹ Cars are banned between the Radio City theater and Chacaito, the pedestrian mall popularly known as the **Bulevar de Sabana Grande.** People of all ages and nationalities come to savor the best cappuccino and conversation in town, from midday to midnight.

Shopping Many of Caracas's sophisticated shops are in modern complexes known as *centros commerciales*, less stocked with imports than formerly, since devaluation has put foreign goods beyond most local shoppers' purses. Caracas is a buyer's market for fine clothing, tailored suits, elegant shoes, leather goods, and jewelry.

For wholesale jewelry go to **Edificio La Francia,**
whose nine floors off Plaza Bolívar hold some 80
gold workshops and gem traders; profit margins
are low, so buys are attractive. Since alluvial
gold is found in Venezuela, nuggets of *cochanos*
are made into pendants, rings, and bracelets.
Expert gold designer **Panchita Labady,** who
originated the popular gold orchid earrings and
pins, works in a small shop at No. 98 Calle Real
de Sabana Grande, opposite Avenida Los
Jabillos (tel. 02/712016).

Devil's masks are much sought after for colorful
souvenirs. Used in ritual dances marking the
Corpus Christi Festival (usually in early June),
they are made of brightly painted papier-mâché.
A good place to find these and other uniquely
Venezuelan gifts is El Taller de La Esquina,
Nivel Galeria, in the Paseo Las Mercedes shopping center. Explore other *artesanía* (folk art)
shops in Paseo Las Mercedes.

Dining *There is a 10% service charge in Venezuelan restaurants, and it is customary to tip the waiter
another 10%.*

$$–$$$ **La Estancia.** Black-and-white photos of famous
bullfighters seem right at home in this traditional Spanish-style restaurant. But despite the ob-
vious Spanish influence, criollo dishes are the
house specialty. Start with the lobster bisque
and move on to the *parillas* (criollo-style grill)
or rabbit or chicken basted in orange sauce. *Av.
Principal de la Castellana, Esquina Urdaneta,
tel. 02/261–2363. AE, MC, V.*

$ **Le Coq d'Or.** This is probably the best French
restaurant for the money in Caracas. The menu
varies, but it's always dependable. *Calle Los
Mangos at Av. Las Delicias (between Bulevar
de Sabana Grande and Av. Francisco Solano),
tel. 02/761–0891. AE. Closed Mon.*

Cozumel, Mexico

Sun-saturated Cozumel, its ivory beaches
fringed with coral reefs, fulfills the tourist's vision of a tropical Caribbean island. More Mexican than Cancún and far less developed,
Cozumel surpasses its better-known, fancier
neighbor to the north in several ways. It has
more—and lovelier—secluded beaches, superi-

or diving and snorkeling, more authentically Mexican cuisine, and a greater diversity of handicrafts at better prices.

Life on this flat jungle island centers on the town of San Miguel. The duty-free shops stay open as long as a ship is in town, and most of the salespeople speak English. With the world-renowned Palancar Reef nearby, San Miguel is also a favorite among divers.

Cozumel has become a mainstay for ships sailing on western Caribbean itineraries. As more and more cruise passengers arrive, the island has grown more commercial. Waterfront shops and restaurants have taken on a more glitzy appearance—gone are the hole-in-the-wall craft shops and little diners, replaced by high-dollar duty-free shops, gem traders, and slick eateries. There are also no less than half a dozen American fast-food chains and a Hard Rock Cafe.

Cruise ships visiting just for the day call at Cozumel; ships staying for two days usually call at Cozumel on one day and anchor off Playa del Carmen, across the channel on the Yucatán Peninsula, on the other. From here, excursions go to Cancún or to the Mayan ruins at Tulum, Cobá, and Chichén Itzá.

Currency In Mexico, the currency is the peso, written N\$ (for nuevo peso). At press time, the exchange rate was about N\$7 to U.S.\$1.

U.S. dollars and credit cards are accepted at most restaurants and large shops. Most taxi drivers take dollars as well. There is no advantage to paying in dollars, but there may be an advantage to paying in cash. To avoid having to change unused pesos back to dollars, change just enough to cover what you'll need for public transportation, refreshments, phones, and tips. Use up your Mexican coins; they can't be changed back to dollars.

Telephones The best place to make long-distance calls is at the Calling Station (Av. Rafael E. Melgar 27 and Calle 3 S, tel. 987/21417), where you'll save 10%–50%. You can also exchange money here. It is open mid-December–April, daily 8 AM–11 PM; the rest of the year, it's open Monday–Saturday 9 AM–10 PM and Sunday 9–1 and 5–10.

Shore   The following are good choices in Cozumel. They
Excursions may not be offered by all cruise lines. Times and
                prices are approximate.

Archaeological **Chichén Itzá.** This incredible and awe-inspiring
Sites   ruin of a great Mayan city is a 45-minute flight
                  from Cozumel or a 12-hour round-trip bus ride
                  from Playa del Carmen. A box lunch is included.
                  Full day. Cost: $130 (by plane), $85 (by bus).

                  Tulum Ruins and Xel-ha Lagoon. An English-
                  speaking guide leads a tour to this superbly pre-
                  served ancient Mayan city, perched on the cliffs
                  above a beautiful beach. A box lunch is usually
                  included. A stop is made for a swim in the glass-
                  clear waters of Xel-ha. The tour leaves from
                  Playa del Carmen. *7–8 hrs. Cost: $70.*

                  San Gervasio and Cozumel Island. If you want to
                  see Mayan ruins but don't want to spend a full
                  day on a tour, this excursion to a local archaeo-
                  logical site is a good alternative. Time is also al-
                  lotted for swimming and snorkeling at the Playa
                  Sol beach. *4 hrs. Cost: $32.*

Undersea **Glass-Bottom Boat.** For those who don't dive, a
Creatures tour boat with a see-through floor takes passen-
             gers to the famed Paraiso and Chankanaab sites
             to view schools of tropical fish. *2 hrs. Cost: $27.*

             Snorkeling. This region has been acknowledged
             by experts from Jacques Cousteau to *Skin Diver
             Magazine* as one of the top diving destinations
             in the world. If your ship offers a snorkeling
             tour, take it. Equipment and lessons are in-
             cluded. *3 hrs. Cost: $30.*

Coming As many as six ships call at Cozumel on a busy
Ashore day, tendering passengers to the downtown pier
            in the center of San Miguel or docking at the in-
            ternational pier 4 miles away. From the down-
            town pier you can walk into town or catch the
            ferry to Playa del Carmen. Taxi tours are also
            available. Sample prices are $6 to the
            Chankanaab Nature Park, $12 to the Playa Sol
            beach, and $35 to the Mayan ruins at San
            Gervasio. An island tour, including the ruins
            and other sights, costs about $60. The interna-
            tional pier is close to many beaches, but you'll
            need a taxi to get into town. Fortunately, cabs
            meet incoming ships, so there's rarely a wait.

Expect to pay $4 for the ride into San Miguel from the pier.

Once in town, you can find a tourist information directory on the main square, immediately across from the downtown pier, and an information office upstairs in the Plaza del Sol mall, at the east end of the square (open weekdays 9 AM–2:30 PM).

Getting Around
By Ferry To get to Playa del Carmen from Cozumel, you can take a ferry or a jetfoil from the downtown pier. It costs about $10 round-trip and takes 40–60 minutes each way. Travelers prone to seasickness should take medications before embarking. Ferries depart every hour; the last ferry back to Cozumel leaves around 8:30 PM, but be sure to double-check because the schedule changes frequently.

By Car or Moped Mopeds are great fun, and you can circumnavigate the island on one tank of gas. The only gas station is at the corner of Avenida Juárez and Avenida 30 (open 7 AM–midnight). Wear a helmet and be careful: Accidents are frequent on Cozumel. Four-wheel drive is recommended if you're planning to explore the many dirt roads around the island. For two- or four-wheel rentals, contact **Auto Rent** (tel. 987/20844, ext. 712), **Budget** (tel. 987/21732), **National Interrent** (tel. 987/23263), or **Rentadora Cozumel** (tel. 987/21429). Rates start at about $50 per day in summer, $75 in winter. Mopeds cost about half the price of a car.

In Playa del Carmen you can rent a car from **PlayaCar Rental** (tel. 987/30241).

By Taxi Taxis are everywhere in Cozumel. Stands are on Avenida Melgar, just north of the downtown pier, and in front of all the major hotels. At Playa del Carmen, you can usually find a cab just off the ferry pier. Taxis to surrounding towns and archaeological sites are not cheap unless you're traveling in a group. Expect to pay about $45 to Cancún and $25 to Tulum or Akumal. Agree on the fare in advance.

Exploring Cozumel San Miguel is tiny—you cannot get lost—and best explored on foot. The main attractions are the small eateries and shops that line the

streets. Activity centers on the ferry and the
main square, where the locals congregate in the
evenings. The lovely **Museo de le Isla de
Cozumel,** with exhibits devoted to the island environment and to the ecosystem of the surrounding reefs and water, is on the main coastal
drag, near the ferry dock. On the second floor
are displays on Mayan and colonial life and on
modern-day Cozumel. *Av. Melgar and Calle 4
N. Admission: $3. Open daily 10–6.*

It's not necessary to go to the mainland to explore ancient Mayan and Toltec ruins because
Cozumel has several sites of archaeological interest. Start with a visit to the **Cozumel Archaeological Park,** five minutes by cab from the
downtown pier/plaza area. Three thousand
years of pre-Columbian Mexican culture and art
are showcased here. More than 65 full-size repli-
cas of Toltec, Mexicas, and Mayan statues and
stone carvings are surrounded by jungle foli-
age. A guided walking tour, included in the admission price, takes about an hour. *65th Av. S,
tel. 987/20914. Admission: $3. Open daily 8–6.*

To see the largest Mayan and Toltec site on
Cozumel, head inland to the jungle. The ruins at
San Gervasio once served as the island's capital
and probably its ceremonial center, dedicated to
the fertility goddess Ixchel. What remains today are numerous ruins scattered around a plaza and a main road leading to the sea (probably a
major trade route). There's no interpretive
signage, so you'll need to hire a guide in order to
get much out of your visit. Guides charge $12 for
groups of up to six, so try to get a group together aboard ship. *Admission: $1 to private road,
$3.50 for ruins. Open daily 8–5.*

To sample Cozumel's natural beauty, head south
out of town on Avenida Melgar; after 6½ miles
your first stop will be the **Chankanaab Nature
Park.** The natural aquarium has been designated an underwater preserve for more than 50 species of tropical fish, as well as crustaceans and
coral. Snorkeling and scuba equipment can be
rented, and instruction and professional guides
are available, along with gift shops, snack bars,
and a restaurant (open 10–5) serving fresh seafood. *Admission: $5. Open daily 6–5:30.*

Shopping San Miguel's biggest industry—even bigger than diving—is selling souvenirs and crafts to cruise-ship passengers. The primary items are ceramics, onyx, brass, wood carvings, colorful blankets and hammocks, reproductions of Mayan artifacts, shells, silver, gold, sportswear, T-shirts, perfume, and liquor. Almost all stores take U.S. dollars.

The shopping district centers on the Plaza del Sol and extends out along Avenida Melgar and Avenida 5 S and N. Good shops for Mexican crafts are **Los Cinco Soles** and **La Concha** (both on Av. Melgar) and **Unicornio** (Av. 5a S1, just off the Plaza del Sol). The most bizarre collection of shops on the island is the **Cozumel Flea Market,** on Avenida 5 N between Calles 2 and 4, which sells reproductions of erotic Mayan figurines, antique masks, rare coins, and Xtabentún, the local anise-and-honey liqueur. Down the street at Avenida 5 N #14, **Arte Na Balam** sells high-quality Mayan reproductions, jewelry, batik clothing, and a typical array of curios. For atmosphere, fresh fruit, and other foods, go to the **Municipal Market** at Avenida 25 S and Calle Salas.

Passengers whose ships dock at the International Pier can shop dockside at a complex selling T-shirts, handicrafts, trinkets, and more.

Sports In Cozumel contact **Yucab Reef Diving and Fish-**
Fishing **ing Center** (tel. 987/24110) or **Club Naútico Cozumel** (tel. 987/20118 or 800/253–2701 in the U.S.)

Scuba Diving Cozumel is famous for its reefs. In addition to
and Snorkeling **Chankanaab Nature Park,** another great dive site is **La Ceiba Reef,** in the waters off La Ceiba and Sol Caribe hotels. Here lies the wreckage of a sunken airplane that was blown up for a Mexican disaster movie. Cozumel's dive shops include **Aqua Safari** (tel. 987/20101), **Blue Angel** (Hotel Villablanca, tel. 987/21631), **Dive Paradise** (tel. 987/21007), and **Fantasia Divers** (tel. 987/22840 or 800/336–3483 in the U.S.) and **Michelle's Dive Shop** (tel. 987/209470).

Dining *Although it is not common in Mexico, a 10%–15% service charge may be added to the bill. Otherwise, a 10%–20% tip is customary.*

$$ **Pancho's Backyard.** A jungle of greenery, trickling fountains, ceiling fans, and leather chairs set the tone at this inviting restaurant, located on the cool patio of Los Cincos Soles shopping center. The menu highlights local standards such as black-bean soup, *carmone al carbon* (grilled prawns), and fajitas. Round out your meal with coconut ice cream in Kahlua. *Av. Rafael Melgar N 27 at Calle 8 N, tel. 987/22141. AE, MC, V. Closed Sun. No lunch Sat.*

$$ **Rincón Maya.** This is the top place on the island for Yucatecan cuisine, and it's a popular spot with locals and divers. Lobster and fresh fish *a la plancha* (grilled) and *poc chuc* (marinated grilled pork) are among the excellent dishes. The decor is festive; a colorful mural, hats, masks, and fans adorn the walls. *Av. 5A S between Calles 3 and 5 S, tel. 987/20467. No credit cards. No lunch.*

$ **Prima Pasta & Pizza Trattoria.** Since Texan Albert Silmai opened this northern Italian diner just south of the plaza, he's attracted a strong following of patrons, who come for the hearty, inexpensive pizzas, calzones, sandwiches, and pastas. The breezy dining area, located on a second-floor terrace above the kitchen, smells heavenly and has a charming Mediterranean mural painted on two walls. *A. Rosado Salas 109, tel. 987/24242. MC, V.*

Nightlife After 10 PM, **Carlos 'n' Charlie's** (Av. Melgar 11 between Calles 2 and 4 N, tel. 987/20191) and **Chilly's** (Av. Melgar near Av. Benito Juarez, tel. 987/21832) are the local equivalent of college fraternity parties. The new **Hard Rock Cafe** (Av. Rafael Melgar 2A near Av. Benito Juarez) is similarly raucous. A favorite with ships' crews is **Scaramouche** (Av. Melgar at Calle Rosada Salas, tel. 987/20791), a dark, cavernous disco with a crowded dance floor surrounded by tiered seating.

Curaçao

Try to be on deck as your ship sails into Curaçao. The tiny Queen Emma Floating Bridge swings aside to open the narrow channel. Pastel gingerbread buildings on shore look like dollhouses, especially from the perspective of a large cruise ship. Although the gabled roofs and red tiles show a Dutch influence, the riotous colors of the facades are peculiar to Curaçao. It is said that an early governor of Curaçao suffered from migraines that were irritated by the color white, so all the houses were painted in colors.

Thirty-five miles north of Venezuela and 42 miles east of Aruba, Curaçao is, at 38 miles long and 2 to 7½ miles wide, the largest of the Netherlands Antilles. Although always sunny, it is never stiflingly hot here, due to the cooling influence of the constant trade winds. Water sports attract enthusiasts from all over the world, and the reef diving is excellent.

History books still don't agree as to whether Alonzo de Ojeda or Amerigo Vespucci discovered Curaçao, only that it happened around 1499. In 1634 the Dutch came and promptly shipped off the Spanish settlers and the few remaining Indians to Venezuela. To defend itself against French and British invasions, the city built massive ramparts, many of which now house unusual restaurants and hotels.

Today, Curaçao's population, which comprises more than 50 nationalities, is one of the best educated in the Caribbean. The island is known for its religious tolerance, and tourists are warmly welcomed and almost never pestered by vendors and shopkeepers.

Currency U.S. dollars are fine, so don't worry about exchanging money, except for pay phones or soda machines. The local currency is the guilder or florin, indicated by "fl" or "NAf" on price tags. The official rate of exchange at press time was NAf 1.77 to U.S. $1.

Telephones The telephone system is reliable, and there's an overseas phone center in the cruise-ship terminal. Dialing to the United States is exactly the same as dialing long distance within the United States.

Shore Excursions The following are good choices in Curaçao. They may not be offered by all cruise lines. Times and prices are approximate.

Island Sights **Country Drive.** This is a good tour if you'd like to see Westpunt and Mt. Christoffel but don't want to risk driving an hour there yourself. Other stops are the Museum of Natural History, Boca Tabla, and Knip Beach. *3½ hrs. Cost: $25.*

Undersea Creatures **Sharks, Stingrays, and Shipwrecks.** Curaçao's seaquarium, a marine park, and two sunken ships reached by a 30-minute submarine trip highlight this tour of the island's marine environment. *3 hrs. Cost: $40.*

Coming Ashore Ships dock at the cruise-ship terminal just beyond the Queen Emma Bridge, which leads to the floating market and the shopping district. The walk from the berth to downtown takes around 10 minutes. Easy-to-read tourist information maps are posted dockside and in the shopping area. The terminal has a duty-free shop, a telephone office, and a taxi stand.

Getting Around Willemstad is small and navigable on foot; you needn't spend more than two or three hours wandering around here. English, Spanish, and Dutch are widely spoken. Narrow Santa Anna Bay divides the city into the Punda, where the main shopping district is, and the Otrabanda (literally, the "other side"), where the cruise ships dock. The Punda is crammed with shops, restaurants, monuments, and markets. The Otrabanda has narrow winding streets full of colonial homes notable for their gables and Dutch-influenced designs.

You can cross from the Otrabanda to the Punda in one of three ways: Walk across the Queen Emma Pontoon Bridge; ride the free ferry, which runs when the bridge swings open (at least 30 times a day) to let seagoing vessels pass; or take a cab across the Juliana Bridge (about $10).

By Car To rent a car, call **Avis** (tel. 599/9–611255), **Budget** (tel. 599/9–683466), or **National** (tel. 599/9–683489). All you'll need is a valid U.S. or Canadian driver's license. Rates begin at $50 per day.

By Bike, Moped, or Scooter If you want to explore farther into the countryside, mopeds are an inexpensive alternative to renting a car or hiring a taxi. Scooters ($20), mopeds ($15), and bikes ($12.50) can be rented from Easy Going (tel. 599/9–695056).

By Taxi Taxis are not metered, so confirm the price before getting in. Taxis meet every cruise ship, and they can be picked up at hotels. Otherwise, call **Central Dispatch** (tel. 599/9–616711). A taxi tour for up to four people will cost about $25 an hour.

Exploring Curaçao

Numbers in the margin correspond to points of interest on the Curaçao map.

Willemstad

❶

A quick tour of downtown **Willemstad** covers a six-block radius. The first landmark that cruise passengers come upon is the **Queen Emma Bridge,** which the locals call the Lady. The toll to cross the original bridge, built in 1888, was 2¢ per person if wearing shoes and free if barefoot. Today it's free, regardless of what is on your feet.

On the Punda side of the city, **Handelskade** is where you'll find Willemstad's most famous sight, the colorful colonial buildings that line the waterfront. The original red roof tiles came from Europe on trade ships as ballast.

At press time, the bustling **floating market** was temporarily located across Waaigat Channel while its traditional location on Sha Caprileskade was undergoing renovation. Each morning, dozens of Venezuelan schooners arrive laden with tropical fruits and vegetables. Any produce bought at the market should be thoroughly washed before eating.

The Wilhelmina Drawbridge connects the Punda with the once-flourishing district of **Scharloo.** The early Jewish merchants built stately homes in Scharloo, and many of these intriguing structures (some dating back to the 17th century) have been meticulously renovated by the government. If you cross the bridge to admire the architecture along Scharlooweg, steer clear of the waterfront end (Kleine Werf) of the district, which is now a red-light district.

The Punda's **Mikveh Israel-Emmanuel Synagogue** was founded in 1651 and is the oldest temple still in use in the Western Hemisphere. It draws 20,000 visitors a year. Enter through the gates around the corner on Hanchi Snoa. A museum in the back displays Jewish antiques and fine Judaica. *Hanchi Di Snoa 29, tel. 599/9–611067. Small donation expected. Open weekdays 9–11:45 and 2:30–5.*

At the end of Columbusstraat lies **Wilhelmina Park.** The statue keeping watch is of Queen Wilhelmina, a popular monarch of the Netherlands who gave up her throne to her daughter Juliana after her Golden Jubilee in 1948. At the far side of the square is the impressive Georgian facade of the McLaughlin Bank and, to its right, the courthouse with its stately balustrade.

Guarding the waterfront at the foot of the Pontoon Bridge are the mustard-color walls of **Ft. Amsterdam;** take a few steps through the archway and enter another century. In the 1700s the structure was actually the center of the city and the most important fort on the island. Now it houses the governor's residence, the Fort Church, the ministry, and several other government offices. Outside the entrance, a series of gnarled wayaka trees has small, fanciful carvings of a dragon, a giant squid, and a mermaid.

Western Curaçao
The road that leads to the northwest tip of the island winds through landscape that Georgia O'Keeffe might have painted—towering cacti, flamboyant dried shrubbery, aluminum-roofed houses. In these parts you may see fishermen hauling in their nets, women pounding cornmeal, and donkeys blocking traffic. Landhouses—large estate homes, most of which are closed to the public—can often be glimpsed from the road.

2 Christoffel Park is a good hour from Willemstad (so watch your time) but worth a visit. This fantastic 4,450-acre garden and wildlife preserve with Mt. Christoffel at its center consists of three former plantations. As you drive through the park, watch for tiny deer, goats, and other small wildlife that might suddenly dart in front of your car. If you skip everything else on the island, it's possible to drive to the park and climb 1,239-foot Mt. Christoffel, which takes from two to three strenuous hours. The island panorama you get from the peak is amazing—on a clear day you can even see the mountain ranges of Venezuela, Bonaire, and Aruba. *Savonet, tel. 599/9–640363. Admission: $9. Open Mon.–Sat. 8–4, Sun. 6–3.*

Curaçao

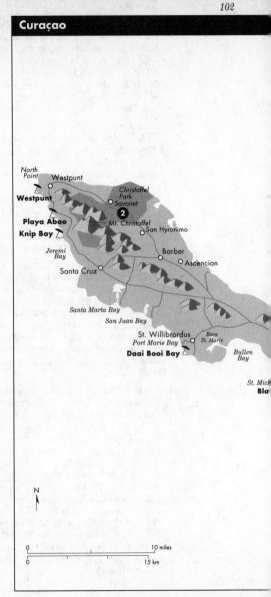

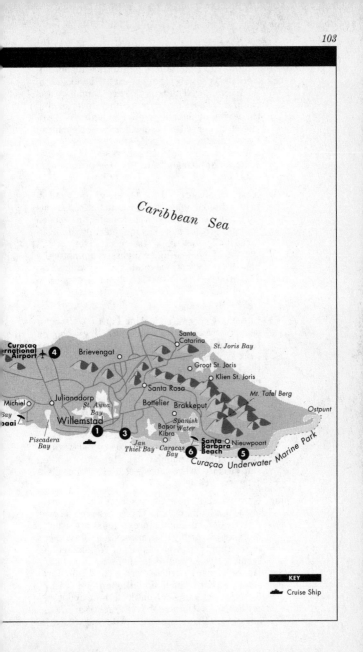

Caribbean Sea

Curaçao International Airport

Brievengat

Santa Catarina

St. Joris Bay

Groot St. Joris

Klien St. Joris

Mt. Tafel Berg

Ostpunt

Michiel

Julianadorp

Santa Rosa

Bottelier

Brakkeput

St. Anna Bay

Bay

aai

Willemstad

Spanish Water

Bapor Kibra

Piscadera Bay

Jan Thiel Bay

Caracas Bay

Santa Barbara Beach

Nieuwpoort

Curaçao Underwater Marine Park

KEY

Cruise Ship

❸ At the **Curaçao Seaquarium,** more than 400 varieties of exotic fish and vegetation are displayed. Outside is a 495-yard-long artificial beach of white sand, well-suited to novice swimmers and children. There's also a platform overlooking the wreck of the steamship SS *Oranje Nassau* and an underwater observatory where you can watch divers and snorkelers swimming with stingrays and feeding sharks. *Tel. 599/9–616666. Admission: $12.50. Open daily 8:30 AM–10 PM.*

❹ Near the airport is **Hato Caves,** where you can take an hour-long guided tour into various chambers containing water pools, a voodoo chamber, fruit bats' sleeping quarters, and Curaçao Falls—where a stream of silver joins a stream of gold. Hidden lights illuminate the limestone formations and gravel walkways. This is one of the better Caribbean caves open to the public. *Tel. 599/9–680378. Admission: $4. Open daily 10–5.*

❺ **Curaçao Underwater Marine Park** (*see* Sports, *below*) is the best spot for snorkeling—though the seabed is sadly litter-strewn in places. The park stretches along the southern shore, from the Princess Beach Hotel in Willemstad to the eastern tip of the island.

Along the southern shore, several private yacht clubs attract sports anglers from all over the world for international tournaments. Stop at Santa Barbara Beach, especially on Sunday, when the atmosphere approaches party time.

❻ **Caracas Bay** is a popular dive site, with a sunken ship so close to the surface that even snorkelers can view it clearly.

Shopping Curaçao has some of the best shops in the Caribbean, but in many cases the prices are no lower than in U.S. discount stores. Hours are usually Monday–Saturday 8–noon and 2–6. Most shops are within the six-block area of Willemstad described above. The main shopping streets are Heerenstraat, Breedestraat, and Madurostraat, where you'll find **Bamali** (tel. 599/9–612258) for Indonesian batik clothing and leather. **Fundason Obra di Man** (Bargestraat 57, tel. 599/9–612413) sells native crafts and curios. If

you've always longed for Dutch clogs, tulips,
delftware, Dutch fashions, or chocolate, try
Clog Dance (De Rouvilleweg 9B, tel. 599/9–
623280).

Arawak Craft Factory (tel. 599/9–627249), con-
veniently located between the Queen Emma
Bridge and the cruise-ship terminal, is open
whenever ships are in port. You can buy a variety of tiles, plates, pots, and tiny landhouse repli-
cas here.

Julius L. Penha & Sons (Heerenstraat 1, tel. 599/
9–612266), in front of the Pontoon Bridge, sells
French perfumes, Hummel figurines, linen
from Madeira, delftware, and handbags from
Argentina, Italy, and Spain. The store also has
an extensive cosmetics counter. **Boolchand's**
(Heerenstraat 4B, tel. 599/9–616233) handles an
interesting variety of merchandise behind a facade of red-and-white-checked tiles. Stock up
here on French perfumes, British cashmere
sweaters, Italian silk ties, Dutch dolls, Swiss
watches, and Japanese cameras. **Little Switzerland** (Breedstraat 44, tel. 599/9–612111) is the
place for duty-free shopping; here you'll find
perfumes, jewelry, watches, crystal, china, and
leather goods at significant savings. Try **New
Amsterdam** (Gomezplein 14, tel. 599/9–612469)
for hand-embroidered tablecloths, napkins, and
pillowcases.

Sports **Christoffel Park** (*see* Exploring Curaçao, *above*)
Hiking has a number of challenging trails.

Scuba Diving The **Curaçao Underwater Marine Park** (tel. 599/
and Snorkeling 9–618131) is about 12½ miles of untouched coral
reef that has been granted national park status.
Mooring buoys mark the most interesting dive
sites. If your cruise ship doesn't offer a diving or
snorkeling excursion, contact **Curaçao Seascape**
(tel. 599/9–625000, ext. 6056), **Peter Hughes Divers** (tel. 599/9–658911), or **Underwater Curaçao**
(tel. 599/9–618131).

Beaches Curaçao doesn't have long, powdery stretches of
sand. Instead you'll discover the joy of inlets:
tiny bays marked by craggy cliffs, exotic trees,
and scads of interesting pebbles and washed up
coral. Westpunt, on the northwest tip of the island, is rocky, with very little sand, but shady in

the morning and with a bay view worth the one-hour trip. On Sunday watch the divers jump from the high cliff. Knip Bay has two parts: Groot (Big) Knip and Kleine (Little) Knip. Both have alluring white sand, and Kleine Knip is shaded by (highly poisonous) manchineel trees. Take the road to the Knip Landhouse, then turn right; signs will direct you.

Dining *Restaurants usually add a 10%–15% service charge to the bill.*

$$$ **Bistro Le Clochard.** This romantic gem is built into the 18th-century Rif Fort and is suffused with the cool, dark atmosphere of ages past. The use of fresh ingredients in consistently well-prepared French and Swiss dishes makes dining a dream. Try the fresh fish platters or the tender veal in mushroom sauce. Save room for the chocolate mousse. *On the Otrabanda Rif Fort, tel. 599/9–625666. AE, DC, MC, V. Closed Sun. No lunch Sat.*

$ **Jaanchi's Restaurant.** Tour buses stop regularly at this open-air restaurant for lunches of mouthwatering native dishes. The main-course specialty is a hefty platter of fresh fish, conch, or shrimp with potatoes or funchi (a starch similar to cornbread) and vegetables. Bring a camera to capture the colorful sugarbirds that swarm Jaanchi's feeder on the terrace. *Westpunt 15, tel. 599/9–640126. AE, DC, MC, V.*

Grand Cayman

The largest and most populous of the Cayman Islands, Grand Cayman is one of the most popular cruise destinations in the western Caribbean, largely because it doesn't suffer from the ailments afflicting many larger ports: panhandlers, hasslers, and crime. Instead, the Cayman economy is a study in stability, and residents are renowned for their courteous behavior. Though cacti and scrub fill the dusty landscape, Grand Cayman is a diver's paradise, with translucent waters and a colorful variety of marine life protected by the government.

Compared with other Caribbean ports, there are fewer things to see on land; instead, the island's most impressive sights are underwater.

Snorkeling, diving, and glass-bottom-boat and submarine rides top every ship's shore-excursion list and also can be arranged at major aquatic shops. Grand Cayman is also famous for the 554 offshore banks in George Town; not surprisingly, the standard of living is high, and nothing is cheap.

Currency The U.S. dollar is accepted everywhere. The Cayman Island dollar (C.I.$) is worth about U.S.$1.20. Prices are often quoted in Cayman dollars, so make sure you know which currency you're dealing with.

Telephones Phone service is better here than on most islands. Calling the United States is the same as calling long distance in the States: Just dial 01 followed by the area code and telephone number.

Shore Excursions The following are good choices in Grand Cayman. They may not be offered by all cruise lines. Times and prices are approximate.

Undersea Creatures **Atlantis Submarine.** A real submarine offers an exciting view of Grand Cayman's profuse marine life. *1 hr 40 min. Cost: $75.*

Seaworld Explorer Cruise. A glass-bottom boat takes you on an air-conditioned, narrated voyage where you sit 5 feet below the water's surface and see sunken ships, tropical fish, and coral reefs. *1 hr. Cost: $29.*

Snorkeling Adventure. Novices can take lessons and experienced snorkelers will find good adventure on this boat trip to one or two snorkeling sites—Sting Ray City is highly recommended. *2 hrs. Cost: $30.*

Coming Ashore Ships anchor in George Town Harbor and tender passengers onto Harbour Drive, placing you in the center of the shopping district. A tourist information booth is located on the pier where tenders land, and taxis line up for disembarking passengers.

Getting Around *By Bicycle, Car, Moped, or Motorcycle* If you want to see more than George Town, you'll need a vehicle. To rent a car, contact **Ace Hertz** (tel. 809/949–2280 or 800/654–3131), **Budget** (tel. 809/949–5605 or 800/527–0700), or **Cico Avis** (tel. 809/949–2468 or 800/228–0668). Bring your driver's license, and the rental agency will issue you a temporary permit ($5). Rental prices for cars range from $40 to $55 a day.

For two-wheeled transportation, try **Bicycles Cayman** (tel. 809/949–5572), **Cayman Cycle** (tel. 809/947–4021), or **Soto Scooters** (tel. 809/947–4363). Mopeds rent for $25–$30 a day, bikes for $10–$15.

By Taxi   Taxis offer island-wide service. Fares are determined by an elaborate rate structure set by the government, and although it may seem expensive, cabbies rarely try to rip off tourists. Ask to see the chart if you want to double-check the quoted fare.

Exploring   George Town is small enough to explore on foot.
Grand   The small but fascinating **Cayman Islands Na-**
Cayman   **tional Museum,** found to the left of the tender landing and just across the street, is well worth visiting. *Tel. 809/949–8368. Admission: C.I.$5. Open weekdays 9–5, Sat. 10–4.*

On Cardinal Avenue is the **General Post Office,** built in 1939, with strands of decorative colored lights and about 2,000 private mailboxes (island mail is not delivered).

Behind the general post office is **Elizabethan Square,** a complex that houses clothing and souvenir stores. At the corner of Fort and Edward streets, notice the small clock tower dedicated to Britain's King George V and the huge fig tree pruned into an umbrella shape.

The **Cayman Maritime and Treasure Museum,** located in front of the Hyatt Hotel, is a real find. Dioramas show how Caymanians became seafarers, boatbuilders, and turtle breeders. Owned by a professional treasure-salvaging firm, the museum displays a lot of artifacts from shipwrecks. A shop offers excellent buys on authentic ancient coins and jewelry. *W. Bay Rd., tel. 809/947–5033. Admission: $5. Open Mon.–Sat. 9–5.*

The **Old Homestead,** formerly known as the West Bay Pink House, is probably the most photographed home in Grand Cayman. This picturesque pink-and-white cottage was built in 1912 of wattle and daub around an ironwood frame. Tours are led by Mac Bothwell, a cheery guide who grew up in the house.

Near the Old Homestead is the tiny village of **Hell,** which is little more than a patch of incredibly jagged rock formations called ironshore. The big attractions here are a small post office, which sells stamps and postmarks cards from Hell (the postcard of bikini beauties emblazoned "When Hell Freezes Over" gives you the idea), and lots of T-shirt and souvenir shops. *W. Bay Rd., tel. 809/949–7639. Admission: $5. Open Mon.–Sat. 8–5.*

The **Cayman Island Turtle Farm** is the most popular attraction on the island. Here you'll see turtles of all ages, from day-old hatchlings to huge 600-pounders that can live to be 100. In the adjoining café, sample turtle soup or turtle sandwiches. *W. Bay Rd., tel. 809/949–3893. Admission: $5. Open daily 9–5.*

Many legends are associated with **Pedro's Castle,** built in 1780 and the oldest structure on Grand Cayman. In 1877 it was struck by lightning, and it remained in ruins until the 1960s, when a restaurateur bought the building.

At **Bodden Town**—the island's original capital—you'll find an old cemetery on the shore side of the road. Graves with A-frame structures are said to contain the remains of pirates, but, in fact, they may be those of early settlers. A curio shop serves as the entrance to what's called the Pirate's Caves, partially underground natural formations that are more hokey than spooky, with fake treasure chests and mannequins in pirate garb.

Queen Elizabeth II Botanic Park is a 60-acre wilderness preserve showcasing the variety of habitats and plants native to the Caymans. Interpretive signs identify the flora along the mile-long walking trail. Halfway along the trail is a walled compound housing the rare blue iguana—it's found only in remote sections of the islands. *Frank Sound Rd., tel. 809/947–9462. Admission: $3. Open daily 7:30–5:30.*

On the way to the East End are the **Blow Holes,** a great photo opportunity as waves crash into the fossilized coral beach, forcing water into caverns and sending geysers shooting up through the ironshore.

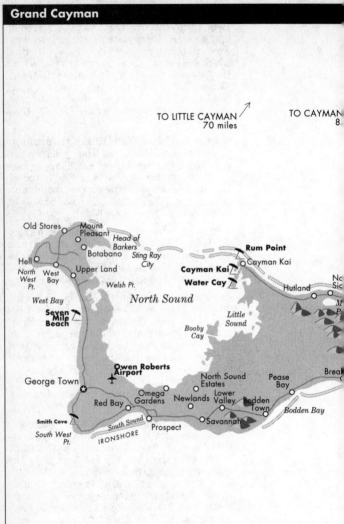

TO LITTLE CAYMAN
70 miles

TO CAYMAN
8.

Old Stores

Mount
Pleasant

*Head of
Barkers*

Botabano

*Sting Ray
City*

Rum Point

Cayman Kai

Hell

*North
West
Pt.*

West
Bay

Upper Land

Cayman Kai

Water Cay

Hutland

Nc
Sic

Welsh Pt.

West Bay

North Sound

*Little
Sound*

M
P

**Seven
Mile
Beach**

*Booby
Cay*

George Town

**Owen Roberts
Airport**

North Sound
Estates

Pease
Bay

Brea

Red Bay

Omega
Gardens

Newlands

Lower
Valley

Bodden
Town

Smith Cove

South Sound

Prospect

Savannah

Bodden Bay

*South West
Pt.*

IRONSHORE

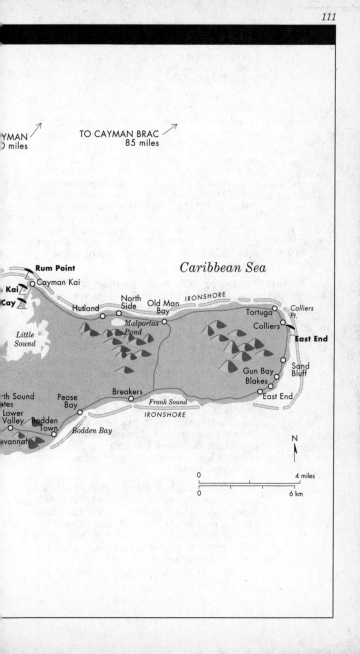

TO CAYMAN BRAC
85 miles

...YMAN
...0 miles

Caribbean Sea

Rum Point

Cayman Kai

Kai

Cay

IRONSHORE

Hutland

North
Side

Old Man
Bay

Tortuga

*Colliers
Pt.*

Colliers

East End

*Malportas
Pond*

*Little
Sound*

Gun Bay

Blakes

Sand
Bluff

...th Sound
...tes

Lower
Valley

Pease
Bay

Breakers

Frank Sound

East End

Bodden
Town

IRONSHORE

...avannah

Bodden Bay

N

0   4 miles

0   6 km

Beyond the Blow Holes is the village of **East End,** the first recorded settlement on Grand Cayman. Farther on, as the highway curves north, you'll come to Queen's View lookout point. There's a monument commemorating the legendary Wreck of the Ten Sails, which took place just offshore.

Shopping   Grand Cayman is known for its turtle and black-coral products, but these are banned in the United States. **Fort Street** and **Cardinal Avenue** are the main shopping streets in George Town. On Cardinal Avenue is **Kirk Freeport Plaza,** with lots of jewelry shops, and the **George Town Craft Market,** with more kitschy souvenirs than crafts. On South Church Street and in the Hyatt Hotel, **Pure Art** (tel. 809/949–4433) features the work of local artists. The **Tortuga Rum Company**'s (tel. 809/949–7701) scrumptious rum cake makes a great souvenir; most shops on Grand Cayman carry it.

Sports
Fishing   For fishing enthusiasts, Cayman waters are abundant with blue and white marlin, yellowfin tuna, sailfish, dolphinfish, bonefish, and wahoo. If your ship does not offer a fishing excursion, about 25 boats are available for charter. Ask at the tourist information booth on the pier.

Scuba Diving
and Snorkeling   Contact **Bob Soto's Diving Ltd.** (tel. 809/947–4631 or 800/262–7686), **Don Foster's Dive Grand Cayman** (tel. 809/949–5679 or 800/833–4837), and **Parrot's Landing** (tel. 809/949–7884 or 800/448–0428). The best snorkeling is off the **Ironshore Reef** (within walking distance of George Town on the west coast) and in the reef-protected shallows of the north and south coasts, where coral and fish are much more varied and abundant.

Beaches   The west coast, the island's most developed area, is where you'll find the famous **Seven Mile Beach.** The white, powdery beach is free of both litter and peddlers, but it is also Grand Cayman's busiest vacation center, and most of the island's resorts, restaurants, and shopping centers are located along this strip. The Holiday Inn rents Aqua Trikes, Paddle Cats, and Banana Rides.

Dining *Many restaurants add a 10%–15% service charge.*

$$$ **Lantana's.** Try the American-Caribbean cuisine at this fine eatery, where the decor is as imaginative and authentic as the food, and both are of top quality. Lobster quesadillas, blackened king salmon over cilantro linguine with banana fritters and cranberry relish, incredible roasted garlic soup, and apple pie are favorites from the diverse menu. *Caribbean Club, W. Bay Rd., Seven Mile Beach, tel. 809/947–5595. AE, D, MC, V. No lunch weekends.*

$$ **Crow's Nest.** With the ocean as its backyard, this secluded seafood restaurant, located about a 15-minute drive south of George Town, is a great spot for snorkeling as well as lunching. The shark du jour, herb-crusted dolphin with lobster sauce, and the shrimp and conch dishes are excellent, as is the chocolate fudge rum cake. *S. Sound Rd., tel. 809/949–9366. AE, MC, V. No lunch Sun.*

Grenada

Nutmeg, cinnamon, cloves, cocoa . . . the aroma fills the air and all memories of Grenada (pronounced gruh-*nay*-da). Only 21 miles long and 12 miles wide, the Spice Island is a tropical gem of lush rain forests, green hillsides, white-sand beaches, secluded coves, and exotic flowers.

Until 1983, when the U.S.–eastern Caribbean intervention catapulted this little nation into the headlines, Grenada was a relatively obscure island hideaway for lovers of fishing, snorkeling, or simply lazing in the sun. Grenada has been back to normal for more than a decade now, a safe and secure vacation spot with enough good shopping, restaurants, historical sites, and natural wonders to make it a popular port of call. Tourism is growing each year, but the expansion of tourist facilities is carefully controlled. New construction on the beaches must be at least 165 feet back from the high-water mark, and no building can stand taller than a coconut palm. As a result, Grenada continues to retain its distinctly West Indian identity.

Currency Grenada uses the Eastern Caribbean (E.C.) dollar. The exchange rate is about E.C.$2.70 to

U.S.$1, although taxi drivers, stores, and vendors will frequently calculate at a rate of E.C.$2.50. U.S. dollars are readily accepted, but always ask which currency is referred to when asking prices. Unless otherwise noted, prices quoted here are in U.S. dollars.

Telephones   U.S. and Canadian telephone numbers can be dialed directly. Pay phones and phone cards are available at the welcome center, on the Carenage in St. George's, where cruise-ship passengers come ashore.

Shore Excursions   The following are good choices in Grenada. They may not be offered by all cruise lines. Times and prices are approximate.

Island Sights   **City and Spice Tour.** Tour St. George's, then ride north along the spectacular west coast, through small villages and lush greenery, to a spice plantation and the nutmeg-processing station in Gouyave. *4 hrs. Cost: $40.*

Nature Tours   **Bay Gardens Tour.** Explore St. George's forts and historical sites, then venture just outside the city to Bay Gardens, a private horticultural paradise, where 450 species of island flowers and plants are cultivated in patterns mimicking their growth in the wild. *2 hrs. Cost: $16.*

Grand Étang Tour. View the sights in the capital, then travel north through Grenada's central mountain range to the rain forest, Crater Lake, and Grand Étang Forest Centre. *3 hrs. Cost: $30.*

Coming Ashore   Big cruise ships anchor outside St. George's Harbour and tender passengers to the east end of the Carenage, a horseshoe-shape thoroughfare that surrounds the harbor. Smaller ships can dock beside the welcome center, where water taxis, cabs, and walking-tour guides ($5 per hour) can be hired. From here, you can easily walk to town or take a taxi ($3 one-way). The capital can be toured easily on foot, but be prepared to climb up and down steep hills.

Getting Around   If you plan to spend your day in port exploring picturesque St. George's, you'll need no more than your feet for transportation. If you want to explore outside the town, hiring a taxi or arranging a guided tour is more sensible than renting a car.

By Minivan Privately owned minivans can be hired just outside the welcome center. Pay E.C.$1, and hold onto your hat.

By Taxi Taxis are plentiful, and fixed rates to popular island destinations are posted at the welcome center on the Carenage. Hiring a cab on an hourly basis runs $15 per hour; island tours cost $16–$50.

By Water Taxi Water taxis are the quickest way to get to the beach. The fare is $4 round-trip to Grand Anse; $10 to Morne Rouge.

Exploring Grenada *Numbers in the margin correspond to points of interest on the Grenada map.*

St. George's **St. George's** is one of the most picturesque and authentic West Indian towns in the Caribbean. Pastel-painted buildings with orange-tile roofs line the Carenage, facing the harbor. Small, rainbow-colored houses rise up from the waterfront and disappear into steep green hills. On weekends, a windjammer is likely to be anchored in the harbor, giving the entire scene a 19th-century appearance.

On the bay side of St. George's, facing the sea and separated from the harbor by the Sendall Tunnel, the **Esplanade** is the location of the open-air meat and fish markets. At high tide, waves sometimes crash against the sea wall. This area is also the terminus of the minibus route.

Ft. George, built by the French in 1708, rises high above the entrance to the harbor. No shots were ever fired from the fort until October 1983, when Prime Minister Maurice Bishop and some of his followers were assassinated in the courtyard. The fort now houses Grenada's police headquarters but is open to the public. The 360-degree view from the fort is magnificent. *Admission free. Open daily during daylight hrs.*

Don't miss picturesque **Market Square,** a block from the Esplanade on Granby Street. It's open weekday mornings but really comes alive every Saturday from 8 AM to noon. The atmosphere is colorful, noisy, and exciting. Vendors sell baskets, spices, fresh produce, clothing, and other items.

Grenada (and Carriacou)

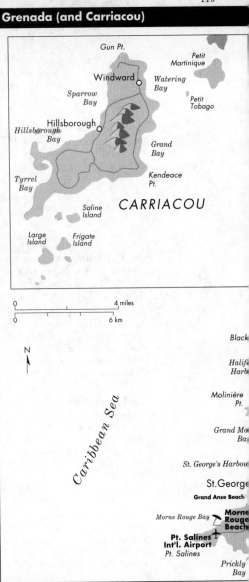

Gun Pt.

Petit
Martinique

Windward

Watering
Bay

Sparrow
Bay

Petit
Tobago

Hillsborough

Hillsborough
Bay

Grand
Bay

Tyrrel
Bay

Kendeace
Pt.

CARRIACOU

Saline
Island

Large
Island

Frigate
Island

0   4 miles
0   6 km

N

Black

Halifa
Harb

Molinière
Pt.

Caribbean Sea

Grand Mo
Ba

St. George's Harbou

St.George

Grand Anse Beach

Morne Rouge Bay

**Morne
Rouge
Beach**

**Pt. Salines
Int'l. Airport**
Pt. Salines

Prickly
Bay

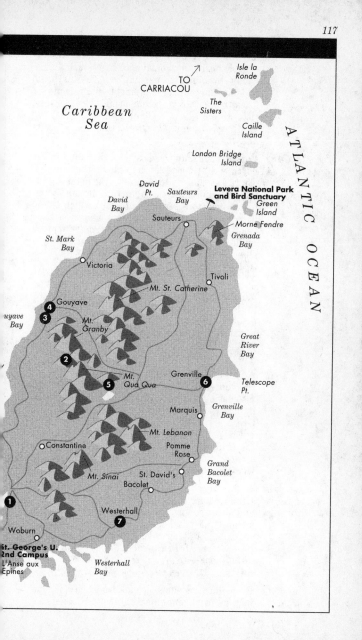

A couple of blocks from the harbor, the **National Museum** has a small, interesting collection of archaeological and colonial artifacts—such as the young Josephine Bonaparte's marble bathtub and old rum-making equipment–and recent political memorabilia documenting the intervention. *Young and Monckton Sts., tel. 809/440–3725. Admission: $1. Open weekdays 9–4:30, Sat. 10–1:30.*

The West Coast **Concord Falls,** up the Coast Road about 8 miles
❷ north of St. George's, is a great spot for hiking. There's a small visitor center at the main waterfall. A 2-mile hike through tropical rain forest brings you to a second waterfall, which thunders down over huge boulders and creates a small natural swimming pool. It's smart to use a guide for the hike. *No phone. Admission: $1. Open daily 9–4.*

❸ The **Dougaldston Estate,** just south of Gouyave, has a spice factory where you can see cocoa, nutmeg, mace, cloves, cinnamon, and other spices in their natural state, laid out on giant trays to dry in the sun. Old women walk barefoot through the spices, shuffling them so they dry evenly. *Coast Rd. just south of Gouyave. No phone. Admission $1. Open weekdays 9–4.*

❹ A tour of the **Nutmeg Processing Cooperative,** in the center of Gouyave, makes a fragrant and fascinating half hour. Workers in the three-story plant, which turns out 3 million pounds of Grenada's most famous export per year, sort nutmegs by hand and pack them in burlap bags for shipping worldwide. *Coast Rd., Gouyave (center of town). No phone. Admission: $1. Open weekdays 10–1 and 2–4.*

The East Coast In the center of this lush, mountainous island is **Grand Étang National Park,** a bird sanctuary
❺ and forest reserve where you can fish, hike, and swim. Crater Lake, in the crater of an extinct volcano, is a 13-acre glasslike expanse of cobalt-blue water. *Main Interior Rd., between Grenville and St. George's, tel. 809/440–6160. Admission: $1. Open weekdays 8:30–4.*

❻ **Grenville,** Grenada's second-largest city, is reminiscent of a French market town. Schooners set

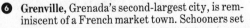

sail from Grenville for the outer islands. The local spice-processing factory is open to the public.

 Westerhall, a residential area about 5 miles east of St. George's, is known for its beautiful villas, gardens, and panoramic views. A great deal of residential development is happening here. European and North American retirees and local businesspeople are building elegant homes with striking views of the sea at prices that compare to those in expensive communities in the United States.

Grand Anse/ South End Most of Grenada's hotels and nightlife are in Grand Anse or the adjacent community of L'Anse aux Epines. There's a small shopping center, too, but beautiful Grand Anse Beach is the main attraction.

Carriacou Some sail-powered cruise ships, such as the vessels of Club Med, Star Clippers, and Windstar, call at Carriacou. A few tall ships, including the *Lili Marleen, Sea Cloud,* and *Yankee Clipper,* stop here, too. Part of the three-island nation of Grenada (Petit Martinique is the third), the 13-square-mile island is 16 miles north of the island of Grenada. Carriacou is the largest and southernmost island of the Grenadines, an archipelago of 32 small islands and cays that stretch from Grenada to St. Vincent.

The colonial history of Carriacou (pronounced kair-ee-uh-koo) parallels Grenada's, but the island's small size has restricted its role in the nation's political history. Carriacou is hilly but not lush like Grenada. In fact, it is quite arid in some areas. A chain of hills cuts a wide swath through the center, from Gun Point in the north to Tyrrel Bay in the south. The island's greatest attraction for cruise passengers is its diving opportunities.

Shopping **Spices** are a best buy. All kinds are grown and processed in Grenada and can be purchased for a fraction of what they would cost back home in your supermarket. Six-packs of tiny handwoven baskets lined with bay leaves and filled with spices (about $8) make good souvenirs. Small bottles filled with fresh nutmeg, cinnamon, curry powder, cloves, peppercorns, and other spices (about $2 each) are an alternative. These are available from vendors along the Carenage and just outside the welcome center.

For Caribbean art and antique engravings, visit **Yellow Poui Art Gallery** (tel. 809/444–3001), at the corner of Cross Street and the Esplanade in St. George's. **Tikal** (Young St., tel. 809/440–2310) is a long-established boutique with exquisite handicrafts, baskets, artwork, jewelry, carvings, batik items, and fashions—both locally made and imported from Africa and Latin America. **Art Fabrik** (Young St., tel. 809/440–0568) is a batik studio where you can watch artisans create the designs by painting fabric with hot wax. You can buy batik by the yard or fashioned into batik clothing and other items.

Stores in St. George's are generally open weekdays 8–4 or 4:30, Saturday 8–1; most are closed on Sunday, though some shops open and vendors appear if ships are in port.

Sports

Golf The **Grenada Golf & Country Club** (tel. 809/444–4128) near Grand Anse has a nine-hole golf course and is open to cruise passengers. Fees are E.C.$7.

Water Sports Major hotels on Grand Anse Beach have watersports centers where you can rent small sailboats, Windsurfers, and Sunfish. For **scuba diving,** contact Dive Grenada at Cot Bam restaurant (tel. 809/444–1092) or Grand Anse Aquatics, Ltd. at Coyaba Beach Resort (tel. 809/444–4129). Both dive operators are on Grand Anse Beach. On Carriacou, try Silver Beach Diving near Hillsborough (tel. 809/443–7882) or Tanki's Watersport Paradise, Ltd. on L'Esterre Bay (tel. 809/443–8406).

Beaches Grenada has 45 white-sand beaches along its 80 miles of coastline. Beaches are all open to cruise passengers, and some great stretches of sand are just 15 minutes from the dock in St. George's. **Grand Anse,** the most spectacular and most popular, is a gleaming 2-mile curve of clear, gentle surf. **Morne Rouge Beach,** a little southwest of Grand Anse, is less crowded and has a reef offshore that's terrific for snorkeling.

Dining *Some restaurants add a 10% service charge to your bill. If not, a 10%–15% gratuity should be added for a job well done.*

$$ **Coconut's Beach, The French Creole Restaurant.** Take local seafood, add butter, wine, and Grenadian herbs, and you have excellent French Creole cuisine. Throw in a beautiful setting at the northern end of Grand Anse Beach, and this West Indian cottage becomes a delightful spot for a meal. Lobster is prepared in a dozen different ways. Coconut's is open daily from 10 AM to 10 PM. The restaurant is set on the north end of Grand Anse Beach; a water taxi is a fun way to arrive. *Grand Anse Beach, tel. 809/444–4644. AE, MC, V.*

$$ **The Nutmeg.** Fresh seafood, homemade West Indian dishes, great hamburgers, and the view of the harbor are reasons why local residents and visitors like the Nutmeg. It's on the second floor, so you can watch the harbor traffic through the large open windows as you eat. *The Carenage, St. George's, tel. 809/440–2539. AE, D, MC, V.*

$$ **Rudolf's.** This informal pub offers fine West Indian fare—such as crab back, *lambi* (conch), and delectable nutmeg ice cream—along with fish-and-chips, sandwiches, and burgers—and the best gossip on the island. *The Carenage, St. George's, tel. 809/440–2241. MC, V. Closed Sun.*

Guadeloupe

On a map, Guadeloupe looks like a giant butterfly resting on the sea between Antigua and Dominica. Its two wings—Basse-Terre and Grande-Terre—are the two largest islands in the 659-square-mile Guadeloupe archipelago. The Rivière Salée, a 4-mile seawater channel flowing between the Caribbean and the Atlantic, forms the "spine" of the butterfly. A drawbridge over the channel connects the two islands.

If you're seeking a resort atmosphere, casinos, and white sandy beaches, your target is Grande-Terre. On the other hand, Basse-Terre's Natural Park, laced with mountain trails and washed by waterfalls and rivers, is a 74,100-acre haven for hikers, nature lovers, and anyone yearning to peer into the steaming crater of an active volcano.

This port of call is one of the least touristy (and least keen on Americans). Guadeloupeans accept visitors, but their economy does not rely on tourism. Pointe-à-Pitre, the port city, is a kaleidoscope of smart boutiques, wholesalers, sidewalk cafés, a pulsating meat and vegetable market, barred and broken-down buildings, little parks, and bazaarlike stores. Though not to everyone's liking, the city has more character than many other island ports.

French is the official language, and few locals speak English—although Guadeloupeans are very similar to Parisians in that if you make an attempt at a few French words, they will usually open up. (It's sensible to carry a postcard of the ship with the name of where it is docked written in French. This will come in handy in an emergency.) Like other West Indians, many Guadeloupeans do not appreciate having their photographs taken. Always ask permission first, and don't take a refusal personally. Also, many locals take offense at short shorts or swimwear worn outside bathing areas.

Currency Legal tender is the French franc, composed of 100 centimes. At press time, the rate was 4.65F to U.S.$1.

Telephones To call the United States from Guadeloupe, dial 191, the area code, and the local number. For calls within Guadeloupe, dial the six-digit number.

Shore Excursions The following is a good choice in Guadeloupe. It may not be offered by all cruise lines. Time and price are approximate.

Pointe-à-Pitre/Island Drive. Grande-Terre's various districts and residential areas are surveyed in this half-day drive that includes a visit to Ft. Fleur d'Epée and a refreshment stop at a hotel. *3 hrs. Cost: $40.*

Coming Ashore Cruise ships dock at the Maritime Terminal of Centre St-John Perse in downtown Pointe-à-Pitre, about a block from the shopping district. To get to the tourist information office, walk along the quay for about five minutes to the

In case you want to see the world.

At American Express, we're here to make your journey a smooth one. So we have over 1,700 travel service locations in over 120 countries ready to help. What else would you expect from the world's largest travel agency?

do more®

AMERICAN
EXPRESS

Travel

In case you want to be welcomed there.

We're here to see that you're always welcomed at establishments everywhere. That's why millions of people carry the American Express® Card – for peace of mind, confidence, and security, around the world or just around the corner.

do more ®

Cards

In case you're running low.

We're here to help with more than 118,000 Express Cash locations around the world. In order to enroll, just call American Express before you start your vacation.

do more

AMERICAN EXPRESS

Express Cash

And just in case.

We're here with American Express® Travelers Cheques and Cheques *for Two*.® They're the safest way to carry money on your vacation and the surest way to get a refund, practically anywhere, anytime.
Another way we help you...

do more

AMERICAN
EXPRESS

**Travelers
Cheques**

Place de la Victoire. The office is across the road at the top of the section of the harbor called La Darse (*see* Exploring Guadeloupe, *below*), just a few blocks from your ship. There's also a small tourist information booth in the terminal, but its hours and the information available are limited.

Getting Around
By Car

Guadeloupe has 1,225 miles of excellent roads (marked as in Europe), and driving around Grande-Terre is relatively easy. Cars can be rented at **Avis** (tel. 590/82–33–47), **Budget** (tel. 590/82–95–58), **Hertz** (tel. 590/82–00–14), or **Thrifty** (tel. 590/91–42–17). Rentals begin at about $60 a day. There is a small Hertz office at the Maritime Terminal.

By Taxi

Taxi fares are regulated by the government and posted at taxi stands. Fares are more expensive here than on other islands. If your French is good, you can call for a cab (tel. 590/82–00–00, 590/83–09–55, or 590/20–74–74). Tip drivers 10%. Before you agree to use a taxi driver as a guide, make sure you speak a common language.

By Moped

Vespas can be rented at **Vespa Sun** in Pointe-à-Pitre (tel. 590/91–30–36).

Exploring Guadeloupe

Numbers in the margin correspond to points of interest on the Guadeloupe map.

❶ **Pointe-à-Pitre,** a city of some 100,000 people, lies almost on the "backbone" of the butterfly, near the bridge that crosses the Salée River. Bustling and noisy, with its narrow streets, honking horns, and traffic jams, it is full of pulsing life. The most interesting area, with food and clothing stalls, markets, tempting pastry shops, and modern buildings, is compact and easy to see on foot.

The **Musée St-John Perse** is dedicated to the Guadeloupean poet who won the 1960 Nobel Prize in literature. Inside the restored colonial house is a complete collection of his poetry, as well as many of his personal effects. *Corner rue Noizières and Achille René-Boisneuf, tel. 590/ 90–07–92. Admission: 10F. Open Thurs.–Tues. 8:30–12:30 and 2:30–5:30.*

Guadeloupe

Guadeloupe Passage

Anse Lab
Anse-Bertra
Souffleur
Port–Louis

Anse du C
Pe
Vieux Bou
*Grand-
Cul-de-Sac-
Marin*
Jo

L
In
Ai

Pointe-à-Pitre

*Petit-
Cul-de-Sac-
Marin*

Goyave

N1

Ste-M

*Anse du
Vieux Fort* Pte. Allègre

Ste-Rose

**La
Grande
Anse**

Deshaies

N2

Lamentin
Destrelen

Pointe-
Noir
*Anse
Caraïbe*

3

2

N1

La Traversée

Petit-
Bourg

D23

Mahaut

Vernou

Malendure
*Pigeon
Island*

Bouillante

BASSE-TERRE

Marigot
Vieux-
Habitants
*Plage de
Rocroy*

Matouba
St-Claude

La Soufrière

Carbet

Capes
Belle-E

Basse-Terre

D11

Gourbeyre **N1** Bananier

Caribbean Sea

Anse Turlet

D6

Trois-
Rivières

D6

Vieux-Fort

0   10 miles
0   15 km

Iles des Saintes Terre-de-H
Place Crav

Terre-O
de-Bas

La Pointe de la Grande Vigie

KEY
Cruise Ship

ATLANTIC OCEAN

rde
nd

D122

N6

N8

Campêche

Gros-Cap

Beauport

Les Mangles

Anse de la Savane Brûlée

nal
t-Canal

N6

D120

N5

Baie du Nord Ouest

g

Morne-à-l'Eau

N5

N7

Le Moule

run du Sud

Jabrun du Nord

GRANDE-TERRE

Anse á la Baie

Abymes

Raizet ernational port
❶

St-François

Tarare

Pte. des Châteaux

Gosier

Ste-Anne

N4

Raisin-Clairs

Anse Kahouanne

Caravelle Beach

Ilet du Gosier

arie

erre-
u

Vieux-Fort

Grosse Pte.

Saint Louis

Baie de St. Louis

Anse Chapelle

Borée

Anse Ballet

Marie-Galante

Capesterre

Grand-Bourg

Petit-Anse

Pte. Des Basses

N

t
en

The **Marketplace** is a cacophonous and colorful place where locals bargain for papayas, breadfruit, christophines, tomatoes, and a vivid assortment of other produce. *Between rues St-John Perse, Frébault, Schoelcher, and Peynier.*

The **Musée Schoelcher** honors the memory of Victor Schoelcher, the 19th-century Alsatian abolitionist who fought slavery in the French West Indies. Exhibits trace his life and work. *24 rue Peynier, tel. 509/82–08–04. Admission: 10F. Open weekdays 8:30–11:30 and 2–5.*

Place de la Victoire, surrounded by wood buildings with balconies and shutters and lined by sidewalk cafés, was named in honor of Victor Hugues's 1794 victory over the British. The sandbox trees in the park are said to have been planted by Hugues the day after the victory. During the French Revolution a guillotine here lopped off the heads of many an aristocrat.

The imposing **Cathedral of St. Peter and St. Paul** has survived havoc-wreaking earthquakes and hurricanes. Note the lovely stained-glass windows. *rue Alexandre Isaac.*

Basse-Terre If you have a car, high adventure is yours by driving across Basse-Terre, which swirls with mountain trails and lakes, waterfalls, and hot springs. Basse-Terre is the home of the Old Lady, as the Soufrière volcano is called, and of the capital, also called Basse-Terre. On the west coast of the island lie the two mountains known ❷ as **Les Mamelles** (The Breasts). The pass that runs between Les Mamelles to the south and a lesser mountain to the north offers a spectacular view. Trails ranging from easy to arduous lace the surrounding mountains.

You don't have to be much of a hiker to climb the stone steps leading from La Traversée to the ❸ **Zoological Park and Botanical Gardens.** Titi the raccoon is the mascot of the park, which also features cockatoos, iguanas, and turtles. *Tel. 590/98–83–52. Admission: 25F. Open daily 9–4:30.*

Shopping For serious shopping in Pointe-à-Pitre, browse the boutiques and stores along **rue Schoelcher, rue Frébault,** and **rue Noizières.** The market square and stalls of **La Darse** are filled mostly with vegetables, fruits, and housewares, but you will find some straw hats and dolls.

There are dozens of shops in and around the cruise terminal, **Centre St-John Perse**. Many stores here offer a 20% discount on luxury items purchased with traveler's checks or major credit cards. You can find good buys on anything French—perfume, crystal, wine, cosmetics, and scarves. As for local handcrafted items, you'll see a lot of junk, but you can also find island dolls dressed in madras, finely woven straw baskets and hats, salako hats made of split bamboo, madras table linens, and wood carvings.

The following shops are all in Pointe-à-Pitre: For Baccarat, Lalique, Porcelaine de Paris, Limoges, and other upscale tableware, check **Selection** (rue Schoelcher), **A la Pensée** (44 rue Frébault, tel. 590/ 82–10–47), and **Rosebleu** (5 rue Frébault, tel. 590/82–93–43). Guadeloupe's exclusive purveyor of Orlane, Stendhal, and Germaine Monteil is **Vendôme** (8–10 rue Frébault, tel. 590/83–42–44). **Tim Tim** (16 rue Henri IV, tel. 590/83–48–71) is an upscale nostalgia shop with elegant (and expensive) antiques; be sure to see the museum-quality displays. For native *doudou* dolls, straw hats, baskets, and madras table linens, try **Au Caraibe** (4 rue Frébault, no phone). The largest selection of perfumes is at **Phoenicia** (8 rue Frébault, tel. 590/83–50–36). You many also want to try **Au Bonheur des Dames** (49 rue Frébault, tel. 590/82–00–30). For discount liquor and French wines, try **Seven Sins** on rue Schoelcher.

Sports

Fishing Contact **Caraibe Peche** (Marina Bas-du-Fort, tel. 590/90–97–51) or **Le Rocher de Malendure** (Pigeon, Bouillante, tel. 590/98–28–84).

Golf **Golf Municipal Saint-François** (St-François, tel. 590/88–41–87) has an 18-hole Robert Trent Jones course, an English-speaking pro, and electric carts for rent.

Hiking Basse-Terre's **Parc Tropical de Bras-David** is abundant with trails, many of which should be attempted only with an experienced guide. Trips for up to 12 people are arranged by **Organisation des Guides de Montagne de la**

Caraibe (Maison Forestière, Matouba, tel. 590/ 81–05–79).

Horseback Riding Beach rides and picnics are available through **Le Criolo** (St-Felix, tel. 590/84–04–06).

Water Sports Windsurfing, waterskiing, and sailing are available at almost all beachfront hotels. The main windsurfing center is at the **UCPA** hotel club (tel. 590/88–64–80) in St-François. You can also rent equipment at **Holywind** (Résidence Canella Beach, Pointe de la Verdure, Gosier, tel. 590/90– 44–00) and at the **Tropical Club Hotel** (tel. 590/ 93–97–97) at Le Moule, blessed with the constant Atlantic trade winds. The **Nautilus Club** (tel. 590/98–89–08) at Malendure Beach is one of the island's top scuba operations and offers glass-bottom-boat and snorkeling trips to Pigeon Island, just offshore—one of the best diving spots in the world.

Beaches Some of the island's best beaches of soft, white sand lie on the south coast of Grande-Terre from Ste-Anne to Pointe des Châteaux. For $5–$10 per passenger, hotels allow nonguests to use changing facilities, towels, and beach chairs. **Caravelle Beach,** just outside Ste-Anne, has one of the longest and prettiest stretches of sand. Protected by reefs, it's a fine place for snorkeling, and water-sports equipment can be rented from Club Med, located at one end of the beach. **Raisin-Clairs,** just outside St-François, offers windsurfing, waterskiing, sailing, and other activities, with rentals arranged through the Méridien Hotel. **Tarare** is a secluded cove close to the tip of Pointe des Châteaux, where locals tan in the buff. There are several secluded coves around **Pointe des Cháteaux,** where the Atlantic and Caribbean waters meet and crash against huge rocks, sculpting them into castlelike shapes. **La Grande Anse,** just outside Deshaies on the northwest coast of Basse-Terre, is a secluded beach of soft, beige sand sheltered by palms. The waterfront Karacoli restaurant serves rum punch and Creole dishes.

Dining *Restaurants are legally required to include a 15% service charge in the menu price. No additional gratuity is necessary.*

$$$ **La Canne à Sucre.** Innovative Creole cuisine has earned this two-story restaurant a reputation for being the best (and most expensive) in Pointe-à-Pitre. Fare at the main-floor Brasserie ranges from crayfish salad with smoked ham to skate in puff pastry with saffron sauce. Dining upstairs is more elaborate and twice as expensive. *Quai No. 1, Port Autonome, tel. 590/82–10–19. AE, V. No lunch Sat.*

$$ **Le Rocher de Malendure.** The setting on a bluff above Malendure Bay overlooking Pigeon Island makes this restaurant worth a special trip for lunch. The tiered terrace is decked with flowers, and the best choices on the menu are fresh fish, but there are also meat selections, such as veal in raspberry vinaigrette and tournedos in three sauces. *Malendure Beach, Bouillante, tel. 590/98–70–84. DC, MC, V. No dinner Sun.*

Jamaica

The third-largest island in the Caribbean, the English-speaking nation of Jamaica enjoys a considerable self-sufficiency based on tourism, agriculture, and mining. Its physical attractions include jungle mountains, clear waterfalls, and unforgettable beaches, yet the country's greatest resource may be its people. Although 95% of Jamaicans trace their bloodlines to Africa, their national origins also lie in Great Britain, the Middle East, India, China, Germany, Portugal, and South America, as well as in many other islands in the Caribbean. Their cultural life is a wealthy one; the music, art, and cuisine of Jamaica are vibrant with a spirit easy to sense but as hard to describe as the rhythms of reggae or the streetwise patois.

Don't let Jamaica's beauty cause you to relax the good sense you would use in your own hometown. Resist the promise of adventure should any odd character offer to show you the "real" Jamaica. Jamaica on the beaten track is wonderful enough, so don't take chances by wandering too far off it.

Currency Currency-exchange booths are set up on the docks at Montego Bay and Ocho Rios whenever a ship is in port. The U.S. dollar is accepted virtually everywhere, but change will be made in local currency. Check the value of the J$ on arrival—it fluctuates greatly. At press time the exchange rate was J$40 to U.S.$1.

Telephones Direct telephone, telegraph, telefax, and telex services are available in communication stations at the ports. Phones take phone cards, which are available from kiosks or variety shops.

Shore Excursions The following are good choices in Jamaica. They may not be offered by all cruise lines. Times and prices are approximate.

Natural Beauty **Prospect Plantation.** The beautiful gardens of Prospect Plantation are the highlight of this tour, with a brief stop at Dunn's River Falls. *3½ hrs. Cost: $39.*

Rafting on the Martha Brae River. Glide down this pristine river in a 30-foot, two-seat bamboo raft, admiring the verdant plant life along the river's banks. *4 hrs. Cost: $45.*

Coming Ashore A growing number of cruise ships are using the city of Montego Bay (nicknamed "Mo Bay"), 67 miles to the west of Ocho Rios, as their Jamaican port of call. The cruise port in Mo Bay is a $10 taxi ride from town. There is one shopping center within walking distance of the Montego Bay docks. The Jamaica Tourist Board office is about 3½ miles away on Gloucester Avenue.

Montego Bay

Ocho Rios Most cruise ships dock at this port on Jamaica's north coast, near the famous Dunn's River Falls. Less than a mile from the Ocho Rios cruise-ship pier are the Taj Mahal Duty Free Shopping Center and the Ocean Village Shopping Center, where the Jamaica Tourist Board maintains an office. Getting anywhere else in Ocho Rios will require a taxi.

Getting Around Neither Montego Bay nor Ocho Rios is a walking port, and driving is not recommended for cruise passengers. Jamaicans are not admired for their driving skills, and driving is on the left. Furthermore, you must reserve a car and send a deposit *before* you reach Jamaica. Rates are about $75–$100 per day.

By Moped Mopeds are available for rent, but as with renting a car, this is not the best Caribbean port for cruise passengers to drive in. Daily rates run from about $45. Deposits of $200 or more or a signed credit card slip are usually required. Ask at the tourist office for rental shops near your port.

By Taxi Some of Jamaica's taxis are metered; rates are per car, not per passenger. Cabs can be flagged down on the street. All licensed and properly insured taxis display red Public Passenger Vehicle (PPV) plates. Licensed minivans also bear the red PPV plates. If you hire a taxi driver as a tour guide, be sure to agree on a price *before* the vehicle is put into gear.

Exploring **Barnett Estates.** Led by a charming guide in
Jamaica period costume who relates poetry and sings
Montego Bay songs of the period as part of the presentation, this great-house tour is one of the best you'll find in Jamaica. The Kerr-Jarrett family has held the land here for 11 generations and still grows coconut, mango, and sugarcane on 3,000 acres; you'll get samples during the plantation tour by jitney. *Granville Main Rd., tel. 809/ 952–2382. Admission: $30. Call for hrs of operation and tour times.*

Greenwood Great House, 15 miles east of Montego Bay, has no spooky legend to titillate visitors, but it's much better than Rose Hall at evoking the atmosphere of life on a sugar plantation. Highlights of Greenwood include oil paintings of the family, china specially made for them by Wedgwood, a library filled with rare books, fine antique furniture, and a collection of exotic musical instruments. *Tel. 809/953–1077. Admission: $10. Open daily 9–6.*

One of the most popular excursions in Jamaica is rafting on the **Martha Brae River** (tel. 809/952–0889 for reservations), a gentle waterway filled with the romance of a tropical wilderness. Wear your swimsuit for a plunge at the halfway point and pick a raft that has a comfortable cushion. The ride costs less than $40 for two people.

Rose Hall Great House, perhaps the most impressive in the West Indies in the 1700s, enjoys its popularity less for its architecture than for the legend surrounding its second mistress. The story of Annie Palmer—credited with murdering three husbands and a plantation overseer who was her lover—is told in two novels sold

Jamaica

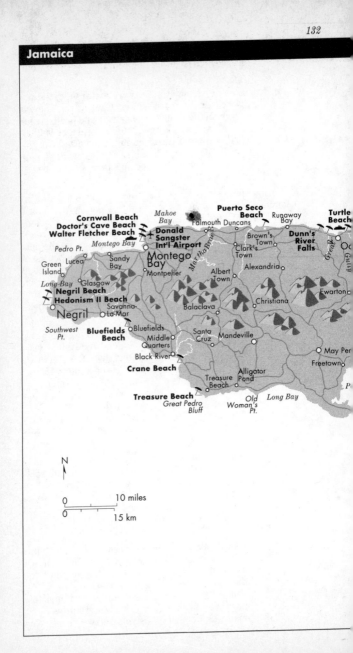

Mahoe Bay

Puerto Seco Beach Runaway Bay

Turtle Beach

Cornwall Beach
Doctor's Cave Beach
Walter Fletcher Beach Falmouth Duncans

Donald Sangster Int'l Airport

Brown's Town

Dunn's River Falls

Pedro Pt. Montego Bay

Clark's Town

Green Island Lucea

Sandy Bay

Montego Bay

Martha Brae

Great

Montpelier

Albert Town

Alexandria

Long Bay Glasgow

Negril Beach
Hedonism II Beach

Savanna-La-Mar

Negril

Balaclava

Ewarton

Christiana

Southwest Pt.

Bluefields Beach Bluefields

Middle Quarters

Santa Cruz

Mandeville

May Pen

Black River

Freetown

Crane Beach

Alligator Pond

Treasure Beach

Treasure Beach
Great Pedro Bluff

Old Woman's Pt.

Long Bay

N

0   10 miles
0   15 km

Turtle
Beach
Mallard's Bay
Galina Pt.
Ocracabessa
Port Maria
Ocho Rios
Great R.
Fern Gully
Annotto
Bay
Troja
St. Margaret's
Bay
Port Antonio
San San Beach
Ewarton
Orange Bay
Berridale
Northeast Pt.
Boston Bay
Priestman's
River
BLUE MOUNTAINS
Moore
Town
Spanish
Town
Kingston
Hectors
River
*Holland
Bay*
May Pen
Port Royal
Gunboat
Beach
White
Horses
Golden
Grove
Freetown
Norman Manley
International
Airport
*Morant
Bay*
Lyssons
Beach
Fort Clarence
Beach
Polink Pt.
*Portland
Bight*
*Kingston
Harbour*

Portland Pt.

Caribbean Sea

KEY
Cruise Ship

everywhere in Jamaica: *The White Witch of Rose Hall* and *Jamaica Witch*. The great house is east of Montego Bay, across the highway from the Rose Hall resorts. *Tel. 809/953–2323. Admission: $15. Open daily 9–6.*

Ocho Rios **Dunn's River Falls** is 600 feet of cold, clear mountain water splashing over a series of stone steps to the warm Caribbean. Don a swimsuit, climb the slippery steps, take the hand of the person ahead of you, and trust that the chain of hands and bodies leads to an experienced guide. The climb leaders are personable, reeling off bits of local lore while telling you where to step. Take a towel and wear tennis shoes. *Tel. 809/974–2857. Admission: $5. Open daily 9–5.*

The tour of **Prospect Plantation** is the best of several offerings that delve into the island's former agricultural lifestyle. It's not just for specialists; virtually everyone enjoys the beautiful views over the White River Gorge and the tour by jitney through a plantation with exotic fruits and tropical trees. Horseback riding through 1,000 acres is available, with one hour's notice, for about $20 per hour. *Tel. 809/974–2058. Admission: $12. Open daily 10:30–3:30; tours at 11, 1:30, and 3:30.*

Shopping Jamaican artisans express themselves in resort wear, hand-loomed fabrics, silk-screening, wood carvings, and paintings. Jamaican rum makes a great gift, as do Tia Maria (Jamaica's famous coffee liqueur) and Blue Mountain coffee. Cheap sandals are good buys (about $20 a pair).

While you should not rule out a visit to the "crafts markets" in Mo Bay and Ocho Rios, you should consider first how much you like pandemonium and haggling over prices and quality. If you're looking to spend money, head for **City Centre Plaza, Half Moon Village, Miranda Ridge Plaza, Montego Bay Shopping Center, St. James's Place,** and **Westgate Plaza** in Montego Bay; in Ocho Rios, the shopping plazas are **Pineapple Place, Ocean Village,** the **Taj Mahal, Coconut Grove,** and **Island Plaza.** Some cruise lines run shore excursions devoted exclusively to shopping.

For Jamaican and Haitian paintings, go to the **Gallery of West Indian Art** (1 Orange La., Montego Bay, tel. 809/952–4547). A corner of the gallery is devoted to hand-turned pottery and beautifully carved birds and jungle animals. Six miles east of the docks in Ocho Rios is **Harmony Hall** (tel. 809/975–4222), a huge house that has been converted into an art gallery, restaurant, and bar. Wares here include arts and crafts, carved items, ceramics, antiques, books, jewelry, fudge, spices, and Blue Mountain coffee.

Sports

Golf The best courses are at the **Half Moon Club** (tel. 809/953–2560) and **Tryall** (tel. 809/956–5681) in Montego Bay or **Runaway Bay** (tel. 809/973–2561) and **Sandal's Golf and Country Club** (tel. 809/974–2528) in Ocho Rios. Rates range from $25 to $50 for 18 holes at the Ocho Rios courses to $110 and higher at Half Moon and Tryall.

Horseback Riding **Chukka Cove** (St. Ann, tel. 809/972–2506), near Ocho Rios, is the best equestrian facility in the English-speaking Caribbean. Riding is also available at **Prospect Plantation** (Ocho Rios, tel. 809/974–2058) and **Rocky Point Stables** (Half Moon Club, Montego Bay, tel. 809/953–2286).

Beaches **Doctor's Cave Beach** at Montego Bay is getting crowded, attracting Jamaicans and tourists alike. The 5-mile stretch of sugary sand has been spotlighted in so many travel articles and brochures that it's no secret to anyone anymore. Two other popular beaches near Montego Bay are **Cornwall Beach,** farther up the coast, which has food and drink options, and **Walter Fletcher Beach,** on the bay near the center of town. Fletcher offers protection from the surf on a windy day and has unusually calm waters for swimming. The recently opened **Rose Hall Beach Club,** east of central Mo Bay near Rose Hall Great House, is a secluded area (far less crowded than beaches in town) with changing rooms and showers, a water-sports center, volleyball and other beach games, and a beach bar and grill. Ocho Rios appears to be just about as busy as Mo Bay these days, and the busiest beach is **Ocho Rios public beach** stretching behind Jamaica Grande and Club Jamaica. Next door is **Turtle Beach,** the islanders' favorite place to swim in Ocho Rios.

Dining *Many restaurants add a 10% service charge to the bill. Otherwise, a tip of 10%–15% is customary.*

Montego Bay **Sugar Mill.** One of the finest restaurants in Ja-
$$$ maica, the Sugar Mill (formerly the Club House) serves seafood with flair on a terrace. Steak and lobster are usually garnished in a pungent sauce that blends Dijon mustard with Jamaica's own Pickapeppa. *At Half Moon Golf Course, Montego Bay, tel. 809/953–2228. AE, DC, MC, V.*

$ **Pork Pit.** Enjoy Jamaica's fiery jerk pork at this open-air hangout. Plan to arrive around noon, when the first jerk is lifted from its bed of coals and pimiento wood. *Gloucester Av. across from Walter Fletcher Beach, Montego Bay, tel. 809/952–1046. Reservations not accepted. No credit cards.*

Ocho Rios **Almond Tree.** This very popular restaurant pre-
$$–$$$ pares Jamaican dishes enlivened by a European culinary tradition. The swinging rope chairs of the terrace bar and the tables perched above a lovely Caribbean cove are great fun. *83 Main St., Ocho Rios, tel. 809/974–2813. Reservations essential. AE, DC, MC, V.*

$–$$ **Evita's.** The setting here is a sensational, nearly 100-year-old gingerbread house high on a hill overlooking Ocho Rios Bay (but also convenient from Mo Bay). More than 30 kinds of pasta are served here, ranging from lasagna Rastafari (vegetarian) and fiery "jerk" spaghetti to rotelle *Colombo* (crabmeat with white sauce and noodles). There are also excellent fish dishes from which to choose. *Mantalent Inn, tel. 809/974–2333. AE, MC, V.*

Key West

The southernmost city in the continental United States was originally a Spanish possession. Along with the rest of Florida, Key West became part of American territory in 1821. During the late 19th century, Key West was Florida's wealthiest city per capita. The locals made their fortunes from "wrecking"—rescuing people and salvaging cargo from ships that foundered on nearby reefs. Cigar making, fishing, shrimping, and sponge gathering also became important industries.

Capital of the self-proclaimed "Conch Republic," Key West today makes for a unique port of call for the 10 or so ships that visit each week. A genuinely American town, it nevertheless exudes the relaxed atmosphere and pace of a typical Caribbean island. Major attractions for cruise passengers are the home of the Conch Republic's most famous citizen, Ernest Hemingway; the birthplace of now-departed Pan American World Airways; and, if your cruise ship stays in port late enough, the island's renowned sunset celebrations.

Shore Excursions The following are good choices in Key West. They may not be offered by all cruise lines. Times and prices are approximate.

Island Sights **Historic Homes Walking Tour.** You'll see three notable Key West residences—the Harry S. Truman Little White House, the Donkey Milk House, and the Audubon House and Gardens—on a short guided stroll through the historic district. *2 hrs. Cost: $16.*

Undersea Creatures **Reef Snorkeling.** The last living coral reefs in continental America are your boat's destination. Changing facilities, snorkeling gear, and unlimited beverages are included. *3 hrs. Cost: $38.*

Coming Ashore Cruise ships dock at Mallory Square or near Truman Annex. Both are within walking distance of Duval and Whitehead streets, the two main tourist thoroughfares. For maps and other tourism information, the Chamber of Commerce (402 Wall St.) is found just off Mallory Square.

Getting Around Key West is easily explored on foot. There is little reason to rent a car or hire a cab; public transportation is virtually nonexistent. If you plan to venture beyond the main tourist district, a fun way to get around is by bicycle or scooter.

By Taxi The **Maxi-Taxi Sun Cab System** (tel. 305/294–2222) and **Five 66666** (tel. 305/296–6666) provide service in and around Key West. Taxis meet ships at the pier, but they are not recommended for sightseeing.

By Bicycle or Moped Key West is a cycling town. In fact, there are so many bikes around that cyclists must watch out for one another as well as for cars. Try renting from **Keys Moped & Scooter** (tel. 305/294–0399) or **Moped Hospital** (tel. 305/296–3344); both can be found on Truman Avenue. Bikes rent for about $3–$5 per day, mopeds cost $10 for three hours.

By Tour Train or Trolley The **Conch Tour Train** (tel. 305/294–5161) provides a 90-minute, narrated tour of Key West that covers 14 miles of island sights. Board at the Front Street Depot every half hour. The first train leaves at 9 AM and the last at 4:30 PM.

Old Town Trolley (tel. 305/296–6688) operates 12 trackless, trolley-style buses for 90-minute, narrated tours of Key West. You may get off at any of 14 stops and reboard later.

Exploring Key West *Numbers in the margin correspond to points of interest on the Key West map.*

❶ **Mallory Square** is named for Stephen Mallory, secretary of the Confederate Navy, who later owned the Mallory Steamship Line. On nearby Mallory Dock, a nightly sunset celebration draws street performers, food vendors, and thousands of onlookers.

❷ Facing Mallory Square is **Key West Aquarium,** which houses hundreds of brightly colored tropical fish and other fascinating sea creatures from local waters. *1 Whitehead St., tel. 305/296–2051. Admission: $6.50. Open daily 9–6; guided tours and shark feeding at 11, 1, 3, and 4:30.*

❸ The **Mel Fisher Maritime Heritage Society Museum** symbolizes Key West's "wrecking" past. On display are gold and silver bars, coins, jewelry, and other artifacts recovered in 1985 from two Spanish treasure ships that foundered in 1622. *200 Greene St., tel. 305/294–2633. Admission: $6. Open daily 9:30–5.*

❹ At the end of Front Street, the **Truman Annex** is a 103-acre former military parade ground and barracks. Also here is the Harry S. Truman Little White House Museum, in the former president's vacation home. *111 Front St., tel. 305/ 294–9911. Admission: $7. Open daily 9–5.*

❺ The **Audubon House and Gardens** commemorates ornithologist John James Audubon's 1832 visit to Key West. On display are a large collection of the artist's engravings. *205 Whitehead*

St., tel. 305/294–2116. Admission: $7.50. Open daily 9:30–5.

6 At **301 Whitehead Street,** a sign proclaims the birthplace of Pan American World Airways, the first U.S. airline to operate scheduled international air service. The inaugural flight took off from Key West International Airport on October 28, 1927.

7 Built in 1851, **Hemingway House** was the first dwelling in Key West to have running water and a fireplace. Ernest Hemingway bought the place in 1931 and wrote eight books here. Descendants of Hemingway's cats still inhabit the grounds. Half-hour tours begin every 10 minutes. *907 Whitehead St., tel. 305/294–1575. Admission: $6.50. Open daily 9–5.*

Up the block from Hemingway House and across the street, behind a white picket fence, is the
8 **Lighthouse Museum,** a 66-foot lighthouse built in 1847 and an adjacent 1887 clapboard house where the keeper lived. You can climb the 98 steps to the top for a spectacular view of the island. *938 Whitehead St., tel. 305/294–0012. Admission: $5. Open daily 9:30–5.*

At the foot of Whitehead Street, a huge concrete marker proclaims this spot to be the
9 **Southernmost Point** in the United States. Turn left on South Street. To your right are two dwellings that both claim to be the Southernmost House. Take a right onto Duval Street, which ends at the Atlantic Ocean, and you will be at the Southernmost Beach.

10 The **Wrecker's Museum** is said to be the oldest house in Key West. It was built in 1829 as the home of Francis Watlington, a sea captain and wrecker. It now contains 18th- and 19th-century period furnishings. *322 Duval St., tel. 305/294–9502. Admission: $3. Open daily 10–4.*

For a look at Key West as it was, visit the re-
11 stored **Old City Hall** (510 Greene St.). Inside is a permanent exhibit of old Key West photographs, dating back to 1845.

12 **Key West Bight,** also known as Harbor Walk, remains the last funky area of Old Key West. Numerous charter boats and classic yachts call its

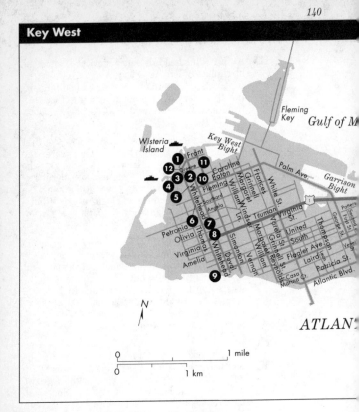

Audubon House
and Gardens, **5**

Hemingway
House, **7**

Key West
Aquarium, **2**

Key West
Bight, **12**

Lighthouse
Museum, **8**

Mallory
Square, **1**

Mel Fisher
Maritime
Heritage Society
Museum, **3**

Old City
Hall, **11**

Southernmost
Point, **9**

301 Whitehead
Street, **6**

Truman
Annex, **4**

Wrecker's
Museum, **10**

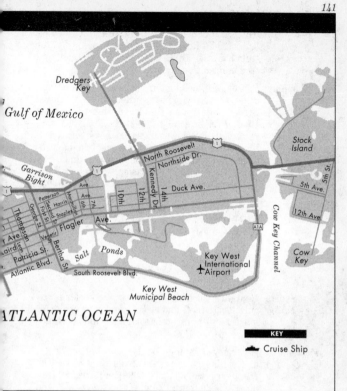

Dredgers
Key

Gulf of Mexico

North Roosevelt
Northside Dr.

Stock
Island

Garrison
Bight

Patterson
Ave.
Harris
Ave.
Staples
6th
7th
Duck Ave.

Kennedy Dr.

10th

12th

14th

5th St.

5th Ave.

12th Ave.

Thompson

George St.

First St.

Second St.

Flagler   Ave.

Cow Key Channel

A1A

Cow
Key

r Ave.

Laird

Vessell

Bertha St.

Patricia St.

Atlantic Blvd.

Salt   Ponds

South Roosevelt Blvd.

Key West
International
Airport

Key West
Municipal Beach

ATLANTIC OCEAN

KEY

Cruise Ship

slips home, and there's a popular waterfront bar called the Schooner Wharf (*see* Pub Crawling, *below*). The Reef Relief Environmental Center (tel. 305/294–3100) has videos, displays, and free information about the coral reef.

Shopping Passengers looking for T-shirts, trinkets, and other souvenirs will find them all along Duval Street and around the cruise-ship piers. **Fast Buck Freddie's** (500 Duval St., tel. 305/294–2007) sells such novelties as battery-operated alligators that eat Muenster cheese, banana leaf–shape furniture, fish-shape flatware, and every flamingo item anyone has ever dreamed up. **H.T. Chittum & Co.** (725 Duval St., tel. 305/292–9002) sells Key West–style apparel and accessories, from aviator hats to fish-cleaning knives. **Key West Island Bookstore** (513 Fleming St., tel. 305/294–2904) is the literary bookstore of the large Key West writers' community, while **Lucky Street Gallery** (919 Duval St., tel. 305/294–3973) carries the work of Key West artists and others.

Sports
Diving **Captain's Corner** (tel. 305/296–8865) leads excursions to reefs and wrecks for spear fishing or lobstering and archaeological and treasure hunting.

Fishing and Boating A variety of fishing vessels, glass-bottom boats, and sailing charters sail from Key West. The ***Discovery*** (tel. 305/293–0099) and ***Fireball*** (tel. 305/296–6293) are two glass-bottom boats, and the ***Wolf*** (tel. 305/296–9653) is a schooner that sails on day and sunset cruises with live music. The ***Linda D III*** and ***Linda D IV*** (tel. 305/296–9798 or 800/299–9798), captained by third-generation Key West seaman Bill Wickers, run full- and half-day sportfishing outings. The Chamber of Commerce on Front Street, by the pier, has a full list of other operators.

Golf **Key West Resort Golf Course** (tel. 305/294–5232) is an 18-hole course on the bay side of Stock Island. Fees are $62 for 18 holes, including a cart.

Snorkeling The northernmost living coral reef in the Americas and clear, warm Gulf of Mexico waters make Key West a good choice for getting your flippers wet (*see* Shore Excursions, *above*, and Beaches, *below*).

Beaches Facing the Gulf of Mexico, **Simonton Street Beach**, at the north end of Simonton Street and near the cruise-ship piers, is a great place to watch the boats come and go in the harbor. On the Atlantic Ocean, **Fort Zachary Taylor State Historic Site** has several hundred yards of beach near the western end of Key West. The beach is relatively uncrowded; snorkeling is good here. **Smathers Beach** features almost 2 miles of coarse sand alongside South Roosevelt Boulevard. Vendors along the road will rent you rafts, Windsurfers, and other beach toys. **Southernmost Beach** is found at the foot of Duval Street (*see* Exploring Key West, *above*).

Dining **Pier House Restaurant.** Steamships from Havana once docked at this pier jutting into the Gulf of Mexico. Now, it's an elegant place to dine, indoors or out, and to watch the boats glide by. The menu highlights American and Caribbean cuisine. Specialties include such dishes as grilled tuna with cracked peppercorns and lobster ravioli in a creamy pesto sauce. *1 Duval St., tel. 305/296–4600. AE, DC, MC, V.*

$–$$ **Half Shell Raw Bar.** "Eat It Raw" is the motto, and even during the off-season this oyster bar keeps shucking. You eat at shellacked picnic tables in a shed, with model ships, life buoys, and old license plates hung overhead. If shellfish isn't to your taste, try the broiled dolphin sandwich or linguine seafood marinara. *Land's End Marina, tel. 305/294–7496. Reservations not accepted. MC, V.*

Pub Crawling Three spots stand out for first-timers among the many local saloons frequented by Key West denizens. **Capt. Tony's Saloon** (428 Greene St.) is where Ernest Hemingway used to hang out when it was called **Sloppy Joe's.** The current **Sloppy Joe's** is found nearby at 201 Duval Street and has become a landmark in its own right. **Schooner Wharf** (Key West Bight; *see* Exploring Key West, *above*) is the most authentically local saloon and doesn't sell T-shirts. All are within easy walking distance of the cruise-ship piers.

Martinique

One of the most beautiful islands in the Caribbean, Martinique is lush with wild orchids, frangipani, anthurium, jade vines, flamingo flowers, and hundreds of hibiscus varieties. Trees bend under the weight of tropical treats such as mangoes, papayas, bright red West Indian cherries, lemons, and limes. Acres of banana plantations, pineapple fields, and waving sugarcane fill the horizon.

The towering mountains and verdant rain forest in the north lure hikers, while underwater sights and sunken treasures attract snorkelers and scuba divers. Martinique is also wonderful if your idea of exercise is turning over every 10 or 15 minutes to get an even tan, or if your adventuresome spirit is satisfied by a duty-free shop.

The largest of the Windward Islands, Martinique is 4,261 miles from Paris, but its spirit and language are decidedly French, with more than a soupçon of West Indian spice. Tangible, edible evidence of that fact is the island's cuisine, a superb blend of classic French and Creole dishes.

Fort-de-France is the capital, but at the turn of the 20th century, St-Pierre, farther up the coast, was Martinique's premier city. Then, in 1902, volcanic Mont Pelée blanketed the city in ash, killing all its residents—save for a condemned man in prison. Today, the ruins are a popular excursion for cruise passengers.

Currency Legal tender is the French franc, which consists of 100 centimes. At press time, the rate was 4.65F to U.S.$1. Dollars are accepted, but if you're going to shop, dine, or visit museums on your own, it's better to convert a small amount of money into francs.

Telephones It is not possible to make collect calls from Martinique to the United States on the local phone system, but you can usually use an AT&T card. There are no coin telephone booths on the island. If you must call home and can't wait until the ship reaches the next port, go to the post office and purchase a Telecarte, which looks like a credit card and is used in special booths marked TELECOM. Long-distance calls made with Telecartes are less costly than operator-assisted calls.

Shore Excursions The following is a good choice on Martinique. It may not be offered by all cruise lines. Time and price are approximate.

Island Sights **Martinique's Pompeii.** By bus or taxi, drive through the lush green mountains, past picturesque villages, to St-Pierre, stopping at the museum there. This is one of the best island tours in the Caribbean. *2½–4 hrs. Cost: $50–$60.*

Coming Ashore Cruise ships that dock call at the Maritime Terminal east of the city. The only practical way to get into town is by cab ($16 round-trip). To get to the Maritime Terminal tourist information office, turn right and walk along the waterfront. Ships that anchor in the Baie des Flamands (*see* Exploring Martinique, *below*) tender passengers directly to the downtown waterfront. A tourist office is just across the street from the landing pier in the Air France building. Guided walking tours ($15 for 1½ hrs.) can be arranged at the nearby open-air marketplace.

Getting Around Martinique has about 175 miles of well-paved roads marked with international road signs. *By Car* Streets in Fort-de-France are narrow and clogged with traffic, country roads are mountainous with hairpin turns, and the Martiniquais drive with controlled abandon. If you drive in the country, be sure to pick up a map from one of the tourist offices; an even better one is the *Carte Routière et Touristique*, available at any local bookstore.

For rental cars, contact **Avis** (tel. 596/70–11–60), **Budget** (tel. 596/63–69–00), or **Hertz** (tel. 596/60–64–64). Count on paying $60 a day.

By Ferry Weather permitting, *vedettes* (ferries) operate daily between Fort-de-France and the marina Méridien, in Pointe du Bout, and between Fort-de-France and the beaches of Anse-Mitan and Anse-à-l'Ane. The Quai d'Esnambuc is the arrival and departure point for ferries in Fort-de-France. The one-way fare is 16F; round-trip, 27F.

By Taxi Taxis are relatively expensive. At press time, metered taxi fares were about to be introduced. Under the old system, rates were regulated by the government. The minimum charge was 10F (about $2.90), but a journey of any distance could easily cost upwards of 50F. Before you agree to use a taxi driver as a guide, make sure his English is good.

Exploring Martinique

Numbers in the margin correspond to points of interest on the Martinique map.

Fort-de-France

On the island's west coast, on the beautiful Baie des Flamands, lies the capital city of **❶ Fort-de-France.** Its narrow streets and pastel buildings with ornate wrought-iron balconies are reminiscent of the French Quarter in New Orleans—but whereas New Orleans is flat, Fort-de-France is hilly.

Bordering the waterfront is **La Savane,** a 12½-acre landscaped park filled with gardens, tropical trees, fountains, and benches. It's a popular gathering place and the scene of promenades, parades, and impromptu soccer matches. Near the harbor is a marketplace where beads, baskets, pottery, and straw hats are sold. The crafts here are among the nicest in the Caribbean.

On rue de la Liberté, which runs along the west side of La Savane, look for the **Musée Départmentale de la Martinique.** Artifacts from the pre-Columbian Arawak and Carib periods include pottery, beads, and part of a skeleton that turned up during excavations in 1972. One exhibit examines the history of slavery; costumes, documents, furniture, and handicrafts from the island's colonial period are on display. *9 rue de la Liberté, tel. 596/71–57–05. Admission: 15F. Open weekdays 8:30–1 and 2:30–5, Sat. 9–noon.*

Rue Schoelcher runs through the center of the capital's primary shopping district—a six-block area bounded by rue de la République, rue de la Liberté, rue Victor Sévère, and rue Victor Hugo (*see* Shopping, *below*).

The Romanesque **St-Louis Cathedral** (west of rue Victor Schoelcher), whose steeple rises high above the surrounding buildings, has lovely stained-glass windows. A number of Martinique's former governors are interred beneath the choir loft.

The **Bibliothèque Schoelcher** (pronounced shell-cher), a wildly elaborate Byzantine-Egyptian-Romanesque public library, is named after Victor Schoelcher, who led the fight to free the slaves in the French West Indies in the 19th century. The eye-popping structure was built for the 1889 Paris Exposition, after which it was dismantled, shipped to Martinique, and reassembled piece by piece on its present site. Inside is a collection of ancient documents recounting Fort-de-France's development. *Corner of rue de la Liberté. Admission free. Open daily 8:30–6.*

The North Martinique's "must do" is the drive north through the mountains from Fort-de-France to St-Pierre and back along the coast. The 40-mile round-trip can be done in an afternoon, although there is enough to see to fill your entire day in port. A nice way to see the lush island interior and St-Pierre is to take the N3, which snakes through dense rain forests, north to Le Morne Rouge; then take the N2 back to Fort-de-France via St-Pierre.

❷ Along the N3 (also called the Route de la Trace), stop at **Balata** to see the **Balata Church,** an exact replica of Sacré-Coeur Basilica in Paris, and the **Jardin de Balata** (Balata Gardens). Jean-Phillipe Thoze, a professional landscaper and devoted horticulturist, spent 20 years creating this collection of thousands of varieties of tropical flowers and plants. There are shaded benches where you can relax and take in the panoramic views of the mountains. *Rte. de Balata, tel. 596/72–58–82. Admission: 30F. Open daily 9–5.*

❸ Continuing north on the N3, you'll reach **Le Morne Rouge,** on the southern slopes of Mont Pelée. This town was, like St-Pierre, destroyed by the volcano and is now a popular resort. Signs will direct you to the narrow road that takes you halfway up the mountain—you won't really have time to hike to the 4,600-foot peak, but this side trip gets you fairly close and offers spectacular views.

❹ Northeast of here on the N3, a few miles south of **Basse-Pointe** on the Atlantic coast, is the flower-filled village of **Ajoupa-Bouillon.** This 17th-century settlement in the midst of pineapple fields

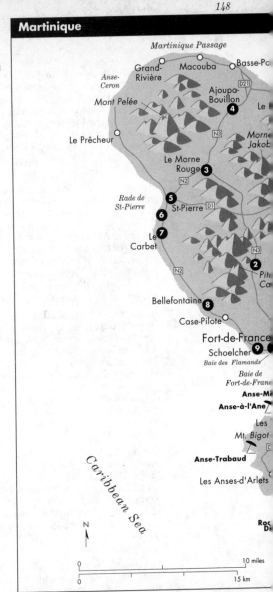

Martinique

Martinique Passage

Grand-
Rivière

Macouba

Basse-Pc

*Anse-
Ceron*

Mont Pelée

Ajoupa-
Bouillon

4

D21

Le

Le Prêcheur

Morne
Jakob

N3

Le Morne
Rouge

3

N2

*Rade de
St-Pierre*

5

St-Pierre

D1

6

7

Le
Carbet

N3

N2

2

Pit.
Ca

Bellefontaine

8

Case-Pilote

Fort-de-France

Schoelcher

9

Baie des Flamands

*Baie de
Fort-de-Fran*

Anse-Mi

Anse-à-l'Ane

Les

Mt. Bigot

Anse-Trabaud

Les Anses-d'Arlets

Caribbean Sea

Roc
Di

N

0   10 miles

0   15 km

asse-Pointe

Le Lorrain

Marigot

Morne
Jakob

Ste-Marie

ATLANTIC OCEAN

Caravelle
Peninsula

Havre de la
Trinité

Tartane

Pointe
Caracoli

La Trinité

Baie du Galion

Gros-Morne

St-Joseph
Pitons du
Carbet

Le Robert

Havre du Robert

Pte. de
la Rose

ance

Lamentin

Le François

Mt. Vauclin

Lamentin
International
Airport

Pointe
du Bout

Ducos

ase-Mitan

Ane

Le Vauclin

Les Trois-Ilets

got

Rivière-
Salée

Rivière-
Pilote

Le
Diamant

rlets

Ste-Luce

Le Marin

Rocher du
Diamant

Pte. Figuier

Cul-de-Sac
du Marin

Pte. Marin

Cap
Chevalier

Les Salines

Ste-Anne

iles

Anse-Trabaud

Pte. des Salines

Pte. d'Enfer

St. Lucia Channel

is a beautiful area, but skip it if you've never seen St-Pierre and are running out of time. From Le Morne Rouge, you'll need a good three hours to enjoy the coastal drive back to Fort-de-France.

5 Take the N2 west a few miles to **St-Pierre,** the island's oldest city. It was once called the Paris of the West Indies, but Mont Pelée changed all that in the spring of 1902, when it began to rumble and spit steam. By the first week in May, all wildlife had wisely vacated the area, but city officials ignored the warnings, needing voters in town for an upcoming election. On the morning of May 8, the volcano erupted, belching forth a cloud of burning ash with temperatures above 3,600°F. Within three minutes, Mont Pelée had transformed St-Pierre into Martinique's Pompeii. The entire town was annihilated, its 30,000 inhabitants calcified. There was only one survivor: a prisoner named Siparis, who was saved by the thick walls of his underground cell. He was later pardoned and for some time afterward was a sideshow attraction at the Barnum & Bailey Circus.

You can wander through the site to see the ruins of the island's first church, built in 1640; the theater; the toppled statues; and Siparis's cell. The Cyparis Express is a small tourist train that runs through the city, hitting the important sights with a running narrative (in French). *Departs from pl. des Ruines du Figuier every 45 mins weekdays 9:30–1 and 2:30–5:30, tel. 596/ 55–50–92. Tickets: 30F.*

While in St-Pierre, which now numbers only 6,000 residents, you might pick up some delicious French pastries to nibble on the way back after stopping in at the **Musée Vulcanologique.** Established in 1932 by American volcanologist Franck Perret, the collection includes photographs of the old town, documents, and excavated relics, including molten glass, melted iron, and contorted clocks stopped at 8 AM, the time of the eruption. *Rue Victor Hugo, tel. 596/ 78–15–16. Admission: 15F. Open daily 9–noon and 3–5.*

A short way south is **Anse-Turin,** where Paul
Gauguin lived briefly in 1887 with his friend and
6 fellow artist Charles Laval. The **Musée Gauguin**
traces the history of the artist's Martinique connection through documents, letters, and reproductions of paintings he completed while on the
island. *Tel. 596/77–22–66. Admission: 15F.
Open daily 9–5:30.*

7 Continuing down the coast, **Le Carbet** is where
Columbus is believed to have landed on June 15,
1502. In 1635 Pierre Belain d'Esnambuc arrived
here with the first French settlers.

On your way back to port, you'll pass two of the
8 island's more interesting towns. **Bellefontaine** is
a small fishing village with pastel houses spill-
ing down the hillsides and colorful boats bob-
bing in the water. Just north of Fort-de-France,
9 **Schoelcher** is home of the University of the
French West Indies and Guyana.

Shopping French products, such as perfume, wines, liquors, designer scarves, leather goods, and crystal, are all good buys in Fort-de-France. In
addition, luxury goods are discounted 20% when
paid for with traveler's checks or major credit
cards. Look for Creole gold jewelry, white and
dark rums, and handcrafted straw goods, pottery, and tapestries.

Small shops carrying luxury items proliferate
around the cathedral in Fort-de-France, particularly on rue Victor Hugo, rue Moreau de
Jones, rue Antoine Siger, and rue Lamartine.
Look for Lalique, Limoges, and Baccarat at **Ca-
det Daniel** (72 rue Antoine Siger, tel. 596/71–
41–48) and at **Roger Albert** (7 rue Victor Hugo,
tel. 596/71–71–71), which also sells perfume. A
wide variety of dolls, straw goods, tapestries,
and pottery is available at the **Caribbean Art
Center** (Centre de Métiers Art, opposite the
tourist office, Blvd. Alfassa, tel. 596/70–32–16).
The **Galerie Arti-Bijoux** (89 rue Victor Hugo,
tel. 596/63–10–62) has some unusual and excellent Haitian art at reasonable prices.

Sports For charter excursions, contact **Bathy's Club**
Fishing (Hôtel Méridien, Anse-Mitan, tel. 596/66–
00–00).

Golf **Golf de l'Impératrice Joséphine** (tel. 96/68–32–81) has an 18-hole Robert Trent Jones course with an English-speaking pro, a pro shop, a bar, and a restaurant. Located at Trois-Ilets, a mile from the Pointe du Bout resort area and 18 miles from Fort-de-France, the club offers special greens fees for cruise-ship passengers.

Hiking **Parc Naturel Régional de la Martinique** (Caserne Bouille, Fort-de-France, tel. 596/73–19–30) organizes inexpensive guided hiking tours. Information is available at the island tourist offices.

Horseback Riding Excursions and lessons are available at the **Black Horse Ranch** (near La Pagerie in Trois-Ilets, tel. 596/68–37–69), **La Cavale** (near Diamant on the road to the Novotel hotel, tel. 596/76–22–94), and **Ranch Jack** (near Anse-d'Arlets, tel. 596/68–37–67).

Water Sports Hobie Cats, Sunfish, and Sailfish can be rented by the hour from hotel beach shacks. If you're a member of a yacht club, show your club membership card and enjoy the facilities of **Club de la Voile de Fort-de-France** (Pointe Simon, tel. 596/70–26–63) and **Yacht Club de la Martinique** (blvd. Chevalier, Ste-Marthe, tel. 596/63–26–76). To explore the old shipwrecks, coral gardens, and other undersea sites, you must have a medical certificate and insurance papers. Among the island's dive operators are **Bathy's Club** (Hotel Méridien, Anse-Mitan, tel. 596/66–00–00) and the **Sub Diamant Rock** (Diamant-Novotel, tel. 596/76–42–42).

Beaches Topless bathing is prevalent at the large resort hotels. Unless you're an expert swimmer, steer clear of the Atlantic waters, except in the area of Cap Chevalier and the Caravelle Peninsula. **Pointe du Bout** has small, white-sand beaches, most of which are commandeered by resort hotels. **Anse-Mitan,** south of Pointe du Bout, is a white-sand beach with superb snorkeling. **Anse-à-l'Ane** offers picnic tables and a nearby shell museum; bathers cool off in the bar of the Calalou Hotel. **Grande-Anse** is less crowded—the preferred beach among people who know the island well. **Les Salines** is the best of Martinique's beaches, whether you choose to be with other sun worshipers or to find your own quiet stretch of sand. However, it's an hour's drive from Fort-de-France and 5 miles beyond Ste-Anne.

Dining *All restaurants include a 15% service charge in their menu prices.*

$$$ **Relais Caraibes.** For a leisurely lunch, a magnificent view of Diamond Rock, and possibly a swim in the pool, head out to this tasteful restaurant and hotel. (A taxi will take you there for about 180F from Fort-de-France, less from Pointe du Bout.) Dishes include a half lobster in two sauces, fresh-caught fish in a basil sauce, and fricassee of country shrimp. *La Cherry (on the small road leading to the Diamant-Novotel), Le Diamant, tel. 596/76–44–65. AE, MC, V. Closed Mon.*

$ **Le Second Soufflé.** The chef uses fresh vegetables and fruits—nutrition is a top priority here—to make soufflés ranging from aubergine (eggplant) to *filet de ti-nain* (small green bananas) with chocolate sauce and other tempting creations, such as eggplant ragout and okra quiche. *27 rue Blénac, Fort-de-France, tel. 596/63–44–11. No credit cards. No lunch Sat.*

St. Croix

St. Croix is the largest of the three U.S. Virgin Islands that form the northern hook of the Lesser Antilles. Its position, 40 miles south of its sisters, is far removed from the hustle and bustle of St. Thomas.

Christopher Columbus landed here in 1493, skirmishing briefly with the native Carib Indians. Since then, the three U.S. Virgin Islands have played a colorful, if painful, role as pawns in the game of European colonialism. Theirs is a history of pirates and privateers, sugar plantations, slave trading, and slave revolt and liberation. Through it all, Denmark had staying power; from the 17th to the 19th century, Danes oversaw a plantation slave economy that produced molasses, rum, cotton, and tobacco. Many of the stones you see in buildings and streets were once used as ballast on sailing ships, and the yellow fort of Christiansted is a reminder of the value once placed on this island treasure.

Currency   The U.S. dollar is the official currency of St. Croix.

Telephones   Calling the United States from St. Croix works the same as within the states. Local calls from a public phone cost 25¢ for every five minutes.

Shore Excursions   The following are good choices on St. Croix. They may not be offered by all cruise lines. Times and prices are approximate.

Island Sights   **Plantation Hike.** At the ruins of this plantation, discovered right outside Frederiksted in 1984, you can get a glimpse into St. Croix's past as you hike through the verdant rain forest. *3 hrs. Cost: $25–$30.*

Tee Time   **Golf at Carambola.** Robert Trent Jones designed this 18-hole, par-72 course, considered one of the Caribbean's finest. Includes shared golf cart and greens fees. *Half day. Cost: $58.*

Coming Ashore   Smaller ships (fewer than 200 passengers) dock in Christiansted, larger ones in Frederiksted. Information centers are found near both piers. In Christiansted, pick up a copy of the "Walking Tour Guide" at the visitor center. Both towns are easily explored on foot; beaches are nearby.

Getting Around
By Car   Driving is on the left-hand side of the road, although steering wheels are on the left-hand side of the car. Rentals are available from **Avis** (tel. 809/778–9355) and **Budget** (tel. 809/778–9636), which are both near the airport; **Caribbean Jeep & Car** (tel. 809/773–4399) in Frederiksted; and **Olympic** (tel. 809/773–2208) in Christiansted. Rates begin at about $50 daily.

By Taxi   Taxis of all shapes and sizes are available at the cruise piers and at various shopping and resort areas; they also respond quickly when telephoned. Taxis do not have meters, so you should check the list of standard rates available from the visitor centers and settle the fare with your driver before you start. Taxi drivers are required to carry a copy of the official rates and must show it to you when asked. Remember, too, that you can hail a taxi that is already occupied. Drivers take multiple fares and sometimes even trade passengers at midpoints. Try **St. Croix Taxi Association** (tel. 809/778–1088) or **Antilles Taxi Service** (tel. 809/773–5020).

It helps to be pushy in airports.

Introducing the revolutionary new TransPorter™ from American Tourister® It's the first suitcase you can push around without a fight. TransPorter's™ exclusive four-wheel design lets you push it in front of you with almost no effort–the wheels take the weight. Or pull it on two wheels if you choose. You can even stack on other bags and use it like a luggage cart.

Stable 4-wheel design.

TransPorter™ is designed like a dresser, with built-in shelves to organize your belongings. Or collapse the shelves and pack it like a traditional suitcase. Inside, there's a suiter feature to help keep suits and dresses from wrinkling. When push comes to shove, you can't beat a TransPorter™ For more information on how you can be this pushy, call 1-800-542-1300.

Shelves collapse on command.

American Tourister®

Making travel less primitive®

©1996 American Tourister®

Your passport around the world.

- Worldwide access
- Operators who speak your language
- Monthly itemized billing

Calling Card

MCI

415 555 1234 2244
J. D. SMITH

Use your MCI Card® and these access numbers for an easy way to call when traveling worldwide.

American Samoa	633-2MCI (633-2624)
Antigua †	#2
(Available from public card phones only)	
Aruba ✛	800-888-8
Argentina ★†	001-800-333-1111
Bahamas (CC)†	1-800-888-8000
Barbados	1-800-888-8000
Belize	815 from pay phones
	557 from hotels
Bermuda ✛†	1-800-888-8000
Bolivia ♦	0-800-2222
Brazil (CC)†	000-8012
British Virgin Islands ✛	1-800-888-8000
Cayman Islands†	1-800-888-8000
Chile (CC)†	
To call using CTC ■	800-207-300
To call using ENTEL ■	123-00316
Colombia (CC)♦†	980-16-0001
Costa Rica ♦†	0800-012-2222
Dominica	1-800-888-8000
Dominican Republic (CC)	1-800-888-8000
Ecuador (CC)✛†	999-170
El Salvador ♦	800-1767
Grenada ✛	1-800-888-8000

Guatemala ♦	189
Guyana	177
Haiti (CC)✛	001-800-444-1234
Honduras ✛	122
Jamaica	1-800-888-8000
(From Special Hotels only)	873
Mexico ▲†	95-800-674-7000
Netherlands Antilles (CC)✛†	
	001-800-950-1022
Nicaragua (CC)	166
(Outside of Managua, dial 02 first)	
Panama†	108
Military Bases	2810-108
Paraguay ✛	008-11-800
Peru	170
Puerto Rico (CC)†	1-800-888-8000
St. Lucia ✛	1-800-888-8000
Trinidad & Tobago ✛	1-800-888-8000
Turks & Caicos ✛	1-800-888-8000
Uruguay	00-412
U.S. Virgin Islands (CC)†	1-800-888-8000
Venezuela ✛♦	800-1114-0

To sign up for the MCI Card, dial the access number of the country you are in and ask to speak with a customer service representative.

MCI

http://www.mci.com

Exploring *Numbers in the margin correspond to points of*
St. Croix *interest on the St. Croix map.*

❶ Next to the cruise-ship pier in **Frederiksted** is
the restored Ft. Frederik, completed in the late
18th century. Here, in 1848, the slaves of the
Danish West Indies were freed by Governor
Peter van Scholten. Down Market Street is the
Market Place, where you can buy fresh fruit and
vegetables early in the morning.

Around the corner on Prince Street is the Old
Danish School, designed in the 1830s and now
part of the Ingeborg Nesbett Clinic. St. Paul's
Episcopal Church, a mixture of classic and Gothic Revival architecture, is two blocks south on
Prince Street; it has survived several hurricanes since its construction in 1812 and became
Episcopal when the United States purchased
the island in 1917. A few steps away, on King
Cross Street, is Apothecary Hall, which survived the great fire of 1878. Walk south and turn
right on Queen Cross Street to the Old Public
Library, or Bell House, which now houses an
arts-and-crafts center and the Dorsch Cultural
Center for the performing arts. Back at the waterfront, walk up Strand Street to the fish market. By the cruise-ship pier is Victoria House,
on your right. Once a private home and the
town's best example of Victorian gingerbread
architecture, it was recently renovated.

❷ South of Frederiksted is the **West End Salt
Pond,** rife with mangroves and little blue herons. In the spring, large leatherback sea turtles
clamber up the white sand to lay their eggs. You
will also see brown pelicans.

❸ If you follow Centerline Road out of town, you'll
soon come to the **Estate Whim Plantation Museum.** The lovingly restored estate, with windmill, cookhouse, and other buildings, gives a
real sense of what life was like for the owners of
St. Croix's sugar plantations in the 1800s. The
great house, with a singular oval shape and high
ceilings, features antique furniture and utensils, as well as a major apothecary exhibit. Note
the house's fresh and airy atmosphere—the waterless moat was used not for defense but for
gathering cooling air.

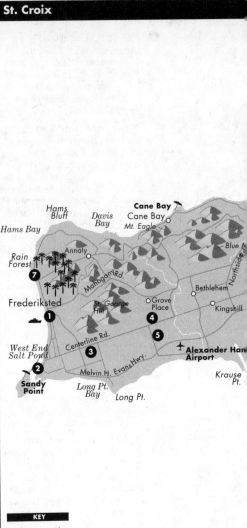

St. Croix

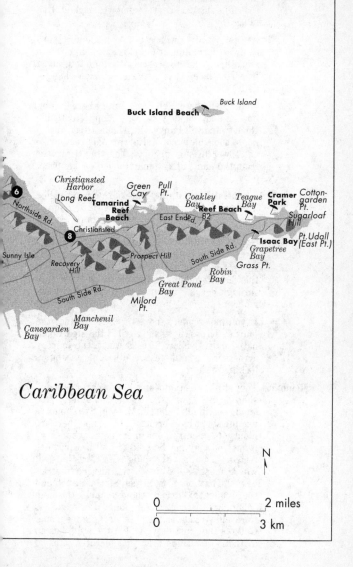

Buck Island

Buck Island Beach

Christiansted Harbor

Green Cay

Pull Pt.

6

Long Reef

Northside Rd.

Tamarind Reef Beach

Coakley Bay

Reef Beach

Teague Bay

Cramer Park

Cotton-garden Pt.

East End Rd.

82

Sugarloaf Hill

8

Christiansted

Pt. Udall (East Pt.)

Isaac Bay

Sunny Isle

Recovery Hill

Prospect Hill

South Side Rd.

Grapetree Bay

Grass Pt.

Robin Bay

Great Pond Bay

South Side Rd.

Milord Pt.

Manchenil Bay

Canegarden Bay

Caribbean Sea

N

0   2 miles

0   3 km

❹ About a mile east of Estate Whim Plantation, on Centerline Road, are the **St. George Village Botanical Gardens,** 17 lush and fragrant acres amid the ruins of a 19th-century sugarcane plantation village.

❺ At the **Cruzan Distillery** rum is made with pure rainwater, making it (so it is said) superior to any other. Visitors are welcome for a tour and a free rum-laced drink (the concoction changes daily).

❻ For a good view of Salt River Bay, where Columbus landed, make your way along Northside Road to **Judith's Fancy.** Once home to the governor of the Knights of Malta, this old great house and tower are now in ruins. The "Judith" comes from the name of a woman buried on the property.

❼ **Sprat Hall Plantation** (Route 63) has been owned and run for generations by the Hurd Family, who has established quite a reputation for home-cooked food. The beautiful great house is the oldest in the Virgin Islands. Pull up a chair at the breezy Sprat Hall Beach Restaurant to sip on a cooling soda or rum drink and munch on the famous pumpkin fritters while you gaze through beach seagrapes at the glistening Caribbean.

❽ If you have come ashore in Frederikstad, the journey across the island to **Christiansted,** dominated by its yellow fort, is worth the journey across the island—especially for passengers looking to shop.

Shopping Though St. Croix doesn't have nearly as many shops as St. Thomas, the selection of duty-free goods is still fairly large. Many of St. Thomas's leading shops have branches here, and there are plenty of independent merchants who carry items you may not be able to find in Charlotte Amalie. The best shopping is in **Christiansted,** where most shops are in the historic district near the harbor. **King Street, Strand Street,** and the arcades that lead off them comprise the main shopping district. The longest arcade is **Caravelle Arcade,** in the hotel of the same name. **Gallows Bay,** just east of Christiansted, has an attractive boutique area that features unusual

island-made silver jewelry and gift items. In
Frederiksted, a handful of shops face the cruise-
ship pier.

Sports

Golf The 18-hole course at the **Buccaneer** (tel. 809/
773–2100) is close to Christiansted. More spectacular is the **Carambola Golf Course** (tel. 809/
778–5638), designed by Robert Trent Jones, in
a valley in the northwestern part of the island.
The **Reef Club** (tel. 809/773–8844), in the northeast, has a nine-hole course. Rates for 18 holes
range from $35 to $77.

Horseback At Sprat Hall (*see* Exploring St. Croix, *above*),
Riding near Frederiksted, **Paul & Jill's Equestrian Stables** (tel. 809/772–2627) offer rides through the
rain forest.

Scuba Diving **Dive Experience** (tel. 809/773–3307) is one of the
and Snorkeling island's best dive specialists. **Mile-Mark Charters** (tel. 809/773–2628) offers a full range of water sports, including sailing, snorkeling, and
scuba diving. Both are in Christiansted.

Beaches **Buck Island** and its reef, which is under environmental protection, can be reached only by boat
from Christiansted but are well worth a visit.
The beach is beautiful, but its finest treasures
are those you see when you plop off the boat and
adjust your face mask, snorkel, and flippers. At
Cane Bay, a breezy north-shore beach, the waters are not always gentle but the diving and
snorkeling are wondrous, and there are never
many people around. Less than 200 yards out is
the drop-off, called Cane Bay Wall. Three miles
north of Frederiksted you'll find **Rainbow
Beach** where you can enjoy the sand, snorkel at
a small nearby reef, and get a bite to eat at the
bar. **Tamarind Reef Beach** is a small but attractive beach with good snorkeling east of
Christiansted. Green Cay and Buck Island seem
smack in front of you and make the view arrest-
ing.

Dining **Le St. Tropez.** A dark-wood bar and soft lighting
$$ add to the Mediterranean feel at this pleasant
bistro, tucked into a courtyard off Frederik-
sted's main thoroughfare. Daily specials high-
light local seafood, while light French cuisine,
such as quiches, brochettes, and crepes, are the

menu's mainstays. *67 King St., Frederiksted, tel. 809/772–3000. AE, D, MC, V. Closed Sun.*

$ **Camille's.** This tiny, lively spot is perfect for lunch or a light supper. Sandwiches and burgers are the big draw, but each day there's a seafood special—often wahoo or mahimahi. *Queen Cross St., Christiansted, tel. 809/773–2985. No credit cards. No lunch Sun.*

St. Lucia

Lush St. Lucia—a ruggedly beautiful island, with towering mountains, a dense tropical rain forest, fertile green valleys, and hundreds of acres of banana plantations—sits in the middle of the Windward Islands. Nicknamed "the Helen of the West Indies" because of its natural beauty, St. Lucia is distinguished from its eastern Caribbean neighbors by its unique geological sites. The Pitons, twin peaks on the island's southwest coast that have become a symbol of this island, soar to more than 2,400 feet above the ocean floor. Nearby, just outside the French colonial town of Soufrière, is a "drive-in" volcano with bubbling sulfur springs that attract visitors for their curative waters. Visitors come to St. Lucia for the ecotouring opportunities and to enjoy resort life at some of the Caribbean's most spectacular properties. The island's offshore reefs attract world-class scuba divers.

Battles between the French and English resulted in St. Lucia changing hands 14 times before 1814, when England finally won possession. In 1979, the island became an independent state within the British Commonwealth of Nations. The official language is English, although most people also speak a French Creole patois.

Currency St. Lucia uses the Eastern Caribbean (E.C.) dollar. The exchange rate is about E.C.$2.65 to U.S.$1. U.S. dollars are readily accepted, but you'll usually get change in E.C. dollars. Major credit cards and traveler's checks are also widely accepted.

Telephones Long-distance connections from St. Lucia are excellent, and numbers can be dialed directly. International telephone and telex services are available at Pointe Seraphine, where most ships dock.

Shore
Excursions The following is a good choice in St. Lucia. It may not be offered by all cruise lines. Time and price are approximate.

Natural Beauty **La Soufrière and the Pitons.** Travel by air-conditioned bus along the winding West Coast Road for a spectacular view of the Pitons; visit La Soufrière volcano and its sulfur springs and nearby Diamond Botanical Gardens and Mineral Baths. A buffet lunch accompanies this scenic overview of the island. *8 hrs. Cost: $45.*

Coming
Ashore Most cruise ships call at the capital city of Castries, on the island's northwest coast. Two docking areas are used: Pointe Seraphine, a duty-free shopping complex and cruise-ship terminal, or the downtown industrial dock across the harbor. Ferry service connects the two dock areas.

On some cruise itineraries, vessels call instead at Soufrière, farther south on the island's west coast. Ships calling at Soufrière drop anchor and tender passengers ashore.

Tourist information offices are located at Pointe Seraphine and along the waterfront, on Bay Street, in Soufrière. Neither Castries nor Soufrière offers much of interest for visitors, although downtown Castries is within walking distance of the pier. Instead, most of St. Lucia's worthwhile attractions are found beyond these two port cities. You can hire a taxi at the docks to see the outlying sights, but the most cost-efficient way to see the island is on a ship-organized shore excursion.

Getting
Around Passengers who choose to explore on their own have the option of renting a car or hiring a taxi.

By Car To rent a car, you must have a valid driver's license and credit card and also buy a temporary St. Lucian license, which costs U.S.$12. Rates begin at about U.S.$50 a day for a Jeep and U.S.$75 for a car with standard transmission. Remember that driving is on the *left* side of the road. Rental agencies at or convenient to Pointe Seraphine include **Avis** (tel. 809/452–2700), **Budget** (tel. 809/452–0233), **Hertz** (tel. 809/452–0679), and **National** (tel. 809/450–8721). In Soufrière, contact **Cool Breeze Jeep/Car Rental,** (tel. 809/459–7729).

By Taxi Taxis are unmetered, but the government has issued a list of suggested fares. From Pointe Seraphine, a 10–20 minute ride north to Rodney Bay should cost about $10–$15. For trips to Soufrière, at least an hour's drive to the south, expect to pay $20 per hour for up to four people. A tour of the entire island takes about six hours and costs about $120. Whatever your destination, negotiate the price with the driver before you depart, and be sure that you both understand whether the rate you've agreed upon is in E.C. or U.S. dollars. Drivers expect a 10% tip.

Exploring *Numbers in the margin correspond to points of*
St. Lucia *interest on the St. Lucia map.*

Castries Area **Government House,** the official residence of the governor-general of St. Lucia, is one of the island's few remaining examples of Victorian architecture. *On Government House Rd., Castries.*

❷ Driving up **Morne Fortune,** the "hill of good fortune," you'll see beautiful tropical plants—frangipani, lilies, bougainvillea, hibiscus, and oleander. *South of Castries.*

Ft. Charlotte, on the Morne, was begun in 1764 by the French as the *Citadelle du Morne Fortune* and completed after 20 years of battling and changing hands. Its old barracks and batteries have been converted to government buildings and local educational facilities, but you can view the remains—redoubts, a guardroom, stables, and cells.

❸ **Gros Islet.** This quiet little fishing village north of Rodney Bay jumps on Friday nights, when a street festival with live music attracts locals and tourists alike.

The Castries **Market** is open every day but most crowded on Friday and Saturday mornings, when farmers bring their produce to town. Across the street, also in a new building, is the Vendor's Arcade, where you can buy souvenirs and handicrafts. *Corner of Jeremie and Peyier Sts., Castries.*

❹ According to island tales, pirate Jambe de Bois (Wooden Leg) used **Pigeon Island** as his hideout. Now a national park, Pigeon Island has a beach,

St. Lucia

St. Lucia Channel — Cap Pt. — **Cariblue Beach**
Pigeon Pt. ➤ 4
Rodney Bay Gros Islet — Anse Lavouette
3 *Esperance Harbour*
Reduit Beach
Choc Bay
Cape Marquis
Vigie Beach
Pte. Seraphine
Vigie Airport
Castries Harbour — Castries — *Grand Anse Bay*
La Toc Bay 1 — Grande Anse
Morne Fortune 2
Grande Cul de Sac Bay — *La Sorcière*
Marigot Bay
Roseau — *Fond d'or Bay*
Anse-la-Raye — Dennery
Grande Caille Pt. — Canaries
Anse Cochon — *Praslin Bay*
Anse Chastanet — Soufrière
Soufrière Harbour — 5 6 — Fond St. Jacques 7
Anse des Pitons 8 — *Petit Piton* — Micoud — *Vierge Pt.*
Gros Piton
Gros Piton Pt. — Gros Piton
Choiseul
Caribbean Sea
Laborie — **Hewanorra International Airport** — *Savannes Bay*
N
0 — 4 miles — *Laborie Bay* — Vieux Fort
0 — 6 km
Vieux Fort — Maria Islands
Honeymoon Beach — *Moule à Chique Peninsula* — *Anse de Sables*

St. Lucia Channel
Barre de L'Isle Ridge
ATLANTIC OCEAN

KEY
⚓ Cruise Ship

calm waters for swimming, restaurants, and picnic areas. On the grounds you'll see ruins of barracks, batteries, and garrisons dating from the French and British battles for control of St. Lucia. The island is easily reached by a causeway. *Pigeon Island, St. Lucia Trust, tel. 809/450–8167. Admission: E.C.$10. Open daily 9–5.*

Soufrière Area

❺ It's an hour's drive on the new, but winding, West Coast Road from Castries to **Soufrière,** a French colonial town that was named for the nearby volcano. The mountainous region of St. Lucia is breathtakingly lush, and the road that snakes along the coast offers spectacular views of the Pitons, the rain forest, and the sea.

❻ In 1713 Louis IV provided funds for the construction of curative baths on this site. Today, you can walk through the **Diamond Mineral Baths and Botanical Garden**'s beautifully kept grounds to Diamond Falls, then slip into your swimsuit for a dip in the steaming sulfur baths. *Soufrière Estate, tel. 809/452–4759. Admission: E.C.$5. Open daily 10–5.*

❼ **La Soufrière,** the drive-in volcano, is southeast of the town of Soufrière. More than 20 pools of black, belching, smelly sulfurous waters bubble, bake, and steam on the surface. *Bay St., tel. 809/459–5500. Admission: E.C.$3, includes guided tour. Open daily 9–5.*

❽ The incredible **Pitons** have become the symbol of St. Lucia. These perfectly shaped pyramidal cones, covered with thick tropical vegetation, rise precipitously out of the azure sea. Petit Piton, at 2,619 feet, is taller than Gros Piton (2,461 feet), although Gros is broader.

Shopping

As tourism is increasing in St. Lucia, so are the options for shopping. Local products include silk-screened fabric and clothing, pottery, wood carvings, cocoa and coffee, and baskets and other straw items. The only duty-free shopping is at Pointe Seraphine.

Artsibit (corner of Brazil and Mongiraud Sts., Castries, tel. 809/452–7865) features works by top St. Lucian artists.

Bagshaw Studios (at Pointe Seraphine and on La Toc Rd., La Bay, tel. 809/452–7570) sells clothing and Toc household items created from unique silk-screened and hand-printed fabrics that are designed, printed, and sold only on St. Lucia.

Caribelle Batik (Old Victoria Rd., The Morne, tel. 809/452–3785) welcomes visitors to watch artisans creating batik clothing and wall hangings.

Eudovic Art Studio (Morne Fortune, 15 mins south of Castries, tel. 809/452–2747) sells trays, masks, and figures that are carved in the studio from mahogany, red cedar, and eucalyptus wood.

Made in St. Lucia (Gablewoods Mall, north of Castries, tel. 809/453–2788) sells only items made on the island—sandals, shirts, hot sauces, costume jewelry, carved wooden items, clay cooking pots, original art, and more—all at reasonable prices.

Noah's Arkade (Jeremie St., Castries and Pointe Seraphine, tel. 809/452–2523) has hammocks, straw mats, baskets and hats, and carvings, as well as books about and maps of St. Lucia.

Pointe Seraphine, the cruise-ship terminal, is a modern, Spanish-style complex where 33 shops sell designer perfume, china and crystal, jewelry, watches, leather goods, liquor, and cigarettes; to get the duty-free price, you must show your boarding pass or cabin key. Native crafts are also sold here.

Soufrière is not much of a shopping port, although there's a small arts center where handicrafts are sold and a batik studio at the Humming Bird Resort. Both are along the waterfront at the north end of town.

Sports
Fishing Among the sea creatures in these waters are dolphin, Spanish mackerel, barracuda, and white marlin. For half- or full-day fishing excursions, contact **Captain Mike's** (Vigie Bay Marina, Castries, tel. 809/452–7044) or **Mako Watersports** (Rodney Bay Marina, tel. 809/452–0412).

Golf The golf courses on St. Lucia are scenic and good fun, but they're not of a professional caliber. Nine-hole courses are at both **Sandals St. Lucia**

(La Toc Rd., Castries, tel. 809/452–3081) and **St. Lucia Golf Club** (Cap Estate, tel. 809/452–8523). A caddy is required at Sandals. Greens fees are about U.S.$20 at either for 18 holes; club rentals are $10.

Hiking St. Lucia is laced with trails, but you should not attempt the challenging peaks on your own. The **Forest and Land Department** (tel. 809/450–2231) can provide you with a guide. The **St. Lucia National Trust** (tel. 809/452–5005) offers tours of several sites, including Pigeon Island (*see* Exploring St. Lucia, *above*).

Horseback Riding For trail rides, contact **International Riding Stables** (Gros Islet, tel. 809/452–8138), **Trim's Riding School** (Cas-en-Bas, tel. 809/452–8273), **North Point Riding Stables** (Gros Islet, tel. 809/450–8853), or **Jalousie Plantation** (Soufrière, tel. 809/459–7666). A half-hour ride runs about U.S.$30.

Scuba Diving **Scuba St. Lucia** (tel. 809/459–7355) is a PADI five-star training facility that offers daily beach and boat dives, resort courses, underwater photography, and day trips. Trips can also be arranged through **Buddies Scuba** (tel. 809/452–5288), **Dive Jalousie** (tel. 809/459–7666), **Moorings Scuba Centre** (tel. 809/451–4357), and **Windjammer Diving** (tel. 809/452–0913).

Tennis **St. Lucia Racquet Club** (adjacent to Club St. Lucia, Cap Estate, tel. 809/450–0551) is one of the top tennis facilities in the Caribbean. **Jalousie Plantation** (Soufrière, tel. 809/459–7666) has four lighted courts open to cruise passengers.

Beaches All of St. Lucia's beaches are public. Many are flanked by hotels where you can rent watersports equipment and have a rum punch, but the resorts are sometimes less than welcoming to cruise-ship passengers. About a 30-minute ride from Pointe Seraphine is **Pigeon Island** (admission E.C.$10), which has a white-sand beach and a small restaurant; it's great for picnicking and swimming. **Reduit Beach,** 20 minutes from Castries, is a long stretch of beige sand next to Rodney Bay. Water-sports equipment can be rented at the two beachfront hotels.

Near Soufrière, **Anse Chastanet** is a gray-sand beach with a backdrop of green hills and the island's best reefs for snorkeling and diving. A dive shop and bar are located on the beach. The black-sand **Anse des Pitons** sits directly between the Pitons and is accessible through Jalousie Plantation or by boat from Soufrière. It, too, offers great snorkeling and diving.

Dining *Most restaurants add a 10% service charge to the bill.*

Castries **Jimmie's.** It's a 10- to 15-minute ride from the
$$–$$$ ship, but worth it for the great views. Popular with locals as well as visitors, Jimmie's specializes in seafood—from Creole stuffed crab for an appetizer to the special seafood platter for an entrée. Dessert lovers had better be in a banana mood—everything from fritters to ice cream is made with St. Lucian "figs." *Vigie Cove, Castries, tel. 809/452–5142. Reservations not accepted. AE, MC, V.*

Soufrière **Dasheene Restaurant and Bar.** The breathtak-
$$$$ ing view—the Pitons look close enough to touch—plus some of the best food on St. Lucia are reasons to make this open-air perch high in the mountains your stop when touring in the area. Fresh-caught fish is always special, but there's an array of inspired salads, sandwiches and even a burger on the luncheon menu. Dinner, of course, is more elaborate. *Ladera Resort, tel. 809/459–7323. AE, DC, MC, V.*

$ **Camilla's.** Just a short walk from the wharf, this friendly, second-floor restaurant serves local dishes, such as the catch of the day curried, Creole-style, or grilled with lemon sauce. The list of tropical cocktails is bigger than the entire restaurant! *12 Boulevard St., tel. 809/459–5379. AE.*

St. Martin/St. Maarten

St. Martin/St. Maarten: one tiny island, just 37 square miles, with two different accents, and ruled by two separate nations. Here French and Dutch have lived side by side for hundreds of years, and when you cross from one country to the next there are no border patrols, no customs. In fact, the only indication that you have crossed a border at all is a small sign and a change in road surface.

St. Martin/St. Maarten epitomizes tourist islands in the sun, where services are well developed but there is still some Caribbean flavor left. The Dutch side is ideal for people who like plenty to do. The French side has more ambience, more fashionable shopping, and much more Continental flair. The combination of the two halves makes an almost ideal port. On the negative side, the island has been thoroughly discovered and completely developed. There is gambling, but table limits are so low that high rollers will have a better time gamboling on the beach. It can be fun to shop, and you'll find an occasional bargain, but many goods (particularly electronics) are cheaper in the United States. At press time, this island was still feeling some aftereffects of the devastating hurricane in fall 1995. Some resorts were closed, and much of the land was left barren—only now is it beginning to fully recover.

Though Dutch is the official language of St. Maarten, and French of St. Martin, almost everyone speaks English. If you hear a language you can't quite place, it's Papiamento, a Spanish-based Creole.

Currency   Legal tender on the Dutch side is the Netherlands Antilles florin (guilder), written NAf; on the French side, it's the French franc (F). In general, the exchange rate is about NAf 1.80 to U.S.$1, and 5F to U.S.$1. There's little need to exchange money, though, as dollars are accepted everywhere.

Telephones   To phone from the Dutch side to the French
Intra-Island   side, dial 06 plus the local number. From the
Calls   French side to the Dutch side, dial 011–5995 plus the local number. Remember that a call from one side to the other is an international call and not a local one.

Overseas Calls   At the Landsradio in Philipsburg, St. Maarten, there are facilities for overseas calls and an AT&T USADirect telephone. On the French side, it's not possible to make collect calls to the United States, but you can make credit-card calls from a phone on the side of the tourist office in Marigot. The operator will assign you a PIN number, valid for as long as you specify. Calls to the United States are about $4 per minute. To call from other public phones, you'll need to go to the special desk at Marigot's post office and buy a Telecarte, which looks like a credit card.

Shore Excursions The following is a good choice in St. Martin/St. Maarten. It may not be offered by all cruise lines. Time and price are approximate.

Undersea Creatures **Snorkel Tour.** Take a boat to a beach, where you will be taught how to snorkel, then given the choice of joining a group or setting off on your own. Refreshments may be served. *3 hrs. Cost: $27.*

Coming Ashore Except for a few vessels that stop on the French side, cruise ships drop anchor off the Dutch capital of Philipsburg or dock in the marina at the southern tip of the Philipsburg harbor. If your ship anchors, tenders will ferry you to the town pier in the middle of town, where taxis await passengers. Next to the pier, on Wathey Square, is the Tourist Bureau, where you can pick up information and maps. If your ship docks at the marina, downtown is a 15-minute taxi ride away. The walk is not recommended.

Getting Around One of the island's best bargains, public buses cost from 80¢ to $2 and run frequently between 7 AM and 7 PM, from Philipsburg through Cole Bay to Marigot.

By Bus

By Car The island's roads are good, and it would be quite difficult to get lost. Because everything is within an easy drive of Philipsburg and taxis are very expensive, this is a good port for renting a car. The cost is about $35 a day. It's best to reserve a car before you leave home, especially at the height of the winter season. Contact **Avis** (tel. 800/331–1212), **Budget** (tel. 800/527–0700), **Hertz** (tel. 800/654–3131), or **National** (tel. 800/328–4567).

By Taxi Taxis are government-regulated and costly. Authorized taxis display stickers of the St. Maarten Taxi Association. Taxis are also available at Marigot.

Exploring St. Martin/ St. Maarten *Numbers in the margin correspond to points of interest on the St. Martin/St. Maarten map.*

Dutch Side The Dutch capital of **Philipsburg**, which stretches about a mile along an isthmus between Great Bay and Salt Pond, is easily explored on

❶

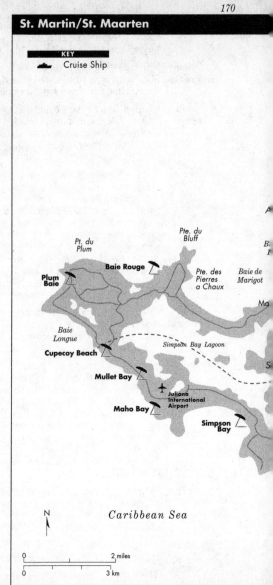

St. Martin/St. Maarten

KEY
Cruise Ship

Pt. du Plum

Baie Rouge

Pte. du Bluff

Pte. des Pierres a Chaux

Baie de Marigot

Plum Baie

Baie Longue

Cupecoy Beach

Simpson Bay Lagoon

Mullet Bay

Maho Bay

Juliana International Airport

Simpson Bay

N

Caribbean Sea

| 0 | | 2 miles |
| 0 | | 3 km |

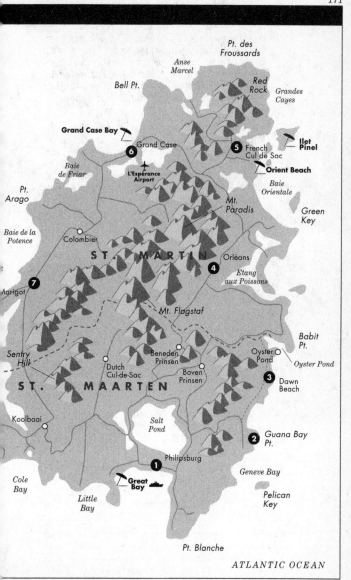

Pt. des
Froussards

Anse
Marcel

Bell Pt.

Red
Rock

Grandes
Cayes

Grand Case Bay

6 Grand Case

5 French
Cul de Sac

**Ilet
Pinel**

Orient Beach

Baie
de Friar

**L'Espérance
Airport**

Baie
Orientale

Pt.
Arago

Mt.
Paradis

Green
Key

Baie de la
Potence

Colombier

S T .   M A R T I N

4 Orléans

Etang
aux Poissons

Aarigot **7**

Mt. Flagstaf

Babit
Pt.

Sentry
Hill

Beneden
Prinsen

Oyster
Pond

Oyster Pond

S T .   M A A R T E N

Dutch
Cul-de-Sac

Boven
Prinsen

3 Dawn
Beach

Koolbaai

Salt
Pond

2 Guana Bay
Pt.

1 Philipsburg

Geneve Bay

Cole
Bay

**Great
Bay**

Pelican
Key

Little
Bay

Pt. Blanche

ATLANTIC OCEAN

foot. It has three parallel streets: Front Street, Back Street, and Pond Fill. Little lanes called *steegjes* connect Front Street (which has been recobbled and its pedestrian area widened) with Back Street, which is considerably less congested because it has fewer shops. Altogether, a walk from one end of downtown to the other takes a half hour, even if you stop at a couple of stores.

The first stop for cruise passengers should be **Wathey Square,** in the middle of the isthmus, which bustles with vendors, souvenir shops, and tourists. The streets to the right and left are lined with hotels, duty-free shops, restaurants, and cafés, most in West Indian cottages decorated in pastels with gingerbread trim. Narrow alleyways lead to arcades and flower-filled courtyards with yet more boutiques and eateries.

To explore beyond Philipsburg, start at the west end of Front Street. The road (which becomes Sucker Garden Road) leads north along Salt Pond and begins to climb and curve just outside town.

2 The first right off Sucker Garden Road leads to **Guana Bay Point,** from which you get a splendid view of the island's east coast, tiny deserted islands, and little St. Barts in the distance.

3 **Dawn Beach,** an excellent snorkeling beach, lies on the east coast of the island, just below Oyster Pond, and has an active sailing community.

French Side Cruise passengers following the main road north out of Philipsburg will come first to **4** **Orléans.** This settlement, also known as the French Quarter, is the island's oldest.

5 North of Orléans is the **French Cul de Sac,** where you'll see the French colonial mansion of St. Martin's mayor nestled in the hills. From here the road swirls south through green hills and pastures, past flower-entwined stone fences.

6 Past L'Espérance Airport is the town of **Grand Case,** known as the "Restaurant Capital of the Caribbean." Scattered along its mile-long main street are more than 20 restaurants serving French, Italian, Indonesian, and Vietnamese fare, as well as fresh seafood. Along the shore, vendors known as *lolos* sell delicious barbecued chicken, beef on skewers, and other delicacies.

❼ The capital of the French side is **Marigot.** (If you're coming from Grand Case, follow the signs south to rue de la République.) Marina Port La Royale is the shopping complex at the port; rue de la République and rue de la Liberté, which border the bay, are also filled with duty-free shops, boutiques, and bistros. The road south from Marigot leads to the official border, where a simple marker, placed here in 1948, commemorates 300 years of peaceful coexistence. This road will bring you back to Philipsburg.

Shopping Prices can be 25%–50% below those in the United States and Canada for French perfume, liquor, cognac and fine liqueurs, crystal, linens, leather, Swiss watches, and other luxury items. However, it pays to know the prices back home; not all goods are a bargain. Caveat emptor: Although most merchants are reputable, there are occasional reports of inferior or fake merchandise passed off as the real thing. When vendors bargain excessively, their wares are often suspect.

In Philipsburg, Front Street is one long strip of boutiques and shops; **Old Street,** near the end of Front Street, is packed with stores, boutiques, and open-air cafés. At Philipsburg's **Shipwreck Shop,** look for Caribelle batiks, hammocks, handmade jewelry, the local guava-berry liqueur, and herbs and spices. You'll find almost 100 boutiques in the **Mullet Bay** and **Maho** shopping plazas. In general, you will find smarter fashions in Marigot than in Philipsburg. In Marigot, wrought-iron balconies, colorful awnings, and gingerbread trim decorate the shops and tiny boutiques in the **Marina Port La Royale** and on the main streets, **rue de la Liberté** and **rue de la République.**

Sports Contact **Sea Brat, Black Fin,** or **Pita** at Bobby's
Fishing Marina, Philipsburg (tel. 599/5–22366) for information on fishing charters.

Golf **Mullet Bay Resort** (tel. 599/5–52801) has an 18-hole championship course. Green fees are $90 for 18 holes and $50 for nine holes.

Water Sports   Myriad boats can be rented at **Lagoon Watersports** (tel. 599/5–52801) and **Caribbean Watersports** (tel. 590/87–58–66). NAUI-, SSI-, and PADI-certified dive centers offer scuba instruction, rentals, and trips. On the Dutch side, try **Trade Winds Dive Center** (tel. 599/5–75176) and **St. Maarten Divers** (tel. 599/5–22446). On the French side, there's **Lou Scuba** (tel. 590/87–22–58) and **Blue Ocean** (tel. 590/87–89–73), both PADI-certified.

Beaches   The island's 10 miles of beaches are all open to the public. Those occupied by resort properties charge a small fee (about $3) for changing facilities, and water-sports equipment can be rented at most hotels. Some of the 37 beaches are secluded; some are in the thick of things. Topless bathing is common on the French side. Nude bathing can be found at Orient Beach, Cupecoy Beach, and Baie Longue. If you take a cab to a remote beach, be sure to arrange a specific time for the driver to return for you. Don't leave valuables unattended on the beach.

Baie Longue, the island's best beach, is a mile-long curve of white sand at the western tip, offering excellent snorkeling and swimming but no facilities. **Cupecoy Beach** is a narrower, more secluded curve of white sand just south of Baie Longue near the border. There are no facilities, but a truck often pulls up with cold beer and sodas. Clothing becomes optional at the western end of the beach. This is also the island's gay beach.

Dining   *By law, restaurants on the French side figure a service charge into the menu prices, so no tips are expected. On the Dutch side, most restaurants add 10%–15% to the bill.*

Dutch Side   **Chesterfield's.** Burgers and salads are served at
$–$$ lunch, but menus are more elaborate for dinner on this indoor/outdoor terrace overlooking the marina. Specialties include French onion soup, roast duckling with fresh pineapple and banana sauce, and chicken Cordon Bleu. The Mermaid Bar is popular with yachtsmen. *Great Bay Marina, Philipsburg, tel. 599/5–23484. AE, MC, V.*

$ **Shiv Sagar.** Authentic East Indian cuisine, emphasizing Kashmiri and Mogul specialties, is served in this small, mirrored room fragrant

with cumin and coriander. Marvelous tandooris
and curries are offered, but try one of the less-
familiar preparations such as *madrasi machi*
(red snapper cooked in a blend of hot spices). A
large selection of vegetarian dishes is also offered. There's a friendly open-air bar out front.
*3 Front St., Philipsburg, tel. 599/5–22299. AE,
D, DC, MC, V. Closed Sun.*

French Side   **Le Poisson d'Or.** At this posh and popular res-
   $$$ taurant set in a stone house, the waters of the
bay beckon from the 20-table terrace as you
feast on hot foie gras salad in raspberry vinai-
grette; smoked lobster boiled in tea with pars-
ley cream sauce; or veal with Roquefort,
hazelnut, and tarragon sauce. The young chef,
François Julien, cooks with enthusiasm, but his
cuisine must compete for attention with the
striking setting. *Off rue d'Anguille, Marigot,
tel. 590/87–72–45. AE, MC, V. No lunch Tues.
in low season.*

$$ **La Crêperie du Soleil.** This charming little
eatery on the beach in quaint Grand Case offers
all kinds of delicious crepes, from sweet to salty.
Owners David and Véronique are most gracious
and helpful in making the decision of which de-
lectable treat to have. They also offer grilled
lobster, fresh fish, chicken kebabs, salads, and
pastas. Don't forget the chocolate fondue for
dessert. *Blvd. de Grand Case, Grand Case, tel.
590/87–92–32. MC, V.*

St. Thomas/St. John

St. Thomas is the busiest cruise port of call in
the world. As many as a dozen ships may visit in
a single day. Don't expect an exotic island experience: One of the three U.S. Virgin Islands
(with St. Croix and St. John), St. Thomas is as
American as any place on the mainland, complete with McDonald's franchises, HBO, and the
U.S. dollar. The positive side of all this development is that there are more tours to choose from
here than anywhere else in the Caribbean, and
every year the excursions get better. Of course,
shopping is the big draw in Charlotte Amalie,
the main town, but experienced travelers remember the days of "real" bargains. Today, so
many passengers fill the stores that it's a seller's
market. One of St. Thomas's best tourist attrac-

tions is its neighboring island, St. John, with its beautiful national parks and beaches. St. Thomas was severely damaged by 1995's Hurricane Marilyn; at press time Coral World—one of the island's most popular attractions—was still closed. Ask at your ship's shore-excursion desk for the current status of this and other island sights.

Telephones It's as easy to call home from St. Thomas as from any city in the United States. And public phones are all over the place, including right on the dock.

Shore Excursions The following are good choices in St. Thomas/ St. John. They may not be offered by all cruise lines. Times and prices are approximate.

Adventure **Helicopter Tour.** If you haven't taken a helicopter tour before, sign up for this exciting aerial tour of St. Thomas and surrounding islands. *1–2 hrs, includes 1-hr flight time. Cost: $50–$100.*

Natural Beauty **St. John Island Tour.** Either your ship tenders you in to St. John in the morning before docking at St. Thomas, or you take a bus from the St. Thomas docks to the St. John ferry. On St. John, an open-air safari bus winds through the national park to a beach for snorkeling, swimming, and sunbathing. (If you have the option, go to Honeymoon Beach instead of Trunk Bay.) All tours end with a ferry ride back to St. Thomas. *4–4½ hrs. Cost: $22–$50.*

Undersea Creatures **Atlantis Submarine.** A surface boat ferries you out to a submarine with large picture windows; the *Atlantis* dives to explore the underwater world, with good accompanying narrative. *2 hrs. Cost: $72.*

Coki Beach Snorkeling. A good choice for novices who want to learn snorkeling (instruction and equipment usually are included) and see a variety of wildlife. *3 hrs. Cost: $21–$22.*

Sailing and Snorkeling Tour. A romantic sail, a snorkeling lesson, and an attractive snorkeling site make this an excellent excursion for experiencing the true beauty of the Virgin Islands. The boat may be a modern catamaran, a single-hull sailing yacht, or a sailing vessel done up to look like a pirate ship. *3½–4 hrs. Cost: $32–$45.*

Scuba Diving. This excursion to one or two choice sites via boat or off a beach may be limited to certified divers, may be open to novices who have been taking lessons on the ship, or may include instruction for beginners. *3 hrs. Cost: $38–$75.*

Coming Ashore Depending on how many ships are in port, cruise ships drop anchor in the harbor at Charlotte Amalie and tender passengers directly to the waterfront duty-free shops, dock at the Havensight Mall at the eastern end of the crescent-shaped bay, or dock at Crown Bay Marina a few miles west of town. The distance from Havensight to the duty-free shops is 1½ miles, which can be walked in less than half an hour, or a taxi can be hired for $5 per person, one-way ($2.50 if there is more than one passenger). Tourist information offices are located at the Havensight Mall (Bldg. No 1) for docking passengers and downtown at the eastern end of the waterfront shopping strip for those coming ashore by tender. Both distribute free island and downtown shopping maps. From Crown Bay, it's also a half-hour walk or a $3 cab ride ($2.50 for more than one passenger).

Getting Around
By Car St. Thomas is an excellent port for cruise passengers to rent a car. Driving is on the left side of the road, though steering wheels are on the left side of the car. Car rentals are available from numerous agencies, including **ABC Rentals** (by Havensight Mall, tel. 809/776–1222), **Budget** (Marriott's Frenchman Reef Hotel, tel. 809/776–5774), and **Hertz** (near the airport, tel. 809/774–1879). Rates for one day range from $55 to $70.

By Ferry You can get to St. John on your own via ferry from Charlotte Amalie. The cost is $7 round-trip. Get ferry schedules and information from the tourist information offices at Havensight or in Charlotte Amalie.

By Taxi Taxis meet every ship. They don't have meters, but rates are set. Check with the shore-excursion director for correct fares and agree on the price before getting in the cab. Most taxis are minivans, which take multiple fares and charge per person. Many of them will give you a guided tour of the island for far less than you'd pay for a ship-sponsored excursion. The most popular destination, Magens Bay, costs $6.50 from town and $7.50 from the Havensight pier, per person, one way.

Exploring St. Thomas *Numbers in the margin correspond to points of interest on the St. Thomas map.*

Charlotte Amalie
❶

Charlotte Amalie is a hilly, overdeveloped shopping town. There are plenty of interesting historic sights here, and much of the town is quite pretty. So while you're shopping, take the time to see at least a few of the sights. For a great view of the town and the harbor, begin at the beautiful Spanish-style Hotel 1829, whose restaurant (*see* Dining, *below*) is one of the best on St. Thomas. A few yards farther up the road is the base of the 99 Steps, a staircase "street" built by the Danes in the 1700s. Go up the steps (there are more than 99) and continue to the right to Blackbeard's Castle, originally Ft. Skysborg. The massive five-story watchtower was built in 1679. It's now a dramatic perch from which to sip a drink and admire the harbor from the small hotel and restaurant.

Government House (on Kongen's Gade) dates back to 1867 and is the official residence of the governor of the U.S. Virgin Islands. Inside are murals and paintings by Pissarro.

Frederick Lutheran Church is the second-oldest Lutheran church in the Western Hemisphere. Its walls date to 1793.

Emancipation Garden honors the 1848 freeing of the slaves and features a smaller version of the Liberty Bell. As you stand in the park facing the water, you'll see a large red building to your left, close to the harbor; this is Ft. Christian, St. Thomas's oldest standing structure (1627–87) and a U.S. national landmark. The building was used at various times as a jail, governor's residence, town hall, courthouse, and church. The clock tower was added in the 19th century. It now houses a museum filled with historical artifacts.

The lime-green edifice on Kings Wharf is the **Legislature Building** (1874), seat of the 15-member U.S.V.I. Senate since 1957.

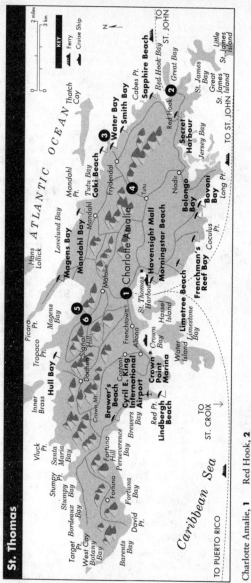

St. Thomas

TO SAINT JOHN

Sapphire Beach

Secret Harbour

TO ST. JOHN

Red Hook

Great Bay

St. James Bay

Great St. James Island

Little St. James Island

Cabes Pt.

Smith Bay

Water Bay

Coki Beach

Frydendal

Mandahl Bay

Mandahl Pt.

Tutu Bay

Mandahl

ATLANTIC OCEAN

Thatch Cay

Lovelund Bay

Magens Bay

Hans Lollick

Havensight Mall

Morningstar Beach

Frenchman's Reef Bay

Bolongo Bay

Boyoni Bay

Coculus Pt.

Long Pt.

Jersey Bay

Nadir

Tutu

Charlotte Amalie

St. Thomas Harbour

Hassel Island

Mafolie

Picara Pt.

Tropaco Pt.

Magens Bay

Signal Hill

Dorothea

Crown Mtn.

Frenchtown

Crown Bay

Cabrita

Crown Point Marina

Cyril E. King International Airport

Brewers Bay

Red Pt.

Lindbergh Beach

Limetree Beach

Limestone Bay

Water Island

Altona

Inner Brass

Hull Bay

Brewer's Beach

Perseverance

Fortuna Bay

Fortuna Hill

Fortuna

Vluck Pt.

Santa Maria Bay

Stumpy Pt.

Stumpy Bay

Bordeaux Bay

Target Pt.

West Cay

Botany Bay

Barents Bay

David Pt.

Caribbean Sea

TO PUERTO RICO

TO ST. CROIX

KEY
Ferry
Cruise Ship

2 miles
3 km

N

Charlotte Amalie, 1   Red Hook, 2
Coral World, 3   Tillett's Gardens, 4
Drake's Seat, 5
Mountain Top, 6

The South   Route 32 brings you into **Red Hook,** which has
Shore and   grown from a sleepy little town, connected to
East End   the rest of the island only by dirt roads, into an
              increasingly self-sustaining village. There's
 luxury shopping at American Yacht Harbor, or
              you can stroll along the docks and visit with sail-
              ors and fishermen, stopping for a beer at The
              Blue Marlin or Larry's Warehouse.

 Coral World has a three-level underwater obser-
              vatory, the world's largest reef tank, and an
              aquarium with more than 20 TV-size tanks pro-
              viding capsulized views of sea life. *Rte. 38, tel.
              809/775–1555. Admission: $14. Open daily 9–6.*

 At **Tillett's Gardens** on Route 38 (*see* Shopping,
              below), local artisans craft stained glass, pot-
              tery, and ceramics. Artist Jim Tillett's paint-
              ings and fabrics are also on display.

North Shore/ In the heights above Charlotte Amalie is
Center Islands **Drake's Seat,** the mountain lookout from which
 Sir Francis Drake was supposed to have kept
              watch over his fleet and looked for enemy ships
              of the Spanish fleet. Magens Bay and Mahogany
              Run are to the north, with the British Virgin Is-
              lands and Drake's Passage to the east. Off to the
              left, or west, are Fairchild Park, Mountain Top,
              Hull Bay, and smaller islands, such as the Inner
              and Outer Brass islands.

 West of Drake's Seat is **Mountain Top,** not only a
              tacky mecca for souvenir shopping, but also the
              place where the banana daiquiri was supposedly
              invented. There's a restaurant here and, at
              1,500 feet above sea level, some spectacular
              views.

Shopping   There are well over 400 shops in Charlotte
              Amalie alone, and near the Havensight docks
              there are at least 50 more, clustered in con-
              verted warehouses. Even die-hard shoppers
              won't want to cover all the boutiques, since a
              large percentage peddle the same T-shirts and
              togs. Many visitors devote their shopping time
              on St. Thomas to the stores that sell handicrafts
              and luxury items.

              Although those famous "giveaway" prices no
              longer abound, shoppers on St. Thomas can still
              save money. Today, a realistic appraisal puts
              prices on many items at about 20% off stateside

prices, although liquor and perfume often are priced 50%–70% less. What's more, there is no sales tax in the U.S. Virgin Islands, and visitors can take advantage of the $1,200-per-person duty-free allowance. Remember to save receipts.

Prices on such goods as linens do vary from shop to shop—if you find a good deal, take it. Prices on jewelry vary the most, and it's here that you'll still run across some real finds. Major credit cards are widely accepted.

Shopping Districts The major shopping area is Charlotte Amalie, in centuries-old buildings that once served as merchants' warehouses and that, for the most part, have been converted to retail establishments. Both sides of **Main Street** are lined with shops, as are the side streets and walkways between Main Street and the waterfront. These narrow lanes and arcades have names like Drake's Passage, Royal Dane Mall, Palm Passage, Trompeter Gade, Hibiscus Alley, and Raadet's Gade. The **Bakery Square Shopping Mall** (1 block north of Main St. off Nye Gade) has about 15 boutiques. The streets adjacent to Bakery Square, notably Back Street, Nye Gade, Garden Street, Kongen's Gade, and Norre Gade, are also very good areas for browsing. At **Havensight Mall,** near the deep-water port where many cruise ships dock, you'll find branches of downtown stores, as well as specialty shops and boutiques.

Charlotte Amalie Unless otherwise noted, the following stores have branches both downtown and in Havensight Mall and are easy to find. If you have any trouble, shopping maps are available at the tourist offices and often from your ship's shore-excursion desk. U.S. citizens can carry back a gallon, or six "fifths," of liquor duty-free.

A.H. Riise Gift Shops: Waterford, Wedgwood, Royal Crown, Royal Doulton, jewelry, pearls, ceramics, perfumes, watches; liquors, cordials, and wines, including rare vintage cognacs, Armagnacs, ports, and Madeiras; tobacco and imported cigars; fruits in brandy; barware from England. **Al Cohen's Discount Liquor** (Havensight only): discount liquors. **Amsterdam Sauer** (downtown only): one-of-a-kind fine jew-

elry. **Blue Diamond** (downtown only): 14-karat
and 18-karat jewelry crafted by European gold-
smiths. **Boolchand's:** cameras, audio-video
equipment.

The **Caribbean Marketplace** (Havensight Mall
only): Caribbean handicrafts, including Caribelle batiks from St. Lucia; bikinis from the
Cayman Islands; Sunny Caribee spices, soaps,
teas, and coffees from Trinidad. **Down Island
Traders** (downtown only): hand-painted cala-
bash bowls; jams, jellies, spices, and herbs; her-
bal teas made of rum, passion fruit, and mango;
high-mountain coffee from Jamaica; Caribbean
handicrafts. The **English Shop:** china and crystal from Spode, Limoges, Royal Doulton,
Portmeirion, Noritaki, and Villeroy & Boch.

The **Gallery** (downtown only): Haitian and local
oil paintings, metal sculpture, wood carvings,
painted screens and boxes, figures carved from
stone, oversize papier-mâché figures. **G'Day**
(downtown only): umbrellas, artwork, sportswear. **Gucci:** wallets, bags, briefcases, totes,
shoes. **H. Stern:** gems and jewelry. **Janine's Boutique** (downtown only): women's and men's apparel and accessories from European designers
and manufacturers, including Louis Feraud,
Valentino, Christian Dior, Pierre Cardin. **Java
Wraps** (downtown only): Indonesian batik,
swimwear, leisure wear, sarongs, ceremonial
Javanese puppets. **The Leather Shop:** Fendi,
Bottega Veneta, other fine leather goods. **Little
Switzerland:** Lalique, Baccarat, Waterford,
Swarovski, Riedel, Orrefors, and other crystal;
Villeroy & Boch, Aynsley, Wedgwood, Royal
Doulton, and other china; Rolex watches.
MAPes MONDe Ltd. (in A.H. Riise, downtown):
old-fashioned maps and engravings of Caribbe-
an scenes. **Opals of Australia** (downtown only):
the name says it all.

Pampered Pirate (downtown only): Caribbean
handicrafts, spices, sauces, jams, and Jamaican
coffee; gold chain by the inch. **Royal Caribbean**
(no affiliation with the cruise line): cameras,
cassette players, audio-video equipment. **Sea
Wench** (Havensight Mall only): swimwear, lin-
gerie. **Traveler's Haven** (Havensight Mall only):
leather bags, backpacks, vests, money belts.

Tropicana Perfume Shoppes (downtown only): fragrances for men and women.

Tillett's Gardens **Tillett's Gardens and Craft Complex** (Estate Tutu, tel. 809/775–1405; *see* Exploring St. Thomas, *above*) is more than worth the cab fare to reach it. Jim Tillet's artwork is on display, and you can watch craftsmen and artisans produce watercolors, silk-screened fabrics, pottery, enamel work, candles, and other handicrafts.

St. John Opportunities for duty-free shopping are more limited and the prices a bit higher on St. John. One popular spot is **Wharfside Village,** an attractive, compact mall of some 30 shops overlooking Cruz Bay Harbor. **Mongoose Junction,** just north of Cruz Bay across from the Park Service visitor center, is one of the most pleasant places to shop in the Caribbean. Built from native stone, the graceful staircases and balconies wind among the shops, a number of which sell handicrafts designed and fashioned by resident artisans.

Sports Call **American Yacht Harbor** at Red Hook (tel. *Fishing* 809/775–6454) if you're interested in some serious angling.

Golf Scenic **Mahogany Run** (tel. 809/775–5000), north of Charlotte Amalie, has a par-70, 18-hole course and a view of the British Virgin Islands. The rate for 18 holes is $85, cart included.

Water Sports **Underwater Safaris** (tel. 809/774–1350) is at the Ramada Yacht Haven Motel and Marina, near Havensight. Other reliable scuba and snorkeling operators are **Chris Sawyer Diving Center** (tel. 809/775–7320) and **Aqua Action** (tel. 809/775–6285).

Beaches All beaches in the U.S. Virgin Islands are pub- *St. Thomas* lic, but occasionally you'll need to stroll through a resort to reach the sand. Government-run **Magens Bay** is lively and popular because of its spectacular loop of white-sand beach, more than a half mile long, and its calm waters. Food, changing facilities, and rest rooms are available. **Secret Harbour** is a pretty cove for superb snorkeling; go out to the left, near the rocks. **Morningstar Beach,** close to Charlotte Amalie, has a mostly sandy sea bottom with some rocks;

snorkeling is good here when the current doesn't affect visibility. **Sapphire Beach** has a fine view of St. John and other islands. Snorkeling is excellent at the reef to the east, near Pettyklip Point, and all kinds of water-sports gear can be rented. Be careful when you enter the water; there are many rocks and shells in the sand.

St. John **Trunk Bay** is the main beach on St. John, mostly because of its underwater snorkeling trail. However, experienced snorkelers may find it tame and picked over, with too little coral or fish. Lifeguards are on duty.

Dining *Some restaurants add a 10%–15% service charge to the bill.*

$$$ **Hotel 1829.** Candlelight flickers over old stone walls and across the pink table linens at this restaurant on the gallery of a lovely old hotel. The award-winning menu and wine list are extensive, from Caribbean rock lobster to rack of lamb; many items, including a warm spinach salad, are prepared table-side. The restaurant is justly famous for its dessert soufflés: chocolate, Grand Marnier, raspberry, and coconut. *Government Hill, a few steps up from Main St., Charlotte Amalie, tel. 809/776–1829. Reservations essential. AE, D, MC, V. No lunch.*

$ **Gladys' Cafe.** Even if the food was less tasty and the prices higher, it would be worth visiting just to see Gladys smile. Antiguan by birth, she won a local following as a waitress at Palm Passage before opening her own restaurant for breakfast and lunch in a courtyard off Main Street in Charlotte Amalie. Try the Caribbean lobster roll, the barbecue ribs, Gladys's hot chicken salad, or one of the filling salad platters. *17 Main St., tel. 809/774–6604. AE. No dinner.*

San Juan, Puerto Rico

Although Puerto Rico is part of the United States, few cities in the Caribbean are as steeped in Spanish tradition as San Juan. Old San Juan has restored 16th-century buildings, museums, art galleries, bookstores, 200-year-old houses with balustrade balconies overlooking narrow, cobblestone streets—all within a seven-block neighborhood. In contrast, San

Juan's sophisticated Condado and Isla Verde areas have glittering hotels, flashy Las Vegas–style shows, casinos, and discos.

Out in the countryside is the 28,000-acre El Yunque rain forest, with more than 240 species of trees growing at least 100 feet high. You can also visit dramatic mountain ranges, numerous trails, vast caves, coffee plantations, old sugar mills, and hundreds of beaches. No wonder San Juan is one of the busiest ports of call in the Caribbean. Like any other big city, San Juan has its share of crime, so guard your wallet or purse, and avoid walking in the area between Old San Juan and the Condado.

Telephones You can use the long-distance telephone service office in the cruise-ship terminal, or call from any pay phone. A phone center by the Paseo de la Princesa charges 40¢ a minute for calls to the United States.

Shore Excursions The following are good choices in San Juan. They may not be offered by all cruise lines. Times and prices are approximate.

Local Flavors **Bacardi Rum Distillery.** After seeing how it is made, you can sample and buy some Bacardi rum. *2 hrs. Cost: $15.*

San Juan Nightlife Tour. Several major hotels (like the Condado Plaza) have very exciting revues, especially those that feature flamenco or Latin dancers. Admission includes a drink or two. *3 hrs. Cost: $26–$34.*

Natural Beauty **El Yunque Rain Forest.** A 45-minute drive heads east to the Caribbean National Forest, where you may walk along various trails, see waterfalls, and climb the observation tower. The trip may include a stop at Luquillo Beach. *4 hrs. Cost: $20.*

Coming Ashore Cruise ships dock within a couple of blocks of Old San Juan. The Paseo de la Princesa, a tree-lined promenade beneath the city wall, is a nice place for a stroll, where you can admire the local crafts and stop at the refreshment kiosks. A tourist information booth and long-distance telephone office are found in the cruise-terminal area. From here a 10- or 15-minute taxi ride to

New San Juan costs $8–$10. A five-minute ride to the Condado costs $3–$4.

**Getting
Around**
By Bus

The **Metropolitan Bus Authority** operates buses that thread through San Juan. The fare is 25¢, and the buses run in exclusive lanes, against traffic, on all major thoroughfares, stopping at yellow posts marked *Parada* or *Parada de Guaguas.* The main terminal is Intermodal Terminal, at Marina and Harding streets in Old San Juan.

By Car

U.S. driver's licenses are valid in Puerto Rico. All major U.S. car-rental agencies are represented on the island. Contact **Avis** (tel. 787/721–4499 or 800/331–1212), **Budget** (tel. 787/791–3685 or 800/527–0700), **Hertz** (tel. 787/791–0840 or 800/654–3131), or **L & M Car Rental** (tel. 787/725–8416). Prices start at $30 a day. If you plan to drive across the island, arm yourself with a good map and be aware that many roads up in the mountains are unmarked, and many service stations require cash. To keep you on your toes, speed limits are posted in miles, distances in kilometers, and gas prices are per liter.

By Taxi

Taxis line up to meet ships. Metered cabs authorized by the Public Service Commission charge an initial $1; each additional ⅒ mile is 10¢. Waiting time is 10¢ for each 45 seconds. Demand that the meter be turned on, and pay only what is shown, plus a tip of 10%–15%.

By Trolley

If your feet fail you in Old San Juan, climb aboard the free open-air trolleys that rumble through the narrow streets. Take one from the docks or board anywhere along the route.

**Exploring
Old San Juan**

Numbers in the margin correspond to points of interest on the Old San Juan map.

Old San Juan

Old San Juan, the original city founded in 1521, contains authentic and carefully preserved examples of 16th- and 17th-century Spanish colonial architecture. Graceful wrought-iron balconies decorated with lush green hanging plants extend over narrow, cobblestoned streets. Seventeenth-century walls still partially enclose the old city. Designated a U.S. National Historic Zone in 1950, Old San Juan is packed with shops, open-air cafés, private homes, tree-shaded squares, monuments, plaques, pigeons, people, and traffic jams. It's faster to walk than to take a cab. Nightlife is quiet, even spooky during the low season; you'll find more to do in New San Juan, especially the Condado area.

❶ **San Cristóbal,** the 18th-century fortress that guarded the city from land attacks, is known as the Gibraltar of the West Indies. San Cristóbal is larger than El Morro (*see below*), and offers spectacular views of both Old San Juan and the new city. *Tel. 787/729–6960. Admission free. Open daily 9–5.*

❷ **Plaza de Armas** is the original main square of Old San Juan. The plaza has a lovely fountain with statues representing the four seasons.

❸ West of the main square stands **La Intendencia,** a handsome, three-story neoclassical building that was home to the Spanish Treasury from 1851 to 1898. *Calle San José at Calle San Francisco. Admission free. Open weekdays 8–noon and 1–4:30.*

❹ On the north side of the Plaza de Armas is **City Hall,** called the *alcaldía.* Built between 1604 and 1789, it was fashioned after Madrid's city hall, with arcades, towers, balconies, and a lovely inner courtyard. An art gallery is on the first floor. *Tel. 787/724–7171, ext. 2391. Open weekdays 8–4.*

❺ The remains of Ponce de León are in a marble tomb near the transept in the **San Juan Cathedral** on Calle Cristo. This great Catholic shrine of Puerto Rico had humble beginnings in the early 1520s as a thatch-top wood structure that was destroyed by a hurricane. It was reconstructed in 1540, when the graceful circular staircase and vaulted ceilings were added, but most of the work on the church was done in the 19th century. *153 Calle Cristo. Open daily 8–4.*

❻ **Casa de los Contrafuertes**—also known as the Buttress House because buttresses support the wall next to the plaza—is one of the oldest remaining private residences in Old San Juan. Inside is the Pharmacy Museum, a re-creation of an 18th-century apothecary shop, and the Latin American Graphic Arts Museum and Gallery. *101 Calle San Sebastián, Plaza de San José, tel.*

N

ATLANTIC OCEAN

TO THE
CONDADO

El Morro

❶❶

❻❼❽❾

Norzagaray

San Sebastián

Sol
Luna

Las Monjas

San Cristo

San José

San Justo

Cruz

San Francisco

Fortaleza

O'Donnell

❶

Muñoz

Rivera

Ponce de Léon

Paseo de

Del Muelle

❺

❸

❷

❹

Tetuán

Recinto Sur

Marina

Calle Recinto
Oeste

❿

Paseo de
la Princesa

Arsenal

Bahía de
San Juan

| 0 | 550 yards |
| 0 | 500 meters |

787/724–5477. Admission free. Open Wed.–
Sun. 9–4:30.

❼ The **Pablo Casals Museum** contains memorabilia
of the famed Spanish cellist, who made his home
in Puerto Rico for the last 20 years of his life. *101
Calle San Sebastián, Plaza de San José, tel.
787/723–9185. Admission: $1. Open Tues.–Sat.
9:30–5.*

❽ In the center of Plaza San José is the **San José
Church.** With its series of vaulted ceilings, it is a
fine example of 16th-century Spanish Gothic architecture. *Calle San Sebastián, tel. 787/725–
7501. Admission free. Open Mon.–Sat. 8:30–4;
Sun. mass at 12:15.*

❾ Next door to the San José Church is the
Dominican Convent. Also built in the 16th century, the building now houses an ornate 18th-
century altar, religious manuscripts, artifacts,
and art. *98 Calle Norzagaray, tel. 787/721–
6866. Admission free. Chapel museum open
Mon.–Sat. 9–5.*

❿ **La Fortaleza,** on a hill overlooking the harbor, is
the Western Hemisphere's oldest executive
mansion in continuous use. Built as a fortress,
the original 16th-century structure has seen numerous changes, including the addition of marble and mahogany, medieval towers, and
stained-glass galleries. Guided tours are conducted every hour on the hour in English, on the
half hour in Spanish. *Tel. 787/721–7000, ext.
2211. Admission free. Open weekdays 9–4.*

⓫ San Juan's most famous sight is undoubtedly **El
Morro** (Fuerte San Felipe del Morro), set on a
rocky promontory on the northwestern tip of
the old city. Rising 140 feet above the sea, the
massive, six-level Spanish fortress is a labyrinth
of dungeons, ramps, turrets, and tunnels. Built
to protect the port, El Morro has a commanding
view of the harbor and Old San Juan. Its small
museum traces the history of the fortress. *Tel.
787/729–6960. Admission free. Open daily 9–5.*

New San Juan In **Puerta de Tierra,** a half mile east of the pier, is
Puerto Rico's white marble Capitol, dating from
the 1920s. Another mile east, at the tip of
Puerta de Tierra, tiny Ft. San Jeronimo perches
over the Atlantic like an afterthought. Added to

San Juan's fortifications in the late 18th century, the structure barely survived the British attack of 1797.

Santurce, the district between Miramar on the west and the Laguna San José on the east, is a busy mixture of shops, markets, and offices. The classically designed Sacred Heart University is home of the Museum of Contemporary Puerto Rican Art (tel. 787/268–0049).

San Juan From San Juan, Route 2 leads west to the
Environs **Caparra Ruins,** where, in 1508, Ponce de León established the island's first settlement. The ruins are those of an ancient fort. Its small Museum of the Conquest and Colonization of Puerto Rico contains historic documents, exhibits, and excavated artifacts. *Km 6.6 on Rte. 2, tel. 787/781–4795. Admission free. Open Wed.– Sun. 9–4.*

Past the Caparra Ruins, Route 2 brings you to **Bayamón.** In the Central Park, across from the city hall, are some historic buildings and a 1934 sugarcane train that runs through the park.

Along Route 5 from Bayamón to Catano, you'll find the **Barrilito Rum Plant.** On the grounds is a 200-year-old plantation home and a 150-year-old windmill, which is listed in the National Register of Historic Places.

The **Bacardi Rum Plant,** along the bay, conducts 45-minute tours of the bottling plant, museum, and distillery, which has the capacity to produce 100,000 gallons of rum a day. (Yes, you'll be offered a sample.) *Km 2.6 on Rte. 888, tel. 787/ 788–1500. Admission free. Tours Mon.–Sat. 9:30–3:30; closed holidays.*

Shopping San Juan is not a free port, and you won't find bargains on electronics and perfumes. However, shopping for native crafts can be fun. Popular souvenirs and gifts include *santos* (small, hand-carved figures of saints or religious scenes), hand-rolled cigars, handmade lace, carnival masks, Puerto Rican rum, and fancy men's shirts called *guayaberas.*

Old San Juan is filled with shops, especially on **Calles Cristo, La Fortaleza,** and **San Francisco.** You can get discounts on Hathaway shirts and clothing by Christian Dior and Ralph Lauren at **Hathaway Factory Outlet** (203 Calle Cristo, tel. 787/723–8946) and on raincoats at the **London Fog Factory Outlet** (156 Calle Cristo, tel. 787/722–4334). For one-of-a-kind local crafts, head for **Puerto Rican Arts & Crafts** (204 Calle La Fortaleza, Old San Juan, tel. 787/725–5596) or the **Haitian Gallery** (367 Calle Fortaleza, tel. 787/725–0986).

Sports

Golf There are four 18-hole courses shared by the **Hyatt Dorado Beach Hotel** and the **Hyatt Regency Cerromar Beach Hotel** (Dorado, tel. 787/796–1234). You'll also find 18-hole courses at **Palmas del Mar Resort** (Humacao, tel. 787/852–6000), **Club Ríomar** (Rio Grande, tel. 787/887–3964), **Punta Borinquén** (Aquadilla, tel. 787/890–2987), and **Bahia Beach Plantation** (Rio Grande, tel. 787/256–5600).

Hiking Dozens of trails lace **El Yunque.** Information is available at the Sierra Palm Visitor Center (Km 11.6, Rte. 191).

Water Sports Virtually all resorts on San Juan's Condado and Isla Verde (*see* Beaches, *below*) strips rent paddleboats, Sunfish, and Windsurfers.

Beaches By law, all of Puerto Rico's beaches are open to the public (except for the Caribe Hilton's artificial beach in San Juan). The government runs 13 public beaches (*balnearios*), which have lockers, showers, and picnic tables; some have playgrounds and overnight facilities. *Admission free; parking $1. Open Tues.–Sun. 8–5 in summer, 9–6 in winter.*

Isla Verde is a white sandy beach close to metropolitan San Juan. Backed by several resort hotels, the beach offers picnic tables and good snorkeling, with equipment rentals nearby.

Dining *A 10%–15% tip is expected in restaurants.*

$$$ **La Chaumière.** Reminiscent of a French inn, this intimate yet bright white restaurant serves a respectable onion soup, oysters Rockefeller, rack of lamb, and veal Oscar, in addition to daily specials. *327 Calle Tetuán, tel. 787/722–3330. AE, DC, MC, V. Closed Sun. No lunch.*

$–$$ **Amadeus.** The atmosphere of this restaurant is gentrified Old San Juan, with an ever-changing menu of 20 appetizers, including *tostones* with sour cream and caviar, plantain mousse with shrimp, and Buffalo wings. Entrées on the nouvelle Caribbean menu range from Cajun-grilled mahimahi, to creamy pasta dishes, to chicken and steak sandwiches. *106 Calle San Sebastián, tel. 787/722–8635. AE, MC, V. Closed Mon.*

Nightlife Almost every ship stays in San Juan late or even overnight to give passengers an opportunity to enjoy the nightlife—the most sophisticated in the Caribbean.

Casinos By law, all casinos are in hotels. Alcoholic drinks are not permitted at the gaming tables, although free soft drinks, coffee, and sandwiches are available. The atmosphere is quite refined, and many patrons dress to the nines, but informal attire is usually fine. Casinos set their own hours, which change seasonally, but generally operate from noon to 4 AM. Casinos are located in the following hotels: **Condado Plaza Hotel, Caribe Hilton, Carib Inn, Clarion Hotel, Dutch Inn, El San Juan, Ramada, San Juan Marriott,** and **Sands.**

Discos In Old San Juan, young people flock to **Lazers** (251 Cruz St., tel. 787/721–4479). In Puerta de Tierra, Condado, and Isla Verde, the thirty-something crowd heads for **Amadeus** (El San Juan Hotel, tel. 787/791–1000), **Isadora's** (Condado Plaza Hotel, tel. 787/721–1000), and **Club Ibiza** (La Concha Hotel, tel. 787/721–6090).

Nightclubs The Sands Hotel's **Calypso Room** has a flamenco show nightly except Monday. El San Juan's **Tropicoro** presents international revues and, occasionally, top-name entertainers. The Condado Plaza Hotel has the **Copa Room,** and its **La Fiesta** sizzles with steamy Latin shows. Young professionals gather at **Egypt** (tel. 787/725–4664 or 787/725–4675), where the design is 1950s and the music mixes oldies and current dance hits.

Panama Canal and Central America

Transit of the Panama Canal takes only one day. The rest of your cruise will be spent on islands in the Caribbean or at ports along the Mexican Riviera. Increasingly, Panama Canal itineraries include stops in Central America; some may also call along the northern coast of South America. Most Panama Canal cruises are one-way trips, part of a 10- to 14-day cruise between the Atlantic and Pacific oceans. Shorter loop cruises enter the canal from the Caribbean, sail around Gatún Lake for a few hours, and return to the Caribbean.

The Panama Canal is best described as a water bridge that "raises" ships up and over Central America, then down again, using a series of locks or water steps. Artificially created Gatún Lake, 85 feet above sea level, is the canal's highest point. The route is approximately 50 miles long, and the crossing takes from 8 to 10 hours. Cruise ships pay more than $100,000 for each transit, which is less than half of what it would cost them to sail around Cape Horn, at the southern tip of South America.

Just before dawn, your ship will line up with dozens of other vessels to await its turn to enter the canal. Before it can proceed, two pilots and a narrator will come on board. The sight of a massive cruise ship being raised dozens of feet into the air by water is so fascinating that passengers will crowd all the forward decks at the first lock. If you can't see, go to the rear decks, where there is usually more room and the view is just as intriguing. Later in the day you won't find as many passengers up front.

On and off throughout the day, commentary is broadcast over ship's loudspeakers, imparting facts and figures as well as anecdotes about the history of the canal. The canal stands where it does today not because it's the best route but because the railroad was built there first, making access to the area relatively easy. The railway had followed an old Spanish mule trail that had been there for more than 300 years.

Panama Canal

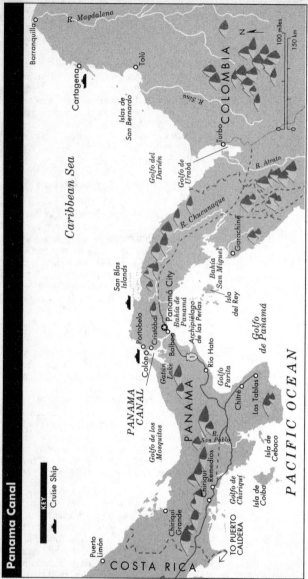

KEY
⬛ Cruise Ship

N
100 miles
150 km

R. Magdalena

Barranquilla

Cartagena

Tolú

COLOMBIA

Islas de San Bernardo

Turbo

Caribbean Sea

Golfo del Darién

Golfo de Urabá

R. Atrato

R. Chucunaque

San Blas Islands

Garachiné

Portobelo

Cristóbal

Panamá City

Bahía de Panamá

Bahía San Miguel

Isla del Rey

Colón

Balboa

Archipiélago de las Perlas

PANAMA CANAL

Gatún Lake

Río Hato

Golfo de Panamá

Golfo de los Mosquitos

Golfo Parita

Chitré

las Tablas

PANAMA

R. San Pablo

PACIFIC OCEAN

Remedios

Isla de Coiba

Golfo de Chiriquí

Isla de Cebaco

Chiriquí

Chiriquí Grande

Puerto Limón

TO PUERTO CALDERA

COSTA RICA

When to Go In spring and autumn a number of cruise ships use the Panama Canal to reposition between the Caribbean and Alaska. However, several ships offer regular transcanal and loop cruises throughout the winter season. (For seasonal itineraries, *see* Chapter 3.)

Currency Passengers won't need to change money to transit the canal, but some ships stop in Costa Rica; in the San Blas Islands, off Panama; and at Cartagena, Colombia. In Costa Rica, the currency is the colón. At press time, one U.S. dollar was worth about 163 colónes. In Panama, the balboa and the U.S. dollar are regular currency and both have the same value. In Colombia, the monetary unit is the peso, with one U.S. dollar worth about 580 pesos.

Passports and Visas No passport or visa is necessary to transit the Panama Canal because passengers do not disembark. A passport is needed for passengers on cruises that call in Costa Rica, the San Blas Islands, or Cartagena.

Cartagena, Colombia

Cartagena, Colombia, is one of the Western Hemisphere's most fascinating cities. Seventeenth-century walls divide Cartagena into the "old" and "new" cities. In the old city, houses are in the Iberian style: thick walls, high ceilings, central patios, gardens, and balconies. The streets are narrow and crooked, designed for protection during assault. The cityscape is filled with historic sites, forts, and museums. Among Cartagena's major exports are coffee and emeralds—Colombia supplies 70% of the world's supply of these gems.

Shore Excursions The best choice in Cartagena for the first-time visitor is the city tour (3½ hrs, $26), which takes you through the city, stopping at a hilltop monastery for a sweeping view, and into the old town for a survey of the historic attractions and shopping.

Costa Rica

Costa Rica is emerging as a popular port of call on Panama Canal itineraries, due to its growing reputation as a land of unspoiled rain forests, abundant wildlife, and friendly locals. Twenty-seven percent of the land is protected wilderness—home to 850 species of birds, 200 species of mammals, and 35,000 species of insects. Some itineraries include a scenic sail into the Golfo Dulce, whose shores are lined with remote beaches and untouched rain forest teeming with wildlife.

Coming Ashore
Most ships call at Puerto Caldera, located 5 miles from Puntarenas on the Pacific Coast, or Puerto Limon, on the Caribbean coast. Both double as cargo ports, and since most attractions are located some distance away or involve guided nature walks, it's a good idea to book a shore excursion. From Puerto Caldera, a local taxi to Puntarenas costs approximately U.S. $12 each way, but its beaches are polluted and there is little of interest for cruise passengers. A small selection of stands at the port sells coffee, souvenir oxcarts, wood, leather and T-shirts.

Shore Excursions
From Puerto Caldera, the best choice for nature lovers is a walk through the Carara Biological Reserve, a half hour from the ship, where you can see crocodiles, toucans, and sloths (4 hrs, $55). (Skip the nine-hour excursion to the more famous Los Angeles Cloud Forest, where you'll spend only about an hour actually in the forest.) Shoppers won't want to miss a trip to the artisan city of Sarchi (5 hrs, $45). A 10-hour tour to the capital city of San Jose, two hours from the ship, costs $95.

Good choices from Puerto Limon include river rafting on the Rio Reventazon (8 hrs, $78) and riding the historic Green Train through banana plantations (2½ hrs, $68).

Puerto Quetzal, Guatemala

Guatemala is home to a vibrant Indian culture, colonial cities, and stunning mountain scenery. Most ships call at **Puerto Quetzal,** a lively cargo and cruise port located on Guatemala's flat Pacific coast. Families and school groups pose for photos in front of the cruise ship, friendly hawkers approach with handcrafted silver belts, and locals slurp ices purchased from a two-wheel cart. You can easily spend a morning bargaining for leather, jewelry, rugs and embroidered belts at the open-air market set up amid sacks of grain at the port. Otherwise, it's a good idea to book a shore excursion. Local taxes aren't necessarily reliable, and it's about U.S.$50 per person each way to the colonial town of Antigua or Guatemala City, a two-hour drive away. The closest town, San Jose, is dirty and offers little of interest to cruise passengers.

Shore Excursions   The Mayan ruins of Tikal are perhaps Guatemala's most famous attraction, and with good reason: They're known as the greatest Mayan site yet discovered, with 3,000 unique buildings nestled in thick jungle. But it's neither cheap nor easy to get there from the ship: The trip involves buses, walking, and a one-hour flight by chartered aircraft (10 hrs, $354). Less costly and complicated options include a tour of historic Antigua, with its cobblestone streets and brightly colored buildings (8 hrs, $104) or an excursion to the Guatemala Highlands and Lake Atitlan, whose crystal-clear waters are ringed by mountains on all sides (9 hrs, $140).

The San Blas Islands

The beautiful islands of the **San Blas** archipelago are home to the Cuna Indians, whose women are famous for handworked stitching. These women are a charming sight, with their embroidered *molas*, strings of necklaces, gold jewelry in their noses, and arm and ankle bracelets. Some cruise lines organize shore excursions to Cuna villages on outlying islands. Travel is by motorized dugout canoe. A native dance performance may be scheduled, and native crafts are usually for sale. If you are wavering between two Panama Canal cruises, take the one that stops at the San Blas Islands.

3   Itineraries

Sailing Schedules

Itineraries begin with fall 1996 and run through summer 1997. Ports of call are described in Chapter 3. Ship deployments and itineraries are subject to change; ports of call may also vary with departure date. Check with your cruise line or travel agent.

American Canadian Caribbean Line

Mayan Prince **Winter:** An 11-night **Panama Canal** transit calls at the San Blas Islands and other ports of call.

Niagara Prince **Winter:** Eleven-night **Virgin Islands** loops depart St. Thomas. Eleven-night **Venezuela** cruises sail between Trinidad and Tobago. Eleven-night **southern Caribbean** cruises call at Aruba, Bonaire, and Curaçao. **Spring–Summer:** Eleven-night **Bahamas** loops depart Nassau.

Carnival Cruise Lines

Carnival Destiny **Year-round:** Seven-night **eastern Caribbean** loops depart Miami, calling at San Juan, St. Croix, and St. Thomas. Seven-night **western Caribbean** loops depart Miami, calling at Cozumel/ Playa del Carmen, Grand Cayman, and Ocho Rios.

Celebration **Fall–mid-Spring:** Seven-night **eastern Caribbean** loops depart Miami, calling at San Juan, St. Thomas/St. John, and St. Maarten/St. Martin. **Mid-Spring–Summer:** Seven-night **western Caribbean** loops depart Tampa or New Orleans, calling at Grand Cayman and Cozumel/Playa del Carmen.

Ecstasy **Year-round:** Three-night **Bahamas** loops depart Miami, calling at Nassau. Four-night **western Caribbean** loops depart Miami, calling at Key West and Cozumel/Playa del Carmen.

Fantasy **Year-round:** Three-night **Bahamas** loops depart Port Canaveral, calling at Nassau. Four-night **Bahamas** loops depart Port Canaveral, calling at Nassau and Freeport/Lucaya.

Fascination **Year-round:** Seven-night **southern Caribbean** loops depart San Juan, calling at St. Thomas, Guadeloupe, Grenada, La Guaira/Caracas, and Aruba.

Imagination **Year-round:** Seven-night **western Caribbean** loops depart Miami, calling at Cozumel/Playa del Carmen, Grand Cayman, and Ocho Rios.

Inspiration **Year-round:** Seven-night **southern Caribbean** loops depart San Juan, calling at St. Thomas, St. Maarten/St. Martin, Dominica, Barbados, and Martinique.

Sensation **Year-round:** Seven-night **eastern Caribbean** loops depart Miami, calling at San Juan, St. Thomas, and St. Maarten/St. Martin.

Tropicale **Early Fall:** A 14-night **Panama Canal** transit from Los Angeles to San Juan calls at Puerto Vallarta, Zihuatenejo/Ixtapa, Acapulco, Puerto Caldera, Curaçao, and St. Thomas. **Late Fall–early Spring:** Ten-night **southern Caribbean** loops depart San Juan, calling at St. Thomas, Martinique, Barbados, Grenada, St. Lucia, St. Barts, Antigua, and St. Maarten/St. Martin. Eleven-night **Panama Canal** loops depart San Juan, calling at St. Thomas, St. Barts, St. Lucia, Aruba, and Ocho Rios. A 16-night Panama Canal transit from Tampa to Vancouver calls at Cartagena, Acapulco, Zihuatenejo/Ixtapa, Puerto Vallarta, Cabo San Lucas, and Los Angeles.

Celebrity Cruises

Century **Year-round:** Seven-night **eastern Caribbean** loops depart Fort Lauderdale, calling at San Juan, St. Thomas, St. Maarten/St. Martin, and Nassau. Seven-night **western Caribbean** loops depart Fort Lauderdale, calling at Ocho Rios, Grand Cayman, Cozumel/Playa del Carmen, and Key West.

Galaxy **Fall–Spring:** Seven-night **western Caribbean** loops depart Fort Lauderdale, calling at Key West, Cozumel/Playa del Carmen, Montego Bay, and Grand Cayman.

Horizon **Fall–Spring:** A 17-night **Panama Canal** transit from Los Angeles to San Juan calls at San Diego, Cabo San Lucas, Acapulco, Puerto Caldera, the San Blas Islands, Cartagena, and Aruba. Seven-night **Caribbean** loops depart San Juan, calling at Catalina Island, Martinique, Barbados, Antigua, and St. Thomas.

Meridian **Fall–Spring:** Ten- and 11-night **Caribbean** and **Caribbean/Panama Canal** loops depart San Juan and include calls at Aruba, Caracas/La Guaira, Grenada, Barbados, St. Lucia, Martinique, St. Maarten/St. Martin, St. Thomas, St. John, Cartagena, and the San Blas Islands. An 11-night **Caribbean** cruise from Fort Lauderdale to San Juan calls at Nassau, Tortola, St. Maarten/St. Martin, Antigua, Martinique, Barbados, Grenada, and St. Thomas.

Zenith **Fall–Winter:** Seven-night **Caribbean** loops depart San Juan, calling at St. Thomas, Guadeloupe, Grenada, Caracas/La Guaira, and Aruba. A seven-night **Caribbean** cruise between San Juan and New York calls at St. Thomas, St. Maarten, and Bermuda.

Clipper Cruise Line

Nantucket Clipper **Winter:** Seven-night **Virgin Islands** loops depart St. Thomas.

Yorktown Clipper **Late Fall–Spring:** Eight-night **Costa Rica/Panama Canal** cruises sail between Colon (Costa Rica) and Puerto Caldera (Costa Rica). Ten-night **Lesser Antilles and Orinoco River (Venezuela)** cruises sail between Curaçao and Trinidad. Seven-night **Caribbean** cruises sail between St. Lucia and St. Kitts.

Club Med

Club Med 1 **Mid-Fall–late Spring:** Seven-night **Caribbean** loops depart Martinique and include calls at Barbados, St. Lucia, Carriacou, St. Thomas, St. Maarten/St. Martin, San Juan, and other islands.

Commodore Cruise Line

Enchanted Isle **Year-round:** Seven-night **western Caribbean** loops depart New Orleans, calling at Cozumel/Playa del Carmen, Grand Cayman, and Montego Bay.

Costa Cruise Lines

CostaClassica **Fall–mid-Spring:** **Caribbean** cruises with port calls to be announced.

CostaRomantica **Fall–mid-Spring:** Seven-night **eastern Caribbean** loops depart Port Everglades, calling at San Juan, St. Thomas, Serena Cay/Casa de Campo, and Nassau. **Western Caribbean** loops call at Key West, Cozumel/Playa del Carmen, Ocho Rios, and Grand Cayman.

CostaVictoria **Fall–mid-Spring:** Seven-night **eastern Caribbean** loops depart Port Everglades, calling at San Juan, St. Thomas, Serena Cay/Casa de Campo, and Nassau. **Western Caribbean** loops call at Key West, Cozumel/Playa del Carmen, Ocho Rios, and Grand Cayman.

Crystal Cruises

Crystal Harmony **Winter:** Ten-, 11-, and 12-night **Panama Canal** transits between Acapulco and New Orleans, San Juan, or Fort Lauderdale include calls at Puerto Limon, Puerto Caldera, the San Blas Islands, Huatulco, Cozumel/Playa del Carmen, Galveston, Grand Cayman, Aruba, St. Maarten/St. Martin, St. Thomas, St. Barts, and Puerto Quetzal.

Crystal Symphony **Fall:** Ten-, 11-, and 12-night **Panama Canal** cruises sail between Acapulco and Barbados, New Orleans, or Fort Lauderdale, and include calls at St. Lucia, St. Vincent, Aruba, Huatulco, Cozumel/Playa del Carmen, Puerto Quetzal, Puerto Caldera, Puerto Limon, and the San Blas Islands. **Winter:** A 12-night **eastern Caribbean** loop from Fort Lauderdale calls at Nassau, Antigua, St. Lucia, Barbados, St. Maarten/St. Martin, and St. John/St. Thomas. A 14-night **Panama Canal** transit from Fort Lauderdale to Los Angeles calls at Grand Cayman, Aruba, and Acapulco. An 11-night **Panama Canal** cruise from Fort Lauderdale to Acapulco calls at Cozumel/Playa del Carmen, Grand Cayman, and Puerto Caldera.

Cunard Line Limited

Cunard Countess **Year-round:** Seven-night **southern Caribbean** loops depart San Juan, calling at St. Maarten/St. Martin, Dominica, Grenada, St. Lucia, St. Kitts, and St. Thomas or Tortola, Antigua, Martinique, Barbados, and St. Thomas.

Cunard Dynasty	**Fall–Spring:** A 14-night **Panama Canal** transit from Los Angeles to Fort Lauderdale calls at Acapulco, Puerto Caldera, Cartagena, Colombia, and Ocho Rios. Ten- and 11-night **Panama Canal** transits between Fort Lauderdale and Acapulco include calls at Cozumel/Playa del Carmen, Grand Cayman, Puerto Caldera, Ocho Rios, and Key West.
Queen Elizabeth 2	**Fall–early Winter:** A 15-night **Caribbean** loop departs New York, calling at Fort Lauderdale, St. Thomas, Aruba, Caracas/La Guaira, Grenada, Barbados, St. Maarten/St. Martin, and Martinique.
Royal Viking Sun	**Late Fall–mid-Winter:** A 14-night **Amazon/Caribbean** cruise from Rio de Janeiro to Fort Lauderdale calls at Salvador de Bahia, Devil's Island, Barbados, and St. Thomas. An 18-night **Panama Canal** transit from Fort Lauderdale to San Francisco calls at Cozumel/Playa del Carmen, Acapulco, Mazatlan, Aruba, and Puerto Caldera.
Sea Goddess II	**Fall:** Ten- and 11-night **Panama Canal** transits between Acapulco and Aruba include calls at Puerto Caldera, the San Blas Islands, Cartagena, and other ports. A 14-night **Panama Canal** transit from Acapulco to St. Thomas also calls at Curaçao and St. Barts. Seven-night **Caribbean** loops depart St. Thomas, calling at St. John, St. Maarten/St. Martin, St. Barts, Antigua, Virgin Gorda, and Jost Van Dyke.
Vistafjord	**Fall:** A 16-night **Caribbean** loop departs Fort Lauderdale, calling at San Juan, St. Croix, Barbados, St. Lucia, Grenada, Caracas/La Guaira, Aruba, and St. Thomas. An 11-night **Caribbean** loop departs Fort Lauderdale, calling at San Juan, St. Thomas, St. Kitts, Aruba, and Grand Cayman. **Spring:** Fifteen-night **Panama Canal** transits between Los Angeles and Fort Lauderdale may call at Acapulco, Puerto Vallarta, Zihuatanejo/Ixtapa, Puerto Caldera, Aruba, Cartagena, and Grand Cayman.

Dolphin Cruise Line

IslandBreeze	**Mid-Fall–early Spring:** Seven-night **Caribbean/Panama Canal** cruises depart Montego Bay (Jamaica), calling at Cartagena, the San Blas Islands, and Puerto Limon.

OceanBreeze **Year-round:** Three-night **Bahamas** loops depart Miami, calling at Nassau and Blue Lagoon Island. Four-night **Mexican Yucatan** loops depart Miami, calling at Cozumel/Playa del Carmen and Key West.

SeaBreeze **Year-round:** Seven-night **eastern Caribbean** loops depart Miami, calling at Nassau, San Juan, and St. Thomas/St. John. Seven-night **western Caribbean** loops call at Grand Cayman, Montego Bay, and Cozumel/Playa del Carmen.

Holland America Line

Maasdam **Late Fall–early Winter:** Ten-night **Panama Canal** transits between Fort Lauderdale and Acapulco include calls at Grand Cayman, Puerto Caldera, and Puerto Quetzal. Ten-night **Panama Canal** transits between New Orleans and Acapulco call at Puerto Quetzal, Grand Cayman and Cozumel/Playa del Carmen.

Nieuw Amsterdam **Fall–mid-Spring:** A 20-night **Panama Canal** transit from Vancouver to New Orleans includes calls at Cabo San Lucas, Acapulco, Puerto Caldera, Aruba, and Ocho Rios. Seven-night **western Caribbean** loops depart New Orleans, calling at Montego Bay, Grand Cayman, and Cozumel/Playa del Carmen. **Mid-Spring–Summer:** A 21-night **Panama Canal** transit from New Orleans to Vancouver includes calls at Grand Cayman, Montego Bay, Cartagena, Puerto Caldera, Acapulco, Zihuatenejo/Ixtapa, Puerto Vallarta, Los Angeles, and Victoria.

Noordam **Fall–mid-Spring:** A 19-night **Panama Canal** transit from Vancouver to Tampa calls at Victoria, San Francisco, San Diego, Cabo San Lucas, Acapulco, Puerto Caldera, Cartagena, and Grand Cayman. Seven-night **western Caribbean** loops depart Tampa, calling at Key West, Cozumel/Playa del Carmen, Ocho Rios, and Grand Cayman. **Late Spring–Summer:** A 12-night **Panama Canal** cruise with ports of call to be announced.

Rotterdam **Winter:** A 14-night **Panama Canal** transit from Fort Lauderdale to Los Angeles includes calls at Curaçao, Puerto Caldera, Acapulco, Cabo San Lucas. **Spring:** A 17-night **Panama Canal** transit from Fort Lauderdale to Los Angeles calls at

Nassau, San Juan, Aruba, Puerto Quetzal, Zihuatanejo/Ixtapa, Acapulco, and other ports.

Ryndam **Early Fall:** A 20-night **Panama Canal** transit from Vancouver to Fort Lauderdale calls at Los Angeles, Puerto Vallarta, Zihuatenejo/Ixtapa, Acapulco, Puerto Caldera, Curaçao, St. Thomas, and Nassau. **Late Fall–mid-Spring:** Ten-night **Caribbean** loops depart Fort Lauderdale, calling at St. Maarten/St. Martin, St. Lucia, Barbados, and Antigua or Guadeloupe, St. Thomas/St. John, and Nassau. **Mid-Spring–Summer:** A 16-night **Panama Canal** transit with ports of call to be announced.

Statendam **Early Fall:** A 21-night **Panama Canal** transit from Vancouver to Fort Lauderdale calls at Victoria, San Francisco, San Diego, Cabo San Lucas, Puerto Vallarta, Acapulco, Puerto Quetzal, the San Blas Islands, Cartagena, and Grand Cayman. **Late Fall–mid-Spring:** Ten-night **southern Caribbean** loops depart Fort Lauderdale, calling at Curaçao, Caracas/La Guaira, Grenada, Dominica, St. Thomas/St. John, and Nassau. A 13-night **Panama Canal** transit with ports of call to be announced.

Veendam **Mid-Fall–Winter:** Seven-night **eastern Caribbean** loops depart Fort Lauderdale, calling at Nassau, San Juan, and St. Thomas/St. John. Seven-night **western Caribbean** loops call at Key West, Cozumel/Playa del Carmen, Ocho Rios, and Grand Cayman. **Winter–mid-Spring:** Seven-night **Caribbean** loops depart Fort Lauderdale, calling at St. Kitts, St. Thomas/St. John and Nassau. **Mid-Spring–Summer:** A 20-night **Panama Canal** transit from Fort Lauderdale to Vancouver calls at Curaçao, Puerto Quetzal, Acapulco, Zihuatenejo/Ixtapa, Puerto Vallarta, San Francisco, Seattle, and other ports.

Westerdam **Fall–Winter:** A 20-night **Panama Canal** transit from Vancouver to New Orleans calls at Los Angeles, Puerto Vallarta, Zihuatenejo/Ixtapa, Acapulco, Puerto Quetzal, Cartagena, Grand Cayman, and Ocho Rios. Seven-night **eastern Caribbean** loops depart Fort Lauderdale, calling at St. Maarten/St. Martin, St. Thomas/St. John, and Nassau. **Spring–Summer:** Seven-night **eastern Caribbean** loops (same as winter). **Western Caribbean** loops depart Fort Lauder-

dale, calling at Key West, Cozumel/Playa del
Carmen, Ocho Rios, and Grand Cayman.

Majesty Cruise Line

Royal Majesty **Late Fall–mid-Spring:** Three-night **Bahamas**
loops depart Miami, calling at Nassau and Key
West. Four-night **Mexican Yucatan** loops depart
Miami, calling at Key West and Cozumel/Playa
del Carmen.

Norwegian Cruise Line

Dreamward **Fall–Spring:** Seven-night **western Caribbean**
loops depart Fort Lauderdale, calling at Grand
Cayman, Cozumel/Playa del Carmen, Cancún,
and Great Stirrup Cay.

Leeward **Year-round:** Three-night **Bahamas** loops depart
Miami, calling at Great Stirrup Cay, and Nas-
sau or Key West. Four-night **Mexican Yucatan**
loops depart Miami, calling at Key West and
Cozumel/Playa del Carmen or Cozumel and
Cancún.

Norwegian **Fall–Winter:** Seven-night **western Caribbean**
Crown loops depart Fort Lauderdale, calling at Grand
Cayman, Cozumel/Playa del Carmen, Great
Stirrup Cay, and Key West.

Norway **Year-round:** Seven-night **eastern Caribbean**
loops depart Miami, calling at St. Maarten/St.
Martin, St. Thomas/St. John, and Great Stirrup
Cay. Seven-night **western Caribbean** loops depart Miami, calling at Ocho Rios, Grand Cayman, Cozumel/Playa del Carmen, and Great
Stirrup Cay.

Seaward **Year-round:** Seven-night **southern Caribbean**
loops depart San Juan, calling at Barbados,
Martinique, St. Maarten/St. Martin, Antigua,
and St. Thomas or at Aruba, Curaçao, Tortola,
and St. Thomas.

Windward **Fall–Winter:** Seven-night **southern Caribbean**
loops depart San Juan, calling at Barbados, St.
Lucia, St. Barts, St. Thomas, and Tortola.

Premier Cruise Lines

Star/Ship **Year-round:** Three- and four-night **Bahamas**
Atlantic loops depart Port Canaveral, calling at Nassau
and Freeport/Lucaya.

Star/Ship   Same as *Star/Ship Atlantic*, above.
Oceanic

Princess Cruises

Crown Princess   **Early Fall:** An 18-night **Panama Canal** transit from Vancouver to Fort Lauderdale calls at San Diego, Cabo San Lucas, Acapulco, Puerto Quetzal, Grand Cayman, and Princess Cays. **Mid-Fall–Spring:** Ten-night **southern Caribbean** loops depart Fort Lauderdale, calling at Nassau, Princess Cays, St. Maarten/St. Martin, Dominica, Barbados, Guadeloupe, and St. Thomas.

Dawn Princess   **Spring:** Seven-night **southern Caribbean** loops depart San Juan, calling at Grenada, Barbados, Guadeloupe, St. Maarten/St. Martin, and St. Thomas.

Pacific Princess   **Winter–Spring:** Fourteen-night **Panama Canal** transits between San Juan and New Orleans call at St. Thomas, Guadeloupe, Grenada, Caracas/La Guaira, Aruba, Puerto Limon, and Cozumel/Playa del Carmen.

Regal Princess   **Fall–Mid-Spring:** Ten-night **Panama Canal** loops depart Fort Lauderdale, calling at Princess Cays, Puerto Limon, Cartagena, and Cozumel/Playa del Carmen. Fifteen-night **Panama Canal** transits between Fort Lauderdale and Los Angeles include calls at Princess Cays, St. Thomas, Cartagena, Puerto Limon, Acapulco, and Cabo San Lucas.

Royal Princess   **Mid-Fall–mid-Spring:** Ten-night **Panama Canal** transits between Acapulco and San Juan call at Puerto Caldera, Cartagena, Aruba, and St. Thomas. Eleven-night **Panama Canal** transits between San Juan and Acapulco call at St. Thomas, Martinique, Grenada, Caracas/La Guaira, and Curaçao.

Star Princess   **Fall–mid-Spring:** An 11-night **Panama Canal** transit from Acapulco to Fort Lauderdale calls at Puerto Limon, Cartagena, St. Thomas, and Princess Cays. Seven-night **eastern Caribbean** loops depart Fort Lauderdale, calling at Nassau, Princess Cays, St. Croix, and St. John/St. Thomas. A 10-night **southern Caribbean** loop departs Fort Lauderdale, calling at Nassau, Princess Cays, St. Thomas, Guadeloupe, Barbados, Dominica, and St. Maarten/St. Martin.

Sun Princess   **Fall–early Spring:** A 16-night **Panama Canal**
transit from Los Angeles to Fort Lauderdale in-
cludes calls at Cabo San Lucas, Acapulco,
Cozumel/Playa del Carmen, Puerto Limon,
Cartagena, Montego Bay, and Grand Cayman.
Seven-night **western Caribbean** loops depart
Fort Lauderdale, calling at Princess Cays, Montego Bay, Grand Cayman, and Cozumel/Playa
del Carmen.

Radisson Seven Seas Cruises

Radisson   **Late Fall–early Spring:** An eight-night **Panama**
Diamond   **Canal** transit from San Juan to Puerto Caldera
(Costa Rica) calls at Curaçao, Cartagena, and
the San Blas Islands. Eleven- or 15-night **Pana-
ma Canal** transits between Puerto Caldera and
Charleston (South Carolina) include calls at
Grand Cayman, Cozumel/Playa del Carmen,
and Fort Lauderdale. Seven-, eight, and nine-
night **Panama Canal** transits between Puerto
Caldera and San Juan or Aruba include calls at
Curaçao, Cartagena, and the San Blas Islands.
Four- and five night **Caribbean** loops depart San
Juan, calling at Tortola, St. Barts, St. Maarten/
St. Martin, and St. Thomas.

Royal Caribbean Cruise Line

Grandeur   **Year-round:** Seven-night **eastern Caribbean**
of the Seas loops depart Miami, calling at Labadee, San
Juan, St. Thomas, and CocoCay.

Legend   **Winter–mid-Spring:** Ten- and 11-night **Panama**
of the Seas **Canal** transits between Acapulco and San Juan
call at St. Thomas, Santo Domingo, Curaçao,
and Puerto Caldera.

Majesty   **Year-round:** Seven-night **western Caribbean**
of the Seas loops depart Miami, calling at Grand Cayman,
Cozumel/Playa del Carmen, Ocho Rios, and
Labadee.

Monarch   **Year-round:** Seven-night **southern Caribbean**
of the Seas loops depart San Juan, calling at Martinique,
Barbados, Antigua, St. Maarten/St. Martin,
and St. Thomas.

Nordic   **Fall:** Three- and four-night **Bahamas** loops de-
Empress part Miami, calling at Nassau and CocoCay.
Four-night cruises also call at Freeport/Lucaya.

Winter–Spring: Three- and four-night **southern Caribbean** loops depart San Juan, calling at St. Thomas/St. John and St. Maarten/St. Martin. Four-night cruises also call at St. Croix. **Summer:** Three- and four-night **Bahamas** loops depart Port Canaveral, calling at Nassau and CocoCay.

Song of America **Winter–mid-Spring:** A 14-night **Panama Canal** transit from Los Angeles to San Juan calls at Acapulco, Puerto Caldera, Aruba, and St. Thomas/St. John.

Song of Norway **Fall–Spring:** A 10-night **Panama Canal** transit from Acapulco to San Juan calls at Puerto Caldera, Curaçao, and St. Thomas/St. John. Ten- and 11-night **southern Caribbean** cruises between Miami and San Juan include calls at CocoCay, St. Barts, St. Lucia, Grenada, Dominica, St. Maarten/St. Martin, and St. Thomas/St. John.

Sovereign of the Seas **Fall:** Seven-night **eastern Caribbean** loops depart Miami, calling at Labadee, San Juan, St. Thomas, and CocoCay. **Winter:** Three- and four-night **Bahamas** loops depart Miami, calling at Nassau and CocoCay. Four-night cruises also call at Freeport/Lucaya.

Splendour of the Seas **Late Fall–Spring:** Seven-night **southern Caribbean** loops depart San Juan, calling at Aruba, Curaçao, St. Maarten/St. Martin, and St. Thomas/St. John.

Royal Olympic Cruises

Stella Solaris **Fall–early Spring:** A 10-night **Caribbean** cruise from Miami to Fort Lauderdale calls at Nassau, San Juan, Curaçao, St. Lucia, and St. Thomas. A 27-night **Caribbean/Amazon** loop departs Fort Lauderdale and includes calls at St. Thomas, St. Lucia, Barbados, Grenada, Tobago, Manaus, Alter de Chao, Antigua, San Juan, and other ports. Twelve-night **Panama Canal** loops depart Galveston (Texas) and include calls at Grand Cayman, the San Blas Islands, Puerto Limon, Cozumel/Playa del Carmen, and Gatun Lake. A 12-night **western Caribbean** loop departs Galveston, calling at Grand Cayman, Cozumel/Playa del Carmen, and other ports. A seven-night **western Caribbean** loop departs Galveston, calling at Cozumel/Playa del Carmen, Mexico, Grand Cayman, and Key West.

Seabourn Cruise Line

Seabourn **Late Fall–Winter:** Fourteen-night **Caribbean/**
Legend **Panama Canal** cruises sail between Fort Lauderdale and Curaçao. A seven-night **Caribbean** loop departs Curaçao. An eight-night **Mexico** loop departs Tampa. A 15-night **Central America** loop departs Tampa and includes calls at Cozumel/Playa del Carmen, Grand Cayman, and other ports. An 18-night **Caribbean/Panama Canal** cruise from Tampa to Antigua calls at Cancún, the San Blas Islands, Cartagena, Curaçao, Barbados, Grenada, St. Lucia, and other ports. A seven-night **Caribbean** cruise from San Juan to Fort Lauderdale calls at St. Barts, St. Maarten/St. Martin, St. Thomas, and Virgin Gorda. A 12-night **Caribbean/Orinoco River** cruise from Curaçao to St. Thomas calls at Barbados, St. Lucia, St. Barts, St. Maarten/St. Martin, and other ports. A seven-night **Caribbean** cruise from St. Thomas to Barbados includes calls at St. Maarten/St. Martin, St. Barts, Antigua, St. Lucia, and Grenada. A nine-night **Caribbean** cruise sails from Barbados to West Palm Beach. **Spring:** A 23-night **Panama Canal** transit from Fort Lauderdale to San Diego calls at Cozumel/Playa del Carmen, the San Blas Islands, Puerto Caldera, Acapulco, Puerto Vallarta, Mazatlan, Cabo San Lucas, and other ports.

Seabourn Pride **Winter:** A 15-night **Amazon/Caribbean** cruise from Manaus to Fort Lauderdale includes calls at ports along the Amazon, Devil's Island, St. John, Antigua, and San Juan.

Seawind Cruise Line

Seawind Crown **Year-round:** Seven-night **southern Caribbean** loops depart Aruba, calling at Curaçao, Grenada, Barbados, and St. Lucia, or Trinidad, Tobago, Barbados, and Martinique.

Silversea Cruises

Silver Cloud **Late Fall–mid-Winter:** A 10-night **Caribbean** cruise from Nassau to Fort Lauderdale calls at Grand Cayman, Aruba, and other ports. Six-night cruises between Fort Lauderdale and Barbados call at St. Maarten/St. Martin, Dominica, St. Lucia, Antigua, and Virgin Gorda. Ten-night **Caribbean/Amazon** cruises between Barbados and Manaus (Brazil) call at Devil's Island and along the Amazon River. A 14-night **Caribbean** loop departs Fort Lauderdale, calling at St. Maarten/St. Martin, Antigua, Martinique, Barbados, St. Lucia, Guadeloupe, and other ports.

Special Expeditions

Polaris **Winter:** Eight-night **Costa Rica and Panama** cruises sail between Colón (Panama) and Puerto Caldera (Costa Rica). Thirteen-night **Panama Canal** transits between Balboa (Panama) and Belize call at the San Blas Islands and ports in Nicaragua and Honduras.

Star Clippers

Star Clipper **Fall–Winter:** Seven-night **Caribbean** loops depart Barbados, calling at Martinique, Dominica, St. Lucia, Tobago, and Bequia or Carriacou, Grenada, Union Island, St. Vincent, and St. Lucia.

Windstar Cruises

Wind Spirit **Late Fall–early Spring:** Seven-, 10-, and 11-night **Caribbean** loops depart St. Thomas and include calls at St. Croix, St. John, St. Lucia, Barbados, Martinique, St. Maarten/St. Martin, Guadeloupe, and other islands.

Wind Star **Late Fall–mid-Spring:** Seven-, nine-, and 12-night **Caribbean** loops depart Barbados and include calls at St. Maarten/St. Martin, Martinique, Carriacou, Grenada, St. Lucia, Guadeloupe, and other islands.

World Explorer Cruises

SS Universe Explorer **Winter:** Fourteen-night **Western Caribbean/Central America/South America** loops depart Nassau, calling at Calica, Puerto Cortes, Puerto Limon, Cristobal, Cartagena, and Ocho Rios.

Index

NOTES

WHEREVER YOU TRAVEL, *H*ELP IS NEVER FAR AWAY.

From planning your trip to providing travel assistance along the way, American Express® Travel Service Offices are always there to help.

Caribbean Ports of Call

Mundy Tours (R)
Suite 20, Regent Center 4
Freeport, Bahamas
809/352-4444

Playtours (R)
303 Shirley Street
Nassau, Bahamas
809/322-2931

Boulevard Travel (R)
811 Peacock Plaza
Key West, Florida
305/251-7454

Southerland Tours (R)
Chandlers Wharf Gallows Bay
St. Croix, USVI
809/773-9500

Caribbean Travel Agency, Inc./Tropic Tours (R)
14AB The Guardian Bldg.
St. Thomas, USVI
809/774-1855

Travel

http://www.americanexpress.com/travel

American Express Travel Service Offices are found in central locations throughout the Caribbean.